COWBOYS & IMAGES

The Watercolors of

WILLIAM MATTHEWS

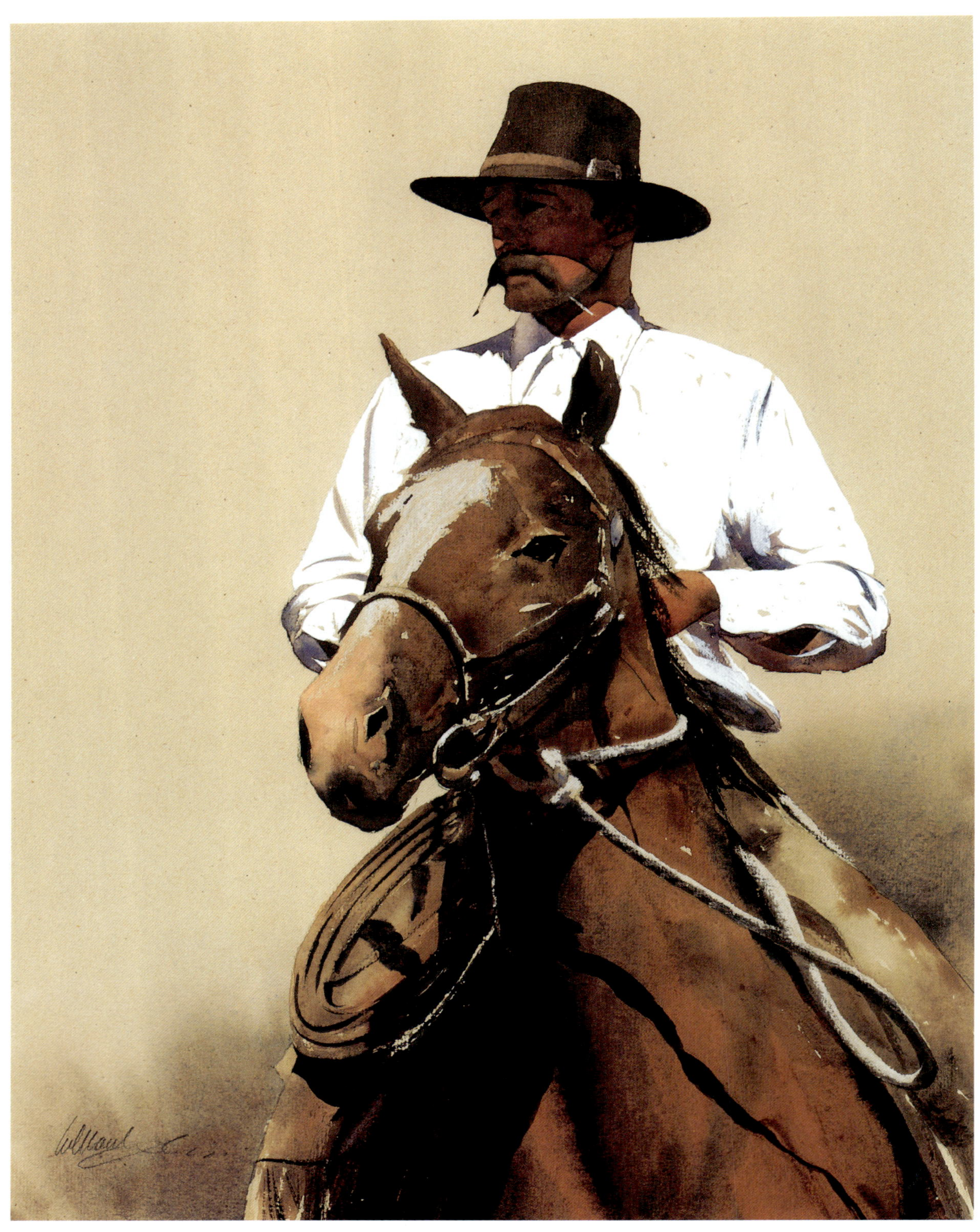

Trail Boss

COWBOYS & IMAGES

The Watercolors of

WILLIAM MATTHEWS

Foreword by William Kittredge

Introduction by Dyan Zaslowsky

CHRONICLE BOOKS

in association with
CALLAWAY EDITIONS

Dedicated to

Austin and Alistair

First published in the United States by Chronicle Books in 1994.

Produced by Callaway Editions, Inc.

Edited by Thomas West, Callaway Editions, Inc.

Designed by Hans Teensma, Impress, Inc.

First Edition

Library of Congress Cataloging-in-Publication Data

Matthews, William, 1949-
Cowboys & Images / William Matthews: foreword by William
Kittredge; introduction by Dyan Zaslowsky
p. cm.

ISBN 0-8118-0768-1

1. Matthews, William, 1949- . 2. Cowboys in art.
I. Matthews, William, 1949- . William Matthews—cowboys and images. II. Title. III. Title: Cowboys and images.
ND 1839.M36A4 1994
94-1187
759.13—dc20
CIP

Distributed in Canada by:

Raincoast Books
112 East Third Avenue
Vancouver, BC VST 1C8

10 9 8 7 6 5 4 3 2 1

Chronicle Books
275 Fifth Street
San Francisco, CA 94103

Printed and bound by Palace Press in Hong Kong

COVER PAINTING: Poet's Brim BACKCOVER PAINTING: Doctoring

C O N T E N T S

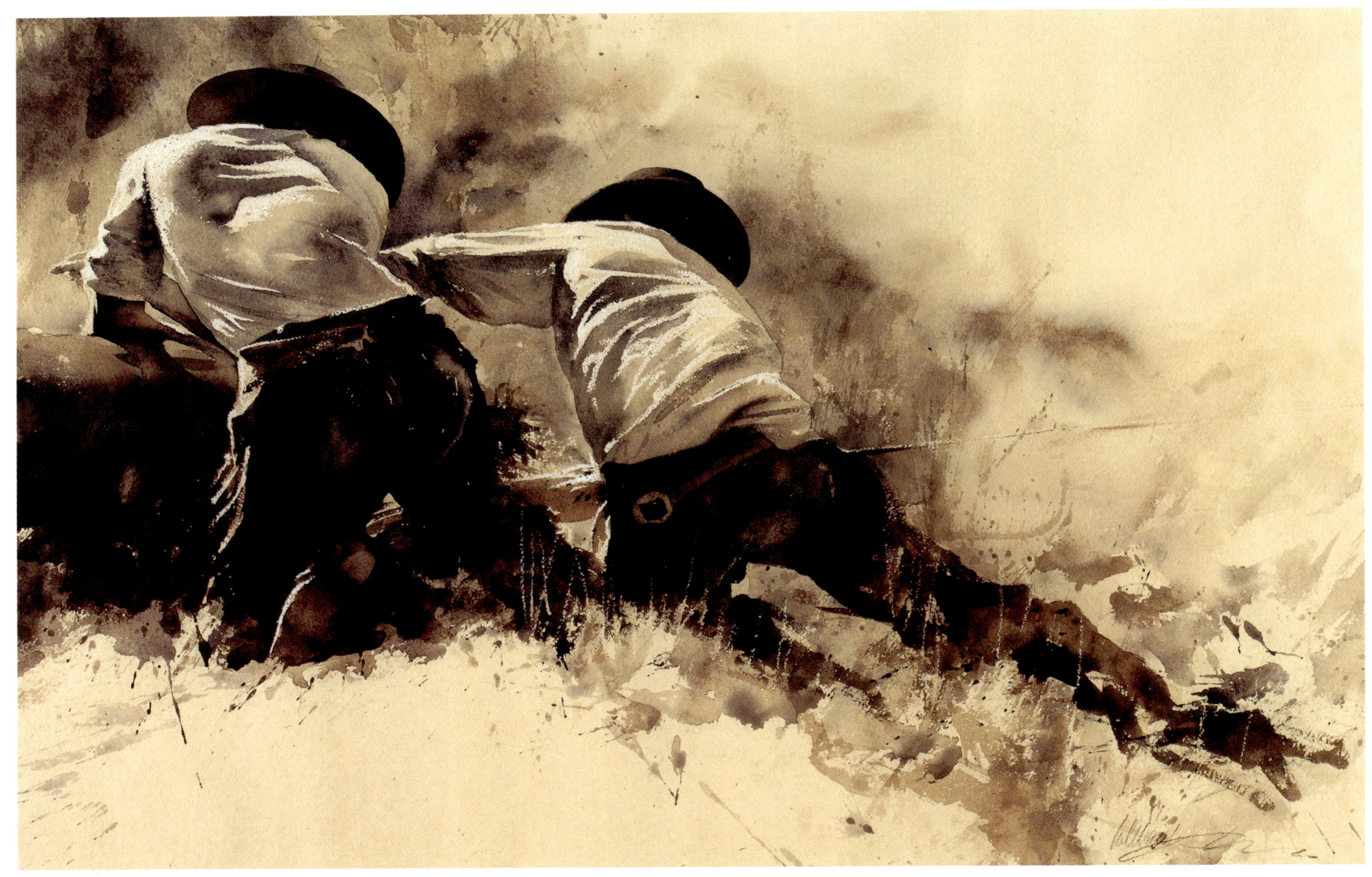

Doctoring

EDITOR'S PREFACE

Many of our images of the American West come from painters active in the nineteenth century. From George Caleb Bingham to Frederic Remington and Charlie Russell, talented artists created a vigorous vernacular tradition that still exerts its power over the popular arts of the western states. In our century, painters like Georgia O'Keeffe and Maynard Dixon have brought a distinctive vision to Western subject matter, but few have reinhabited the imaginative territory carved out in the golden age of Western painting, and none have sent that tradition off in a new direction.

William Matthews had already made a name for himself as a watercolorist when he began to paint cowboys and their world in 1985. As he explored the terrain and its people, both literally and figuratively, he showed how a fresh and unexpected view of a classic American subject could transform our understanding of it and alter all our expectations.

In *Cowboys & Images* we present a selection of watercolor paintings executed during the last ten years. Combining understated tonal values and thoughtful composition, Matthews depicts the cowboy as a rural hero whose gestures create a quiet poetry more in keeping with the reality of a cowpuncher's life than with traditional images of action and derring-do. An outsider living at the margins of society, Matthews's cowboy savors a world joined by connections that many of us may have forgotten — with the land, with tradition, and most importantly with themselves. Short texts by the artist about some of the people and places he has painted suggest how experience and imagination are meshed in his art. In the introductory essay, Dyan Zaslowsky takes us further into Matthews's world and tells the story of his art and of how he came to paint these images.

A memoir by the writer William Kittredge, who grew up on the MC Ranch in the buckaroo country of southeastern Oregon, directs us to the heart of Matthews's subject matter. The cowboys Kittredge grew up with belonged to the working people who invented civilization in the desert West. They were people of integrity and character whom big business and big land owners later threatened with extinction. The characters and life that Kittredge recalls with nostalgia are those that Matthews has sought out and painted. They are the heroes of the West and of *Cowboys & Images*.

— Thomas West

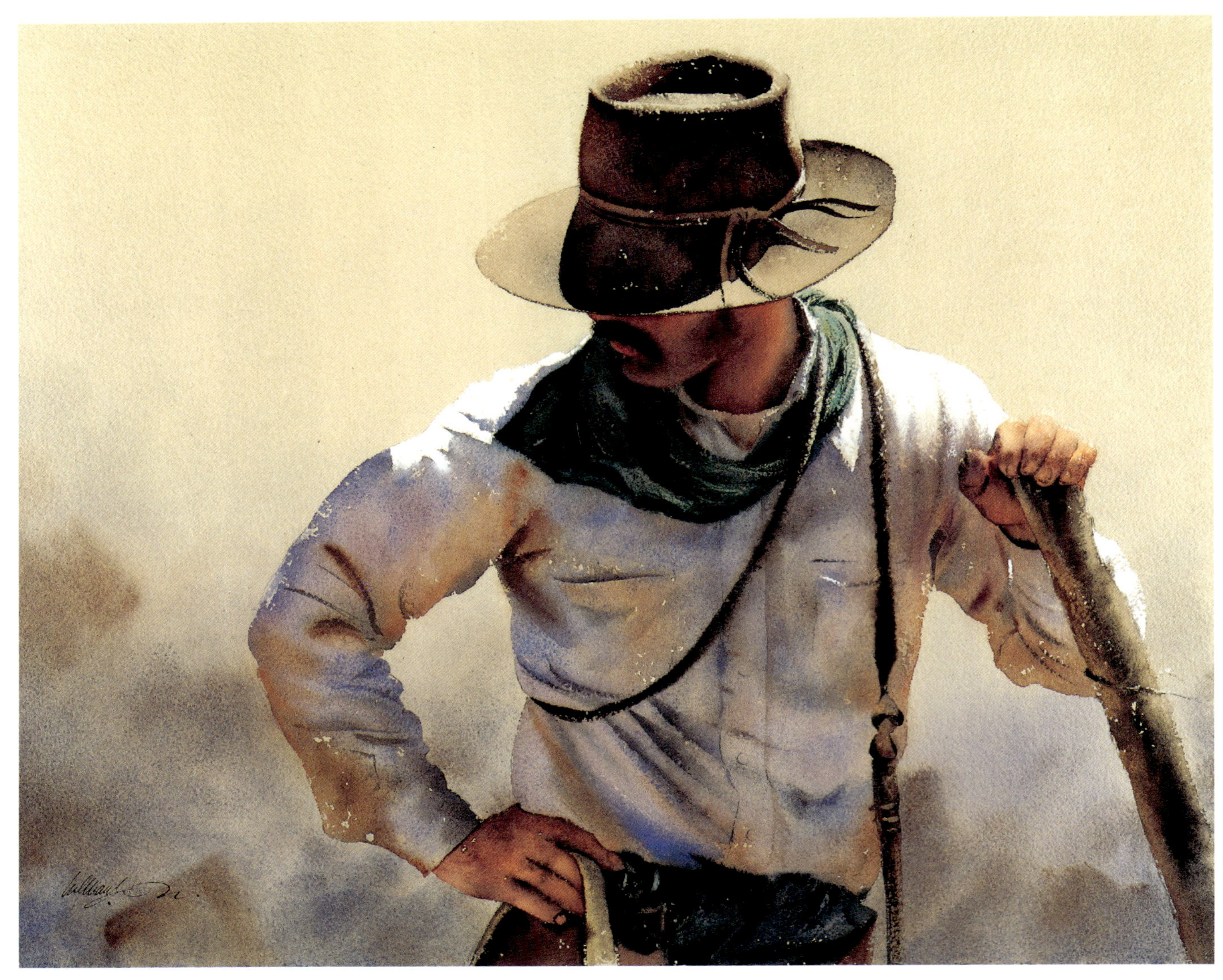

Clover Creek

(FOLLOWING SPREAD)

Navajo Rodeo Ground

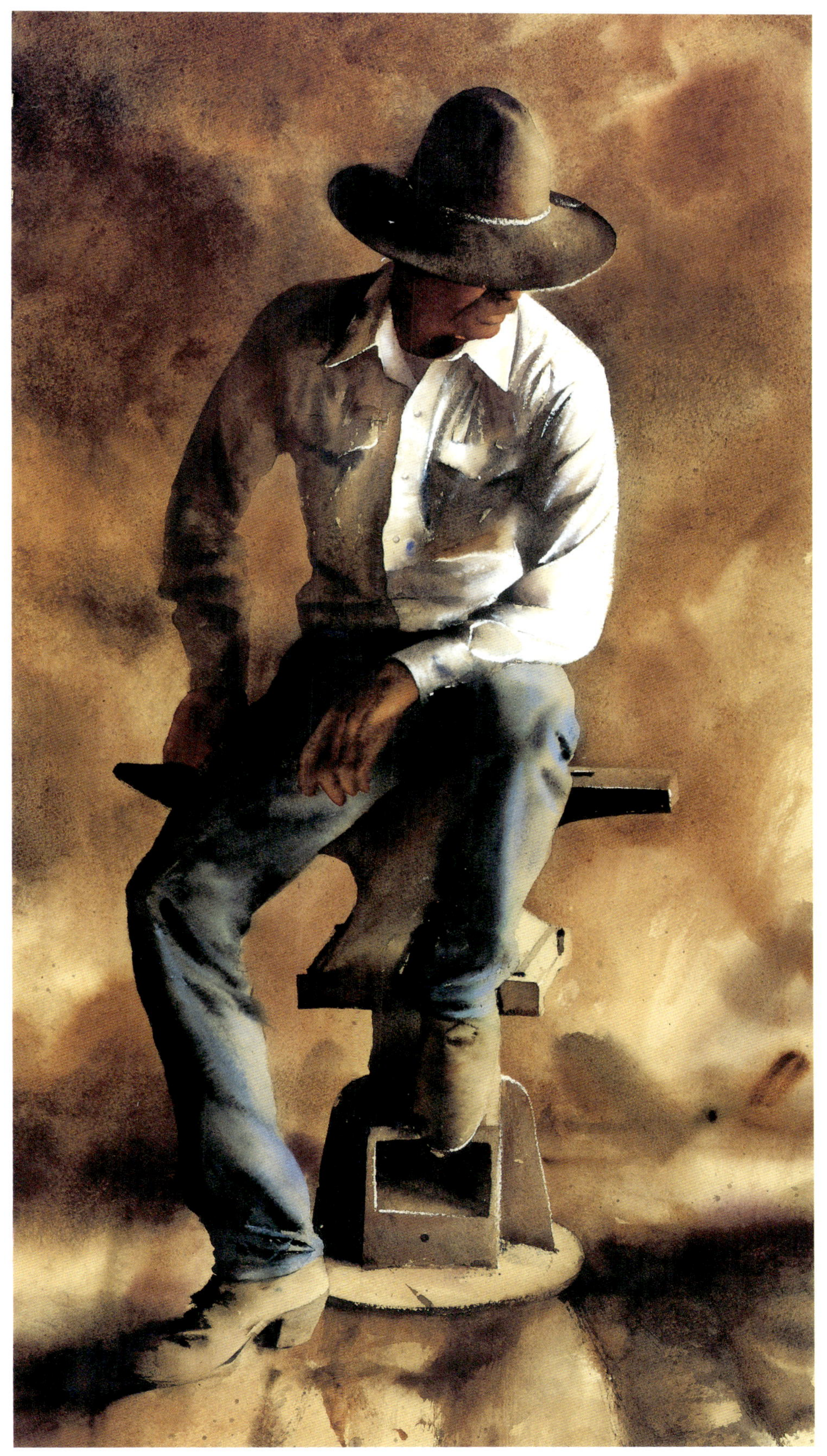

The Farrier

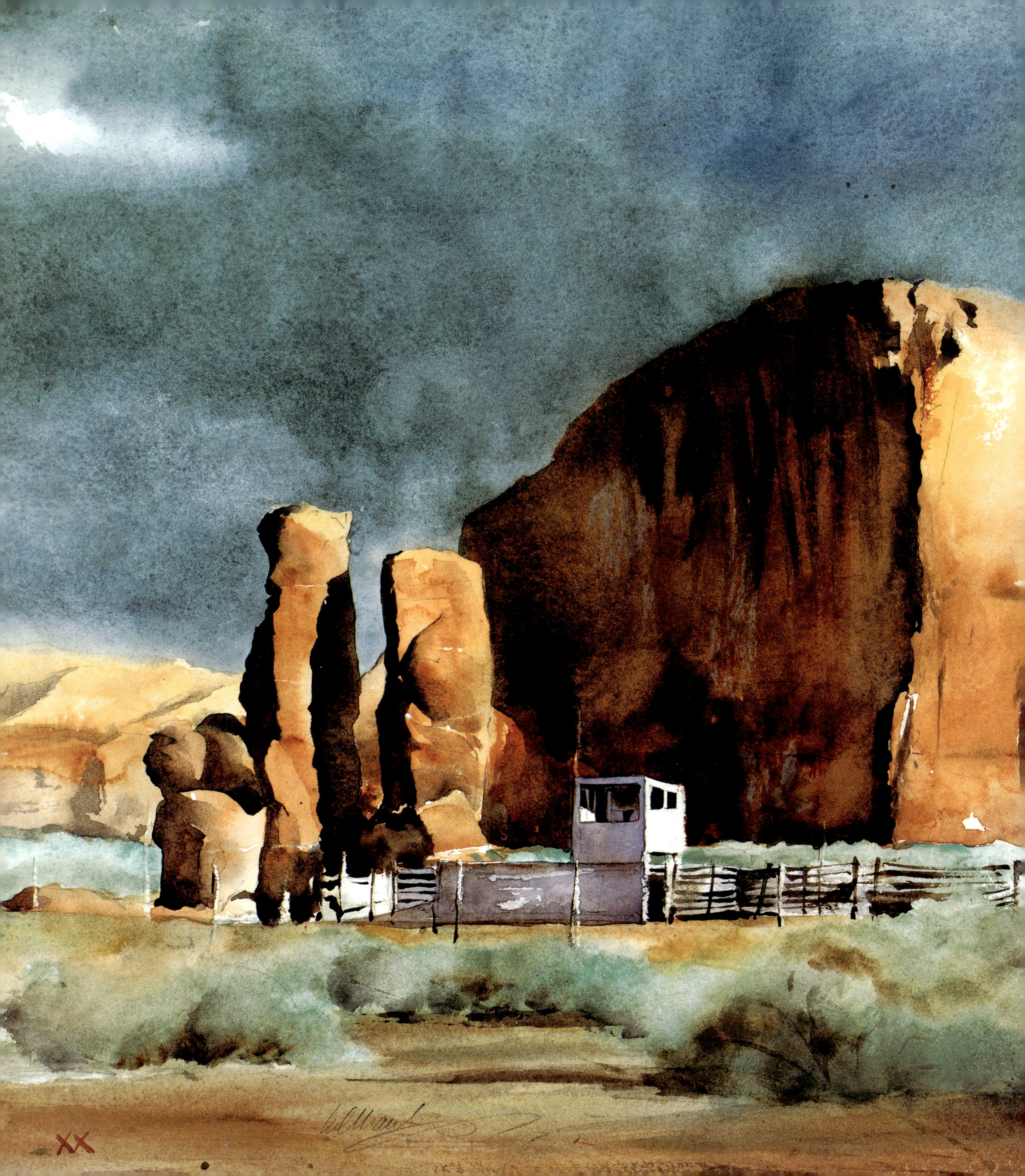

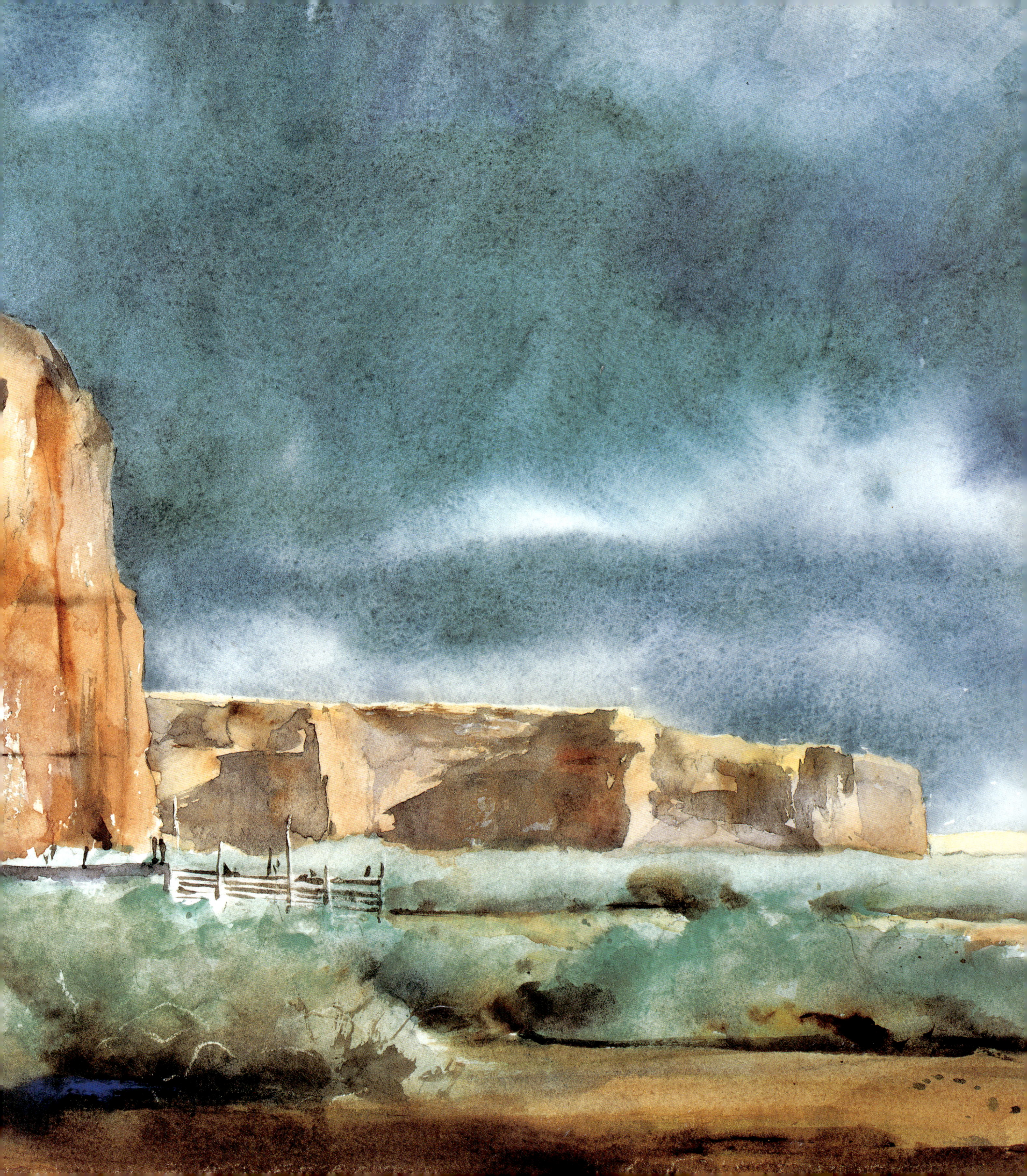

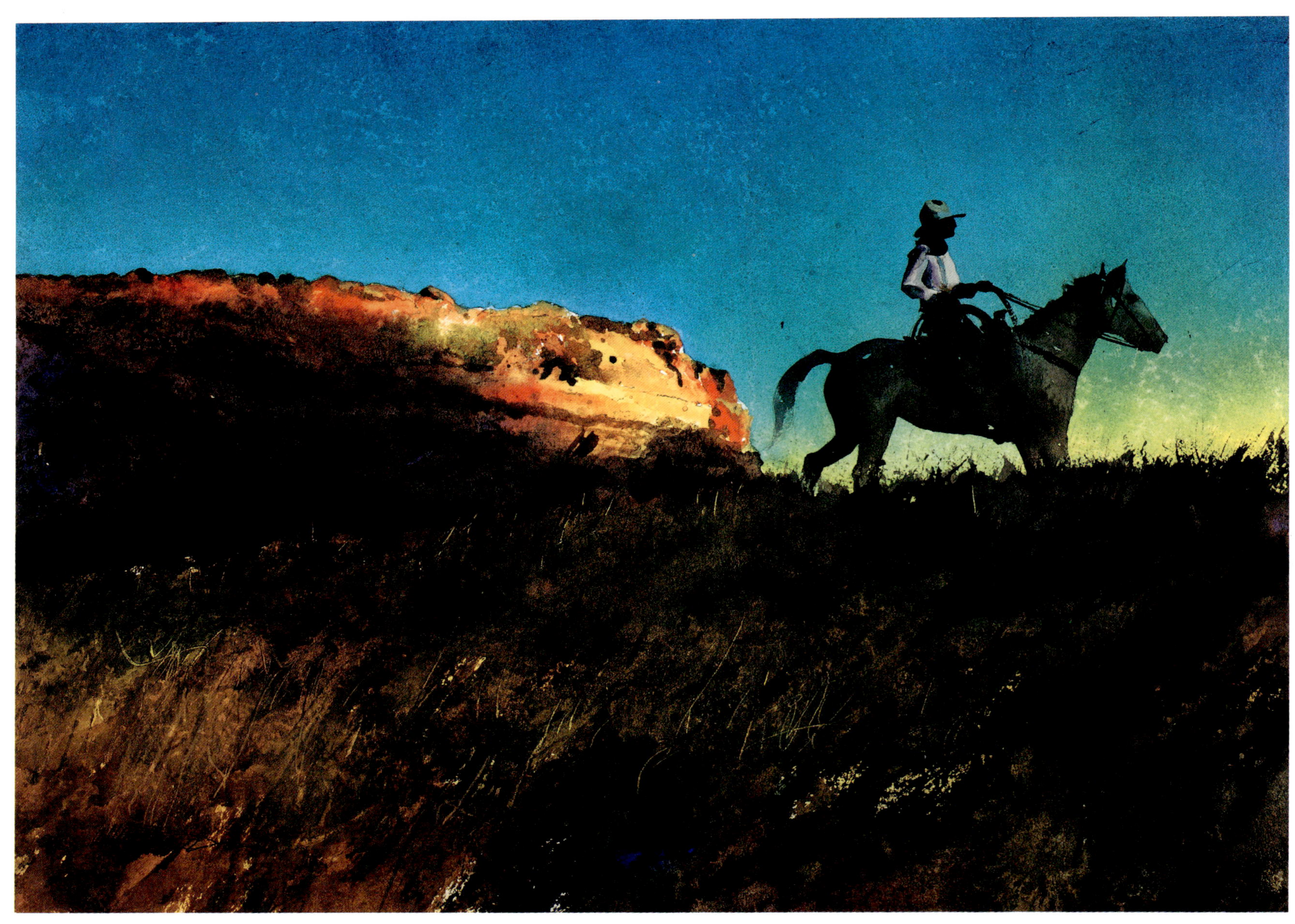

Dusk

Running Horses

By William Kittredge

In the long-gone days of my childhood, the highland desert country of southeastern Oregon was an enclave of unsettled territory, lava-rock and sagebrush flats, fault-block mountains, and swampland valleys echoing with the call of white pelicans and sand hill cranes and Canada geese and thousands of ducks like the green-winged teal and the redheads and canvasbacks nobody sees so often any more. In such country, expansiveness of the personality was commonplace. Children grew up addicted to running horses, as I did, a manifestation of high spirits that adults claimed to see as a disease to be cured (even if they themselves once in a while staged a race). A running horse, I was told, was not a toy.

My cousins and I grew up understanding that horses were creatures with their own complex sensibilities, which could not only be broken (that terrible name for training) but spoiled — ruined — by cheap-shit frivolity such as pointless galloping — a boy coming heedlessly downcountry along a country road with his horse in a lather.

But we were the children of the people who owned ranches, and could sometimes get away with things, so I listened to what I was told but galloped anyway, down long secret lanes through the willows and sloughs, before sunup in the endlessness of midsummer, on my way to visit the hay camps where the old men in the round corrals were lassoing their buckrake teams.

Then, in 1940, the summer I turned nine years old, an older cousin and I were deemed big enough to be useful and sent to ride with my grandfather's crew of buckaroos on the vast sea of deserts east of the ranch, where our family summered several thousand mother cows. We began this serious education under the boss of the buckaroos for my grandfather, a legendary horseman, Ross Dollarhide (everybody knew the story of how he'd ridden to the White Horse Ranch on a flat-tired bicycle, sixteen years old and looking for his first cowhand job, and how he'd ridden a tough horse to death that long-ago morning; his abilities had gone unquestioned ever since).

What a thing it was to be a frightened child, watching Dollarhide step onto some spooky, stocking-footed traveling horse in the light of early morning, knowing you were expected to keep up with him for the rest of the day.

For a long time my cousin and I weren't much use to anybody, that summer and most of the next (I was learning to do things like never cry), then we grew and toughened as boys will. By 1943 we were, we thought, almost cowhands. We learned to shoe our own horses, and braid rawhide on rainy days, and to travel like grownups, at a long trot. We were close to the end of secret galloping; we were becoming little men.

But you have to stay playful to survive. That was another thing we were taught, by clear example, watching the men around us, in whom a certain childish recklessness (at least in the best of them, the finest hands) had never died.

Then, one burning afternoon, that playfulness got us crossways with old man Dollarhide. There for a moment we left him afoot, without a horse. I think he thought we had made him look like a fool.

Just at daybreak one bright morning in June while we were rolling our beds, making ready to move the four-horse chuckwagon from the mountainside camp at Ackley to Sagehen Springs, my cousin and I were detailed to help the wrango boy move the seventy-some-odd saddle horses in the MC remuda. Once we'd turned them out of the willow corral at Ackley they'd be ours as we herded them twenty miles down country across the alkaline flats to the fenced-in field where the wet-weather creek at Sagehen got lost in tall brush. There wasn't much at Sagehen, no sign of a house, just a hog-wire corral and field built of rusty barbed wire and crooked juniper posts. That corral was a small target in a vast territory (nowadays there's a highway called Winnemucca to the Sea just south of Sagehen Springs; in those days there weren't any internal combustion engines in that almost empty country).

Dollarhide told us to take it easy. What we were to do was graze the herd on Ackley Mountain through the morning, and then ease them on down to Sagehen in the late afternoon.

Dollarhide made it real clear: If we got those horses running with their heads, and lost them, there wasn't a fence to turn them within fifty miles. As an afterthought Dollarhide sent along a man named Merle Dodson to keep an eye on us.

What is there to say about Merle Dodson? He was known as "Tarzan," a barroom tag given him because he was, according to my father when I asked him years later, close to animal if he was drinking, huge-handed and barrel-chested, stronger than he knew, impossible to wound, nobody to fight as strangers had found out any number of times, but willing and happy to be entertained.

"That damned Tarz," people would say. "If he ain't something, you tell me, what is?"

What he was on this day was full of vinegar when we eased our drifty grazing herd of bay horses, all of them geldings, over the crest of Ackley Mountain to encounter the mustangs that were also drifting along in their shaggy spotted-horse way.

There were maybe twenty or so mustangs, mares, and colts, a half-dozen branded geldings that had got away from some ranch in the long-ago past, and no doubt a stud horse even if I don't recall any such creature. What I recall is the way we let them drift into the remuda and mix, the way we fell in after them; I recall running horses.

"We've got to go mustanging," Tarz Dodson whispered. Something like that. It was his plan. It frightened us, but we never thought of refusing.

Besides, if I learned something that day, which is the point of this story, it had nothing to do with caution but rather with the splendor of running with the wind. That was the lesson of the summer.

We were going to ease our great herd of horses along the road slow as we could through the afternoon, then stir them into a long run just at the end, and turn them into corral at Sagehen Springs before they came to any sense of what was happening. We were going to have those mustangs inside fences before they realized they had been trapped.

We were going to own those mustangs. That was Tarz Dodson's idea; the whole buckaroo crew could turn some money on the side. It wasn't a plan my grandfather or Ross Dollarhide would have endorsed.

(I have no memory of what those remnant animals were worth at that time. Their herds grew during World War II, when their natural predators, the young able-bodied cowhands, were off to war. After the war they were cleaned out of that country, run with airplanes, and rounded up in great swirling herds; most of them were eventually shot and processed into chicken feed.)

We brought it off, my cousin and I and the MC wrango boy and Tarz Dodson, we got the mustangs running with the remuda, we circled our herd in a great sweep through the afternoon while somebody got the corral gate open at Sagehen. It was about then when I realized something was very wrong.

The chuckwagon tent was up, and everybody on the crew but us had turned their horses loose into the field. Which meant our worn-out horses were it; lose the herd and everybody was afoot. Which was no joke in that country, sure as hell not in a buckaroo outfit. Old man Dollarhide was standing out in front of that chuckwagon tent with a coffee cup in his hand, studying our performance with amazement, looking like an old eagle contemplating a final kill.

The rest of what I recall doesn't take long to tell. We hit that corral gate perfectly; those mustangs circled maybe twice, then went right out the other side, scattering hog-wire; they circled in the little field a time or two and went right on through that fence at a long run, the MC remuda following, horses flowering out into their freedom and starting to spill off in all directions, still running, and there was nothing we could do because we were still back trying to get through the corral gate.

What I remember is somebody took my horse, maybe old man Dollarhide himself, leaping up into my short-legged saddle, and somebody took my cousin's horse, and the wrango boy's horse. What had seemed like play ended abruptly. I remember that it was hours before those men came back driving a remnant of the remuda before them. This was a serious disgrace; the MC buckaroo crew was going to be the laughingstock of the country.

What I think I remember is standing around the cook fire like a fool. Maybe Tarz Dodson was fired and rode off into the night. I don't know.

What matters most in this memory is the feeling I took away from the moments we turned those running horses in that long sweep outside the corral at Sagehen Springs while somebody opened the gate. It was a kind of pleasure Dollarhide no doubt knew more intimately than I ever would.

Maybe we disgraced his buckaroo crew; maybe I got my ass whipped. I don't think so; I don't think old man Dollarhide ever touched me; he taught me to never actually give a shit about small change; it's been an operative principle with me in my good moments ever since. I'd been along for a big ride, and part of a story that would be told for years, and in that if nothing else I was like Dollarhide, who was the real thing all his life.

In 1848, after service in the Mexican War, a young medical doctor from Virginia named Hugh Glenn began driving great herds of cattle over the difficult trails from the midwest to the vast inland valleys of California. In time Hugh Glenn was able to establish himself on a Spanish land-grant ranchero near the present-day town of Willows on the Sacramento River.

I went by his home place on a narrow Glenn County road along the levee above the riverbank about a dozen years ago. All that was left was a driveway lined with exotic imported trees and shrubs. His mansion, the long verandas overlooking the vast fields, and the barns were gone.

I was interested in Glenn because he had great influence in the high desert country of southeastern Oregon where I grew up. In the spring of 1872, free grazing land in California mostly claimed, Glenn turned 1,200 shorthorn cows over to a 23-year-old cowhand named Peter French. He sent French, seven vaqueros, and a Chinese cook north into mostly unmapped territory in the Great Basin to find new ranchlands.

The Chinese cook was named Charlie On Long. He stayed with French until he was killed in the Bannock uprising of 1878. The vaqueros, Vicente Ortega, Juan Ortega, Jesus Charris, Joaquin Berdugo, Francisco Carataguey, Juan Charris, Primo Ortega — Tebo, Chino, Chico — lived out their lives in that country; they were legendary in the cow camps in my part of the world, fifty years ago, when I was a child and knew old men who had known them.

Pete French led the vaqueros up the Pit River, across the Warner Range into Surprise Valley, almost on the Nevada border, north across the southern fringes of Warner Valley where I grew up, and across the high deserts south of the Beatty Buttes, to camp in Catlow Valley below the long western slope of the great 10,000-foot fault block that is Steens Mountain. They were in an almost empty, forgotten enclave in the West, mostly passed by in the rush to settlement in the coastal valleys of California and Oregon.

Other than Shoshoni natives, there were John Devine and his blooded racing stock over at the Whitehorse Ranch, trappers camped at the Sod House on the southern edge of Malheur Lake, and the military at Fort Harney. The rest of that huge territory was unclaimed by whites except for miners at Silver City, Idaho, and the railroad down south at Winnemucca. Our frontier was closing on its remnants as Peter French drove Glenn's cattle into the oasis valley that he made into his true home in the world.

The long string of that herd came down through the breaks south of the Beatty Buttes and out onto the fine bunchgrass country of Catlow Valley while the long ridge of Steens Mountain there to the east was still bright with snow. French had been on the trail two months, and tiny yellow and orange flowers bloomed amid the lava rocks and stunted sage.

At Roaring Springs along the western base of the Steens they rested the cattle on good grazing and water. French bought his brand with a few head of cows from a drifter named Porter, a huge P on the left hip, the first thing French was to own in Oregon.

The next morning before daybreak, according to the legends, French rode out of Catlow Valley, over the ridge to the north, and looked down on the great wetland valley of the Donner and Blitzen River for the first time. Those meadows were for the taking, and Pete French took them. He fit into that part of the world like a lost piece in a puzzle.

It's easy to imagine that morning was the beginning of his manhood as French would understand it, alone in the boulders and brush, looking down into the enclosed reach of swampy, willow-lined sloughs and meadows which lay in the landlocked valley below the rimrocks. Above him lay the high rangelands of the Steens, where the summer grass would never fail. All of it was enclosed by an immensity of sagebrush desert, a buffer against outsiders.

It's easy to imagine snow-geese, the sounds of their wings as he saw the place, knowing it was his, all that he could see, the creek-side reach of high ground where he would build his white house and his barns and the willow corrals and, spreading all around, the finest ranching property in the West.

The great landholders like Peter French were, for a long time, the people we imagined when we imagined kings of the mountain in my part of America. But they turned out, I think, to be living inside the wrong dream — they found a paradise, they thought it could be theirs; they yearned to possess it, and their generosities dissolved before that yearning. For a long time we believed in their pomp and their circumstance; we revered them. It was a mistake.

We should have looked for our heroes among our hay camp cooks and schoolteachers and florists and buckaroos and barbers and haberdashers. They did the endless work, they took the care, theirs was the tradition of civility, they were the people who invented our civilization in the desert West.

Those men who came north with French, the first buckaroos in that country — Tebo, Chino, and Chico — horseback artists who brought the rawhide riata and the Spanish silver-sided bits, quick-handed men who mostly never dreamed they could own much beyond a saddle and a bedroll and a good pocket knife: they were our nobility; like old man Dollarhide, I think, they dreamed of capabilities and beauty. They knew better than to imagine you could ever own anything beyond a coherent self.

Those men, and the men I rode with on those deserts when I was a boy, lived in an ancient horseback world that is mostly gone. The nineteenth century lasted in our part of the universe until the spring of 1946, when my grandfather traded off some two hundred matched work teams for a fleet of John Deere tractors. Everybody thought it was a bold step into the future. We didn't know what we were losing, our ancient proximity with animals, with running horses. The shadows of clouds went on swiftly without us.

— Missoula, Montana

The Watercolors of William Matthews

By Dyan Zaslowsky

William Matthews had been painting for some time when he left the United States for Europe. He toured Britain, Spain, and North Africa, using a makeshift device welded to his motorbike as an easel. He rambled for five years, making watercolors of the places and people he encountered. Painting and travel, two different kinds of inquiry, have always been his passion.

Then one day in 1979, on a wet road in County Kerry, Ireland, the instinct that sent him packing in the first place suddenly called him home, to Evergreen, Colorado, where he still lives today. Since returning from Europe he has used Evergreen as his base, although he continued to travel for several years in search of the things he loved to paint.

In 1985 Matthews discovered the subject that would become the most important element in his painting. The discovery came as a surprise since he found it not thousands of miles away but, by Western measurements, almost in his backyard — six hundred miles from Evergreen. The new theme was anything but exotic. On the contrary, it felt a bit worn or anachronistic; the fact that, as an icon, it still loomed large in the American consciousness gave him pause. Painting it required some cheek, if not foolhardiness. The subject Matthews first embarked upon nine years ago, now the subject of this book, is the American cowboy.

Matthews's involvement with cowboys began shortly after he visited the high desert town of Elko in northeastern Nevada. There he traveled over immense plains of white sagebrush divided into vast cattle ranches, some the size of a small eastern state, and met some of the cowboys in this book. They're not Texas cowpunchers or Plains wranglers, but Nevada buckaroos, highly skilled and very isolated. The Nevada buckaroo maintains a distinct tradition of horsemanship and dress that to other cowboys is synonymous with the Great Basin. This includes a preference for colorful silk scarves or rags and ornate saddles and bits, all of which descend from the old Mexican cowboy, the vaquero or californio.

Matthews was born in New York City but grew up in the Pacific Heights neighborhood of San Francisco when the city's atmosphere was decidedly more Western than it is today. Like others of his generation, Matthews matured thinking he knew all about cowboys from the way they swaggered and shot their way through TV and movie scripts. But what he and other Americans were seeing was, for the most part, based on lurid accounts of the Wild West that first appeared in the dime novels of the 1870s and were later drawn upon by the painters Frederic Remington and Charlie Russell. In the late nineteenth century, artists and writers transformed the lone horseman and herder from a Territorial lowlife into the shining hero of the country's greatest drama, its westward progress.

Russell crammed his paintings with details, in part because he feared that the artifacts of the brief cowboy era would go unrecorded. According to Peter Hassrick, Director of the Buffalo Bill Historical Center in Cody, Wyoming, Remington portrayed the cowboy as a lone agent who had to prove his fitness as a survivor in a world colored by social Darwinism. The cowboy also appeared in his work as a gentle knight errant, although Remington always thought of him as a man of mythic proportions. Both painters, says Hassrick, "intentionally created images that were bigger than life." The Remington and Russell cowboy image became so ingrained in the vernacular tradition that it remains the touchstone of almost all cowboy art.

Hassrick sees an important departure from this tradition in the work of Matthews. "He's not just slogging along in the footsteps of all those others," he notes. "Matthews's paintings offer a more generalized view of the cowboy and suggest a cloudy, reverential vision that is far more cerebral. When you stand back and look at one of Matthews's cowboy paintings, it defines a very powerful piece of visual iconography. You walk away from the painting feeling differently. The strength and uniqueness of his technique and style make a genuine contribution to our visual understanding of cowboy life."

Matthews heard the authentic cowboy voice at one of the first Cowboy Poetry Gatherings in Elko, Nevada. As these gatherings have proliferated in the West, the performances have grown more polished. But at the time they were pretty informal get-togethers where cowboys and ranchers told stories, strummed the guitar, and recited old poems. Matthews listened and realized immediately that he had chanced across a treasure.

The first thing Matthews noticed in Elko was that the modern cowboy is a taciturn but highly focused person, dedicated to making his living from the land and avoiding dependency on others. He was drawn to the buckaroos' love of solitude and moved by the way they equated personal freedom with wide open spaces. Matthews also discovered that cowboys possessed remarkable powers of introspection, humility, and spirituality. This made him revise his ideas about the fabled American icon.

Matthews's cowboy is vulnerable. We never see him with a six-shooter and rarely even with a rope. For Matthews, the drama of the cowboy lies in body language that speaks about a relationship with the land, with horses, or with other people: a rider hobbling his horse, a cowpuncher turning in his saddle to survey the land for water, a buckaroo opening a gate or pointing to a sick cow. He studied the men as they studied their land, or brewed coffee on a frigid morning, or pulled a calf from its mother's body. Matthews painted the people and their gestures, but rarely as figures in a landscape.

"I see the cowboy culture as one of the last vestiges of a genuine rural tradition in America," Matthews notes. "The cowboy allows many people to fantasize about their own inherent need to feel tied to the land. He's a living metaphor for what most of us have lost. What interested me most about Nevada buckaroos was the way they are insulated from everything. To me, they are more interesting than cowboys from some other places because they are much less affected by this century than by their surroundings. The independent, sometimes arrogant attitude of the Nevada cowboy makes other cowboys see them as renegades." He adds: "I guess I'm attracted to the type of renegade who tries to live on his own and make his own way."

Matthews's earliest cowboy portraits have a more nostalgic aspect than those he paints today. Looking at their brown and sepia tones gives one a feeling of peering through smoked glass at a time gone by. Later, a small amount of color enlivened the figures and gave them a more contemporary feel. A stroke of red suggested a saddle blanket; blue creases set off the brilliant whiteness of a shirt.

Many people are struck by the way Matthews paints a cowboy hat. These hats occupy a middle ground that is at once familiar and abstract. One recognizes the hat for what it is, and yet the shape inspires many sculptural associations and feelings. Sometimes the hat is used as a visual pivot in a painting, like the center of a wheel. At other times its dimples and creases look like sad and familiar furrows on the face of an old friend. As he paints in his studio, Matthews frequently draws inspiration from his own collection of hats that hang on the wall above him.

The hat, the gesture, the memorable pose: These are the ingredients of almost all his figure paintings. In *Vital Signs* (page 80) Matthews turns the portrait of Manuel Palomino crouching into a study of contained energy, a pose perfectly balanced between action and contemplation. In another painting, *The Packer* (page 72), a moment of intense exertion yields an image of meditation. We sense that neither the individual identity of the cowboy nor the original pretext of the image is important. What's important are the forces and the emotions the pose brings together.

When Matthews talks he looks people straight in the eye, longer than custom usually dictates. It's the sort of engaging glance that makes one respond. Yet in his paintings the goal is quite different. Faces are invariably portrayed from an obscuring angle or in a shadow. "I prefer mystery," he explains. "I don't want to paint someone straight on, I don't want to tell the whole story or be direct. I want to leave things open." Then, reflecting on the personalities of his models, he adds: "Buckaroos are pretty shy. You have to get to know them in a roundabout way, as though you are observing them out of the corner of your eye."

It is notoriously difficult to understand a painter's work through his personality, and this is especially true of William Matthews. Exuberant and opinionated, Matthews is more like a politician than an artist in public. He ought, one reasons, to be a painter of epic murals, full of brash tonal contrasts and dramatic effects. The man one meets in the studio is utterly different. William Matthews is a loner, a man who, despite appearances, is much more at home painting than working a crowd.

Matthews's assertive presence could have become a problem in his dealings with Elko County cowboys. Their dispositions are diametrically opposed to his own. "Willy was outgoing," remembers Waddie Mitchell, a Nevada buckaroo turned poet. (Mitchell is portrayed in *Poet's Brim* on the cover of this book.) "By cowboy standards, very outgoing. I guess you could say that Willy is just about half-hyper."

The two men were introduced at a Cowboy Poetry Gathering in Elko by a mutual friend, the photographer Kurt Markus, who knew many of the buckaroos Matthews would later paint. Mitchell invited Matthews to come out to the ranch where he was cowboss, and Matthews readily accepted. Mitchell was struck by Matthews's worldliness, but he also recognized the painter's real admiration for the cowboys at the ranch. "Willy came not to take over, but to take part," he says.

Scott Brown, one of the cowboys Matthews frequently paints (see pages 25 and 31), admired how Matthews focused on the quiet moments in a cowboy's day. "That was real different," Brown recalls. "Most of 'em who come out want to photograph or paint action scenes, but Willy liked it best when, if we were out riding, I'd stop to give my horse a break."

Brown, who is a master saddlemaker when not cowboying, says he can tell in a glance whose saddle Willy was painting. "He puts in just enough detail, like the little things tied to a saddle, so you know which cowboy a particular outfit belonged to. You know someone from the way his saddle looks just like you'd know a person from the back by the way he stands. Willy noticed that."

Apart from their saddle, boots, hat, and horse, most buckaroos don't own much of anything. They are poor and are typically employed on family-owned or corporate-owned ranches that have been around for generations, cattle empires cobbled together from hundreds of thousands of acres of privately owned and federally leased lands.

Matthews painted and sketched at the Church Ranch, the Wine Cup, the IL, the YP, the Gamble, and the Spanish Ranch. Some paintings he completed on site. On others he scribbled notes about details to be added in the studio. Still others were based on photographs he took. Matthews kept out of the men's way while they worked, waiting for the cowboys to invite him to come take a closer look at what they were doing. At night he spread his canvas bedroll on the ground near the cowboys, or crawled into the tent he had brought.

Matthews's art is more closely tied to his studio than it was in his traveling days. Clusters of dry brushes resemble brown and buff bouquets in jam jars on a long countertop. On the floor several large paintings await completion. Matthews moves from one painting to the next, working on a detail here, fleshing out the head of a horse there. His studio is full of trophies acquired over the years, everything from a velvet curtain brought back from Ireland to mecate ropes made by buckaroo Larry Schutte (pictured on page 97) and a hand-tooled, silver-trimmed saddle by Jeremiah Watt. Matthews values the scrolls of Chinese ideograms that hang in his studio as much as his cowboy hats. He can lose himself in the Chinese calligraphy for minutes, searching for "the expression without intention" that master calligraphers in China strive for: "Fix the thoughts to direct the regard to the wrist," one seventeenth-century calligrapher instructs. Matthews has transferred to his cowboy paintings techniques learned from copying Chinese calligraphy.

Yet we sense nothing self-aware about Matthews's watercolor style. In fact, the last thing he wants is to draw attention to style. Success in painting comes, he feels, when brush technique goes unnoticed and instead conjures up shapes that people believe in.

Matthews enjoys watercolor in particular because of its unpredictability. Learning how to work with adversity is the main challenge. The best watercolorists, he maintains, know how to turn accidents to their advantage, to transform a misplaced stroke into a visual discovery. He prefers a spontaneous stroke, which brings him close to what he thinks is important in art. Although Matthews conceives of a painting long before he reaches for a brush, he enjoys following a narrow line between chaos and recognizable form: "I am prepared in my head, I know what I'm looking for, but I have to stay open and take risks. Watercolor is more interesting if you give it some rein." Freshness and spontaneity are the qualities he admires most. "Visually the painting either comes together quickly or it doesn't make it. Since it is born in the flash of an idea, it won't be improved by being overworked."

Matthews commissioned Twinrocker, a small handmade-paper mill, to create for him beige watercolor paper based on that used by the great English watercolorists. In the British tradition, Matthews prefers using blends of ultramarine blue and burnt umber instead of black, and he also avoids pure white, letting the lightest values emerge from the unpainted surface of the paper. But using colored stock necessitated adding in white, however. Matthews also noticed in the watercolors of John Singer Sargent that wax could be used to resist pigment and he began to use white crayons in his paintings.

Although he has devoted much of his life to painting, Matthews says he still finds a blank piece of paper humbling. "Just because I am on today doesn't mean I'll paint well tomorrow. Watercolors are as fragile as my old snowplow. I never know from one day to the next if they'll work for me." Painting, he says, is the only activity that is incompatible with self-doubt.

Matthews credits contemporary painters Russell Chatham, Ned Jacob, James Havard, and Howard Hodgkin, but it is art by nineteenth-century British and American artists — John Sell Cotman, Richard Bonington, Sargent, Winslow Homer — as well as by the twentieth-century Wyeth family that has always inspired him. His early interest in watercolor was encouraged by an artistic mother, Joan Matthews, and grandfather, Abbott Kimball, who took him to museums and on painting outings of their own. Nevertheless, both his mother and his father were distraught when they realized their son was intent on becoming a painter. They encouraged him to look for something more secure financially, like business or advertising, but to no avail.

Discovering watercolors was undoubtedly a turning point in his young life, as later his European sojourn and his first trip to Elko would be. Hal Cannon, the founding director of Elko's annual Cowboy Poetry Gathering, recalls that Matthews's attraction to buckaroo culture was immediate and encompassing. "When Willy sees a vision he likes, he wants to be part of it," says Cannon. Toward that end Matthews helped Cannon promote the new event and painted enormous backdrops for the stage. He was drawn to the cowboy spirit, as expressed in poetry, in song, in solitary existence, in self-sufficiency, and sometimes in recklessness. Matthews marveled at the way his new cowboy friends made their own gear during the lonesome, sub-zero winter months, and at the beauty of well-made, hand-twisted rope, quirts, bosals, and headstalls braided from rawhide or hitched from horsehair.

Matthews admired the way cowboys were in control of their lives. "If you make your own saddle, you know the cinch isn't going to break," he says. "You feel you can handle what happens, because you know how things are made, and how they work." When Larry Schutte told Matthews that every day he thanked the Lord for letting him be born with the craving to be outside, and for letting him live in a house from which he could look north to summer country and south to winter country, Matthews understood the buckaroo's sense of place. He expressed the same feeling the best way he could — by painting.

"I keep coming back to certain themes," Matthews reflected. Then suddenly he hit upon the word "folk," as if it summed up everything he was trying to do. "Folk art, folk music, folk life. Anthropology. History. The way people have lived, the way they continue to live, and the magic and beauty that is sometimes born out of necessity . . . . Cowboys appeal to me in one sense, but it's really more about the honesty and artifacts of certain cultures that resist change, of people who are close to their native elements."

None of this comes across as literary or self-conscious in his painting, and that is one of Matthews's most important achievements. To paraphrase Henry James, who was writing of the painting of John Singer Sargent, Matthews "sees deep into his subject: undergoes it, absorbs it, discovers in it new things that were not on the surface, becomes patient with it, and almost reverent, and, in short, enlarges, and humanizes the technical problem."

The buckaroo poet Waddie Mitchell puts it a bit differently: "Willy came to Elko as an outsider, as a man who knew nothing about the way cowboys live. What he painted gave us the truth of ourselves."

— Evergreen, Colorado

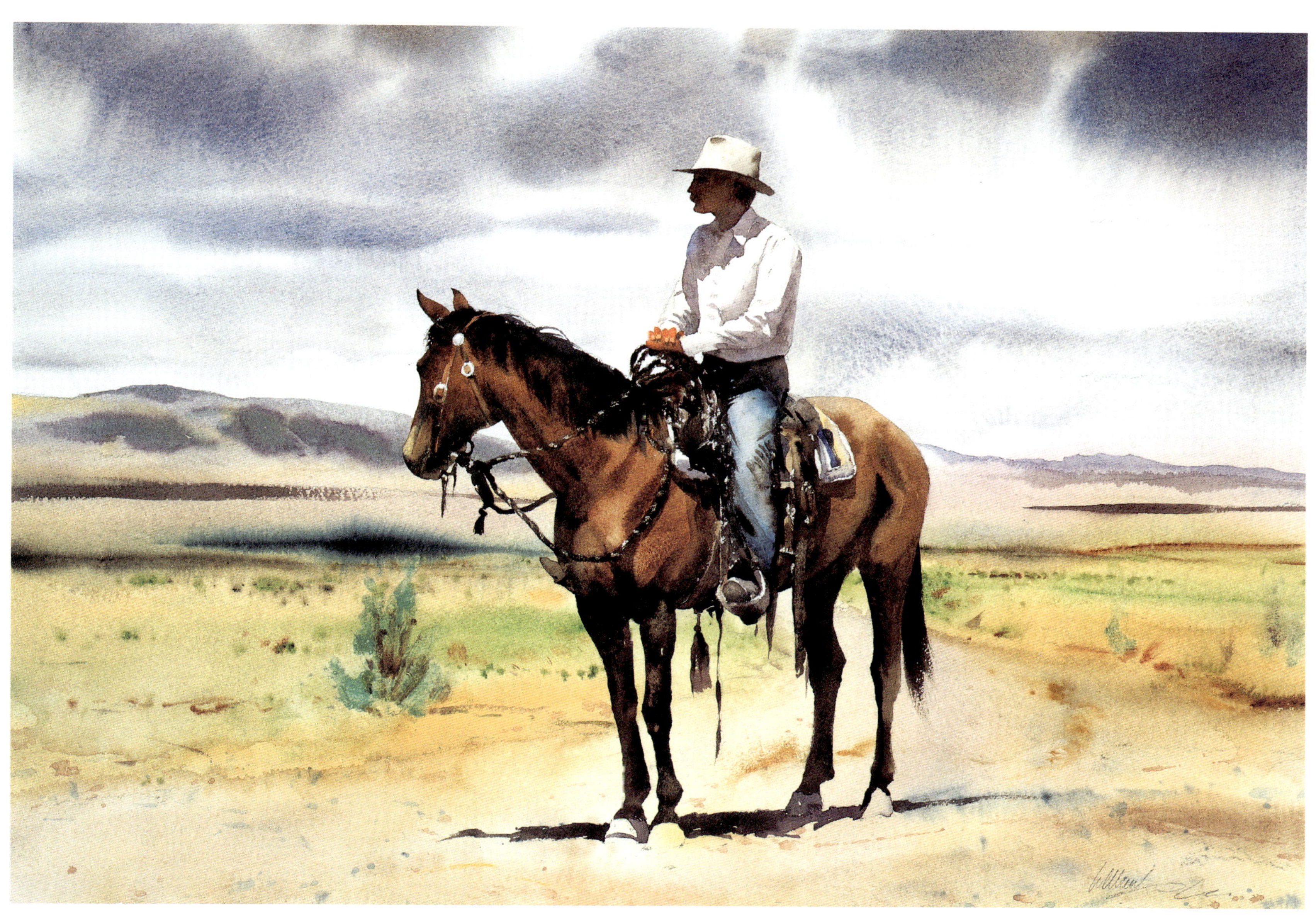

Scott Brown

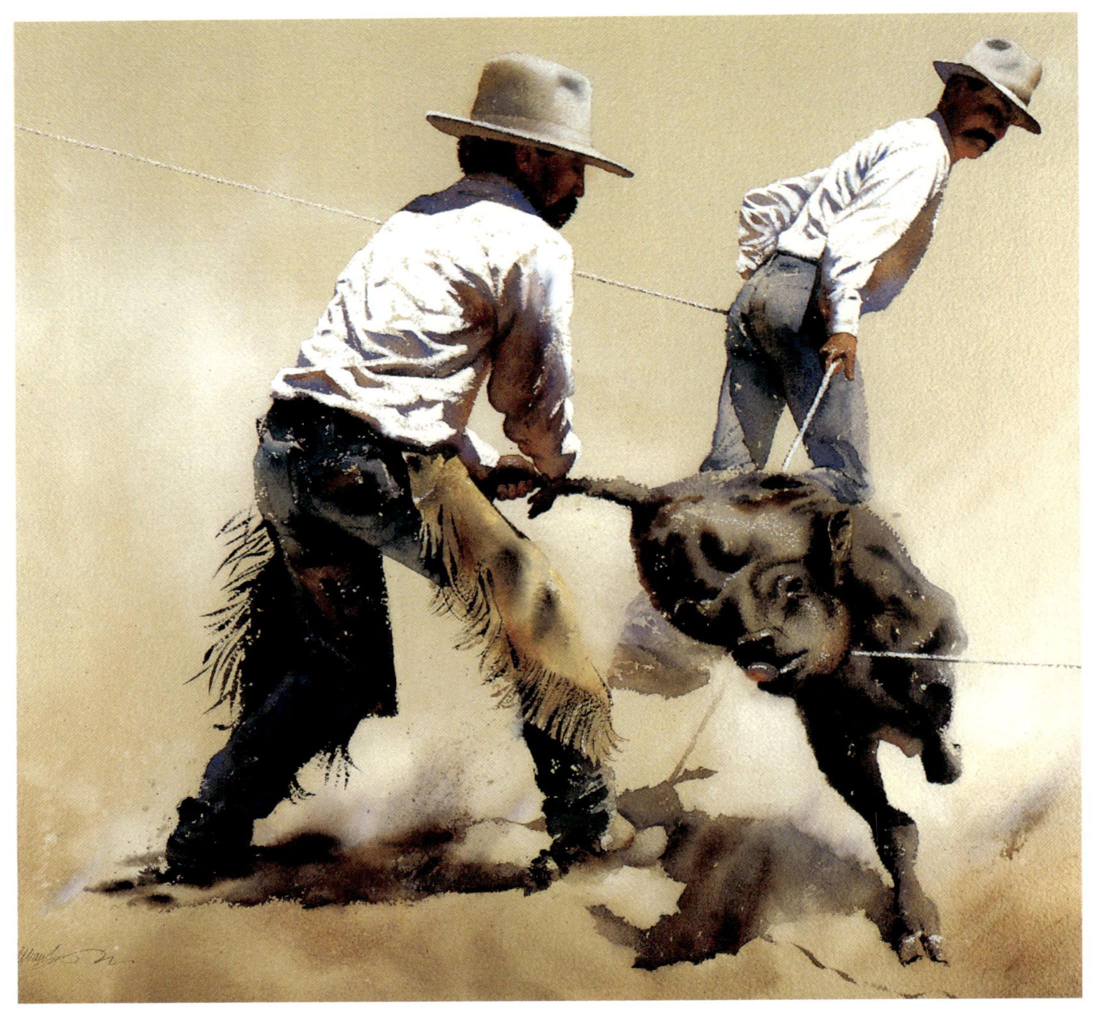

Pirouette

(OPPOSITE)
Branding

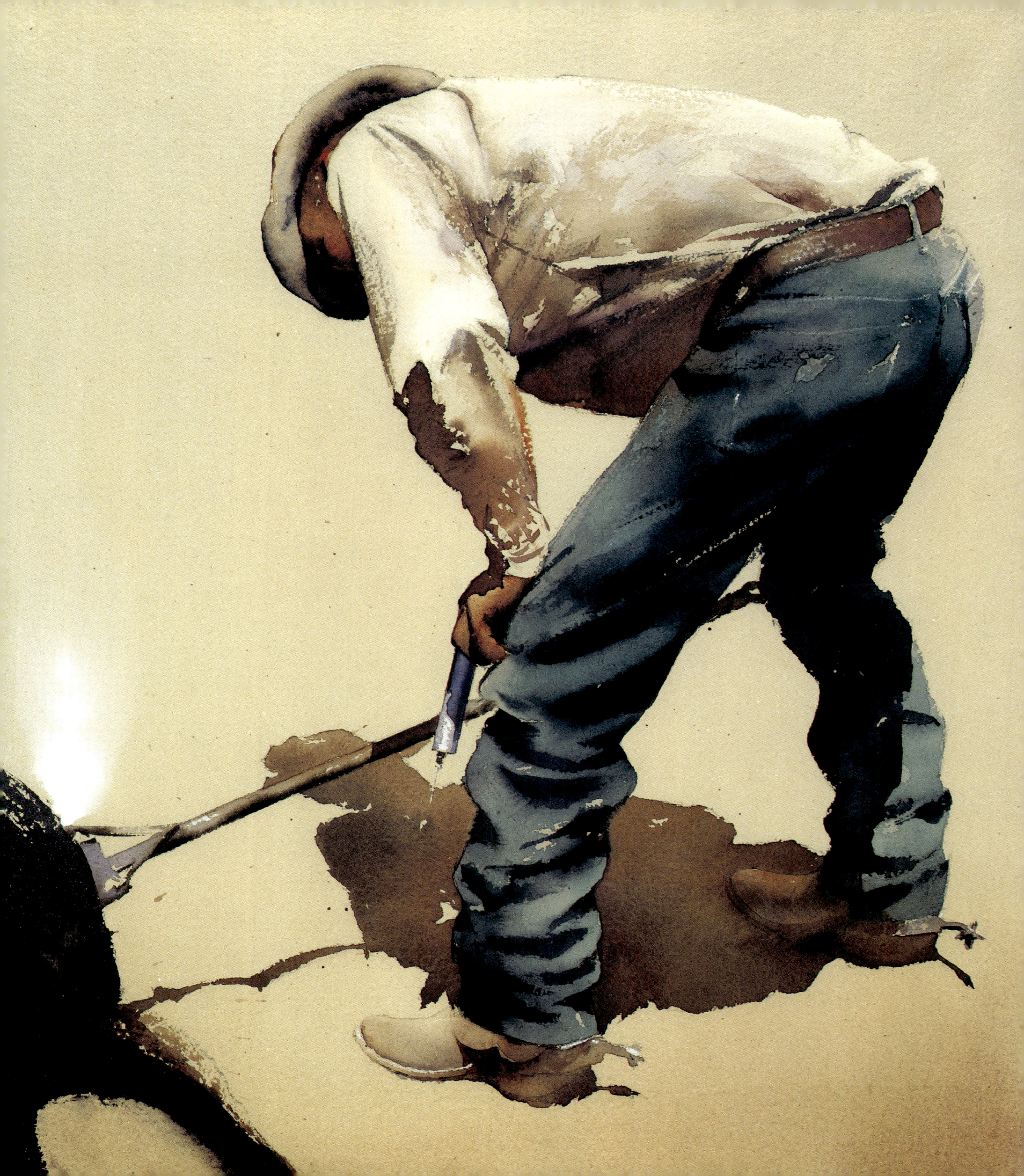

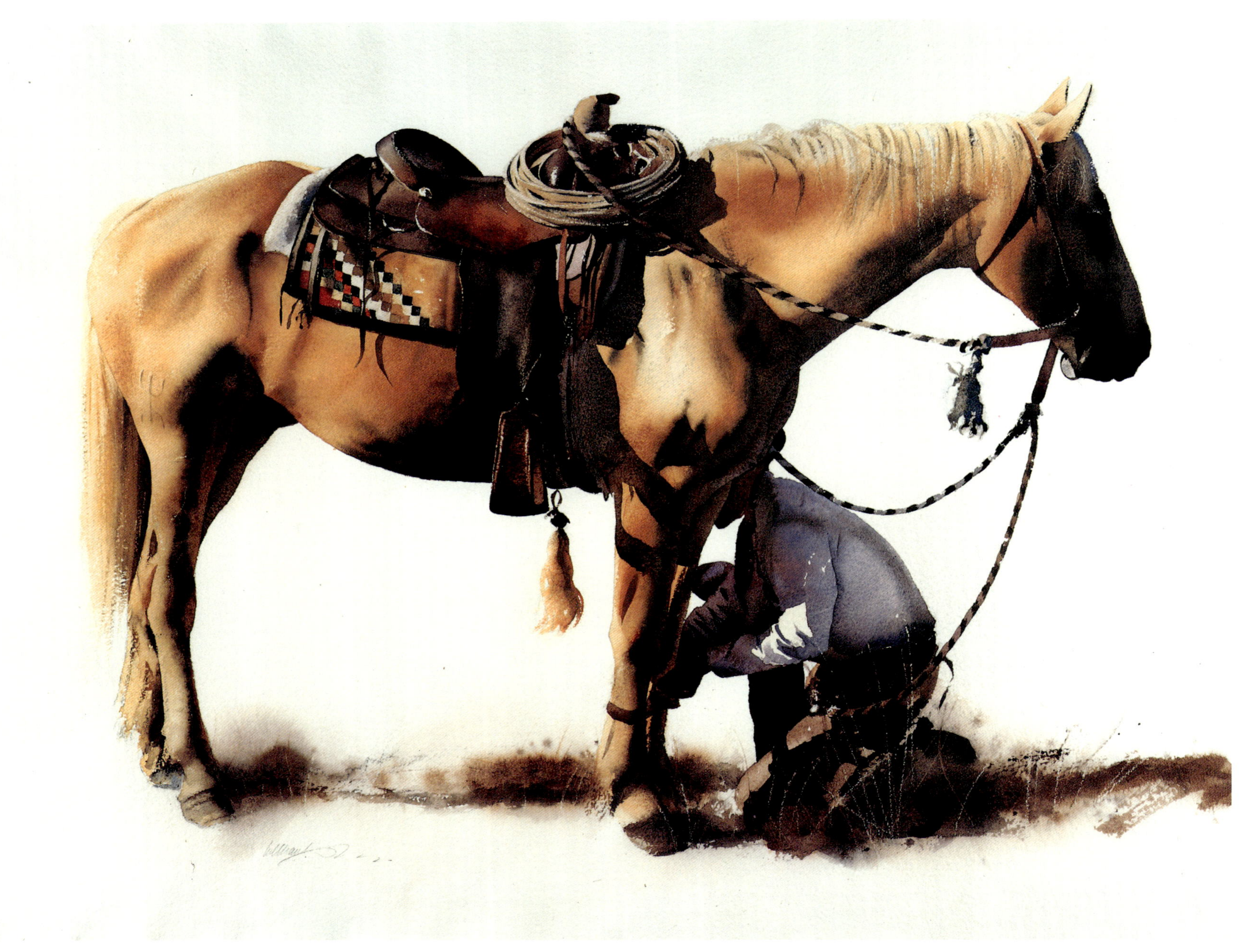

Hobbling

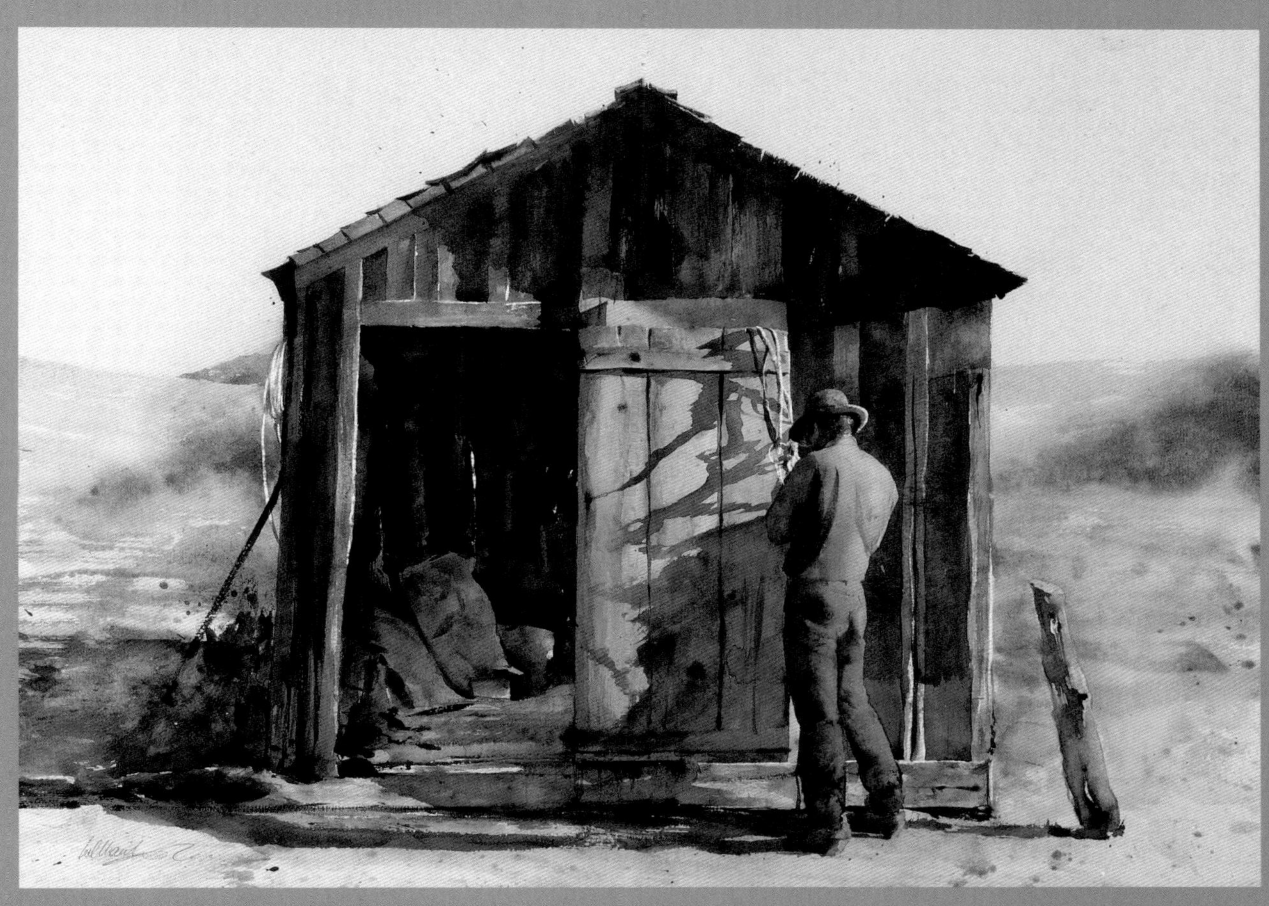

The Barn

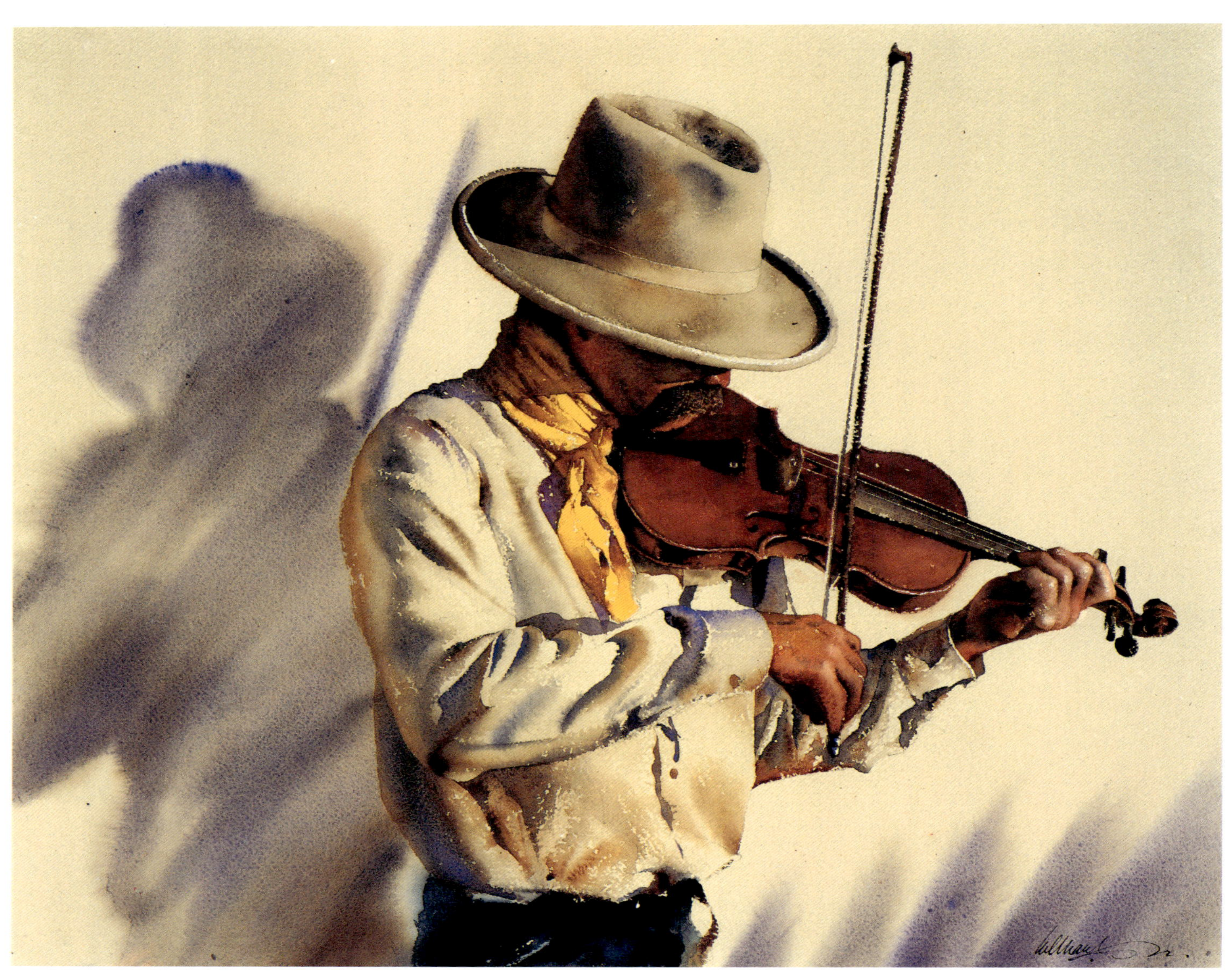

The Red Haired Boy

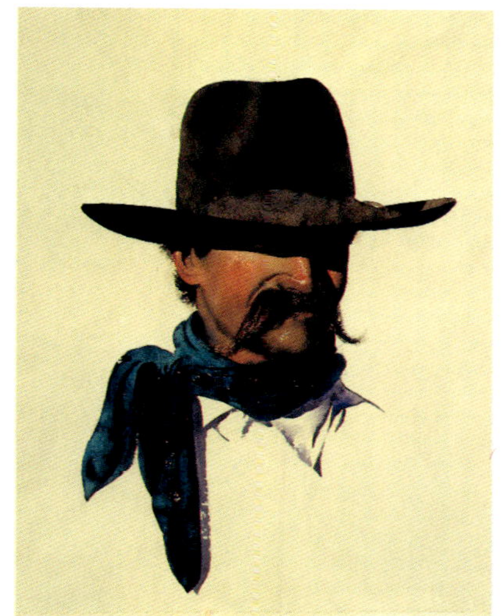

COWBOY culture has its own distinct musical tradition in which the favored instruments are the guitar, banjo, and fiddle. When you hear cowboys play, the campfire or the kitchen table never feels far away. Scott Brown is not only a great saddlemaker but also a fine fiddler who loves traditional Texas fiddle tunes.

(ABOVE)

Scott Brown, Quien Sabe Ranch

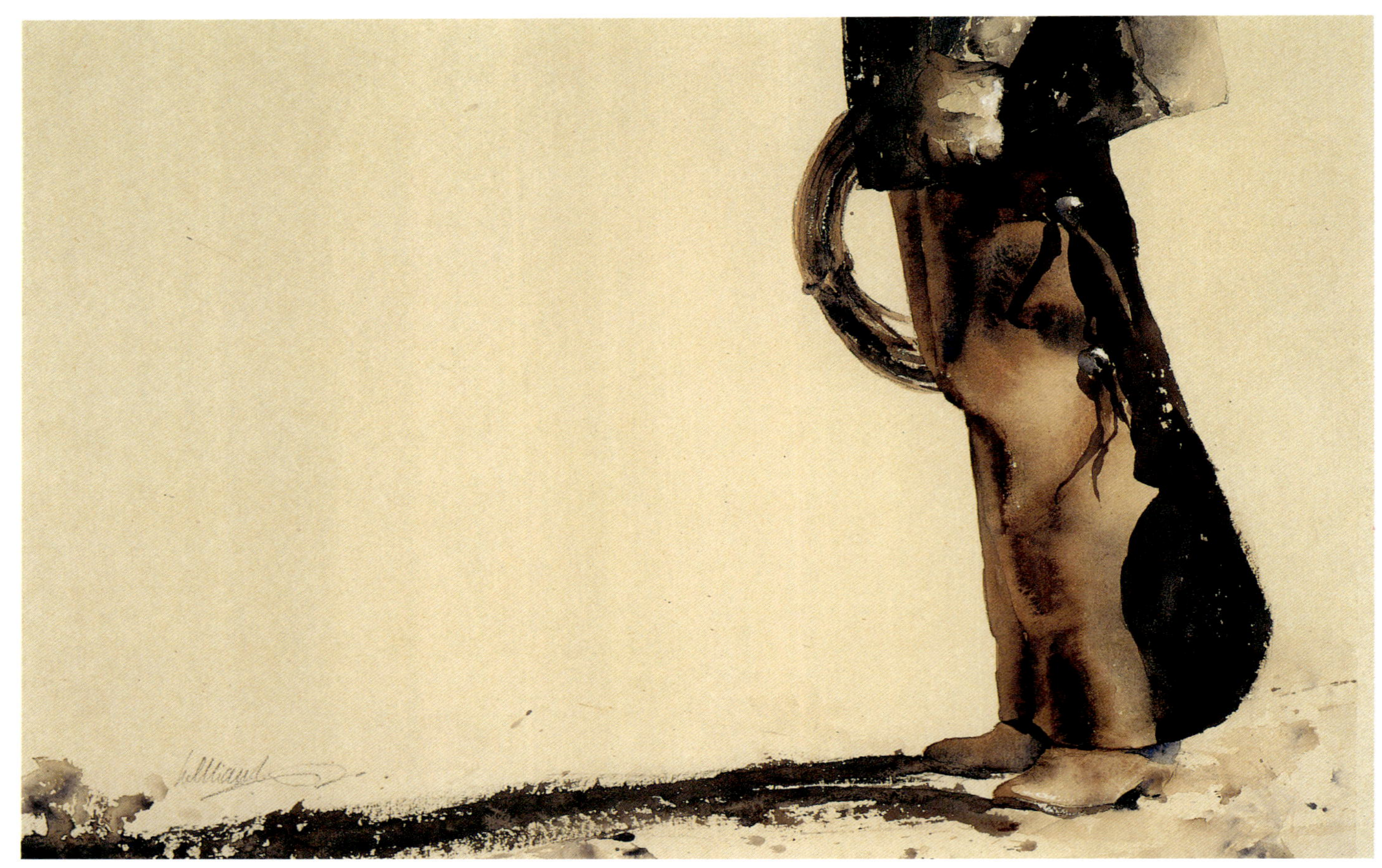

La Reata

(OPPOSITE)

Desert Dust

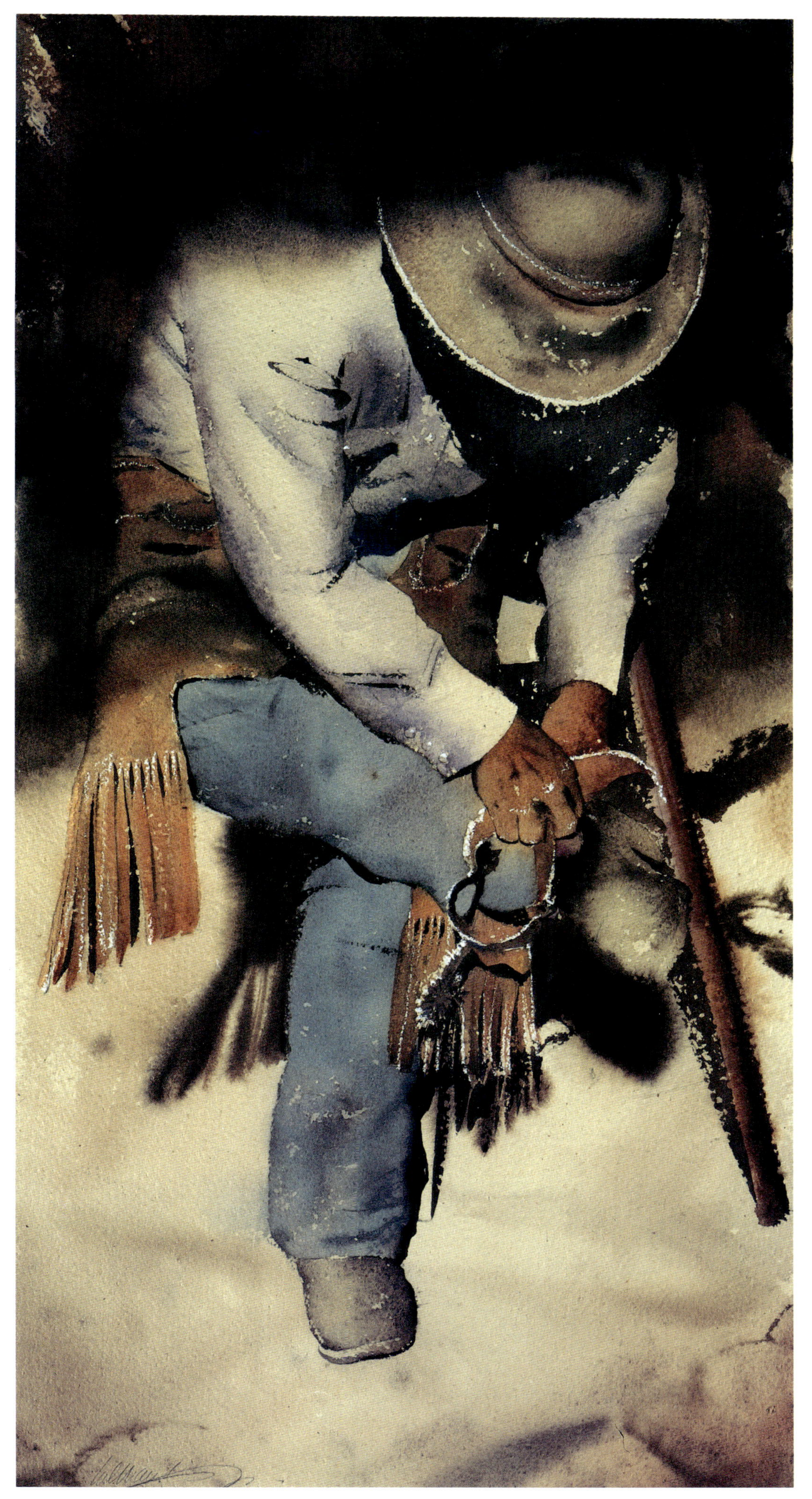

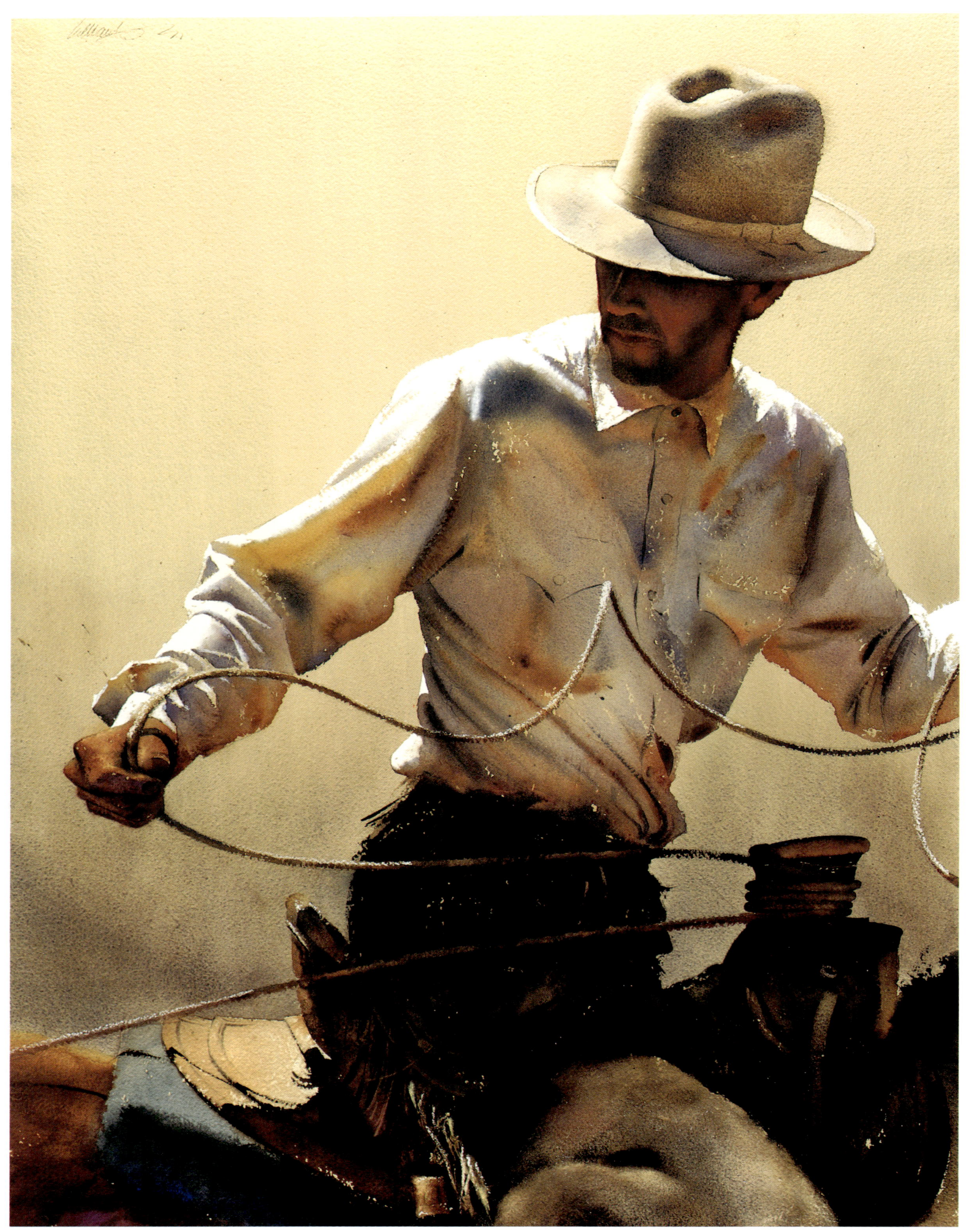

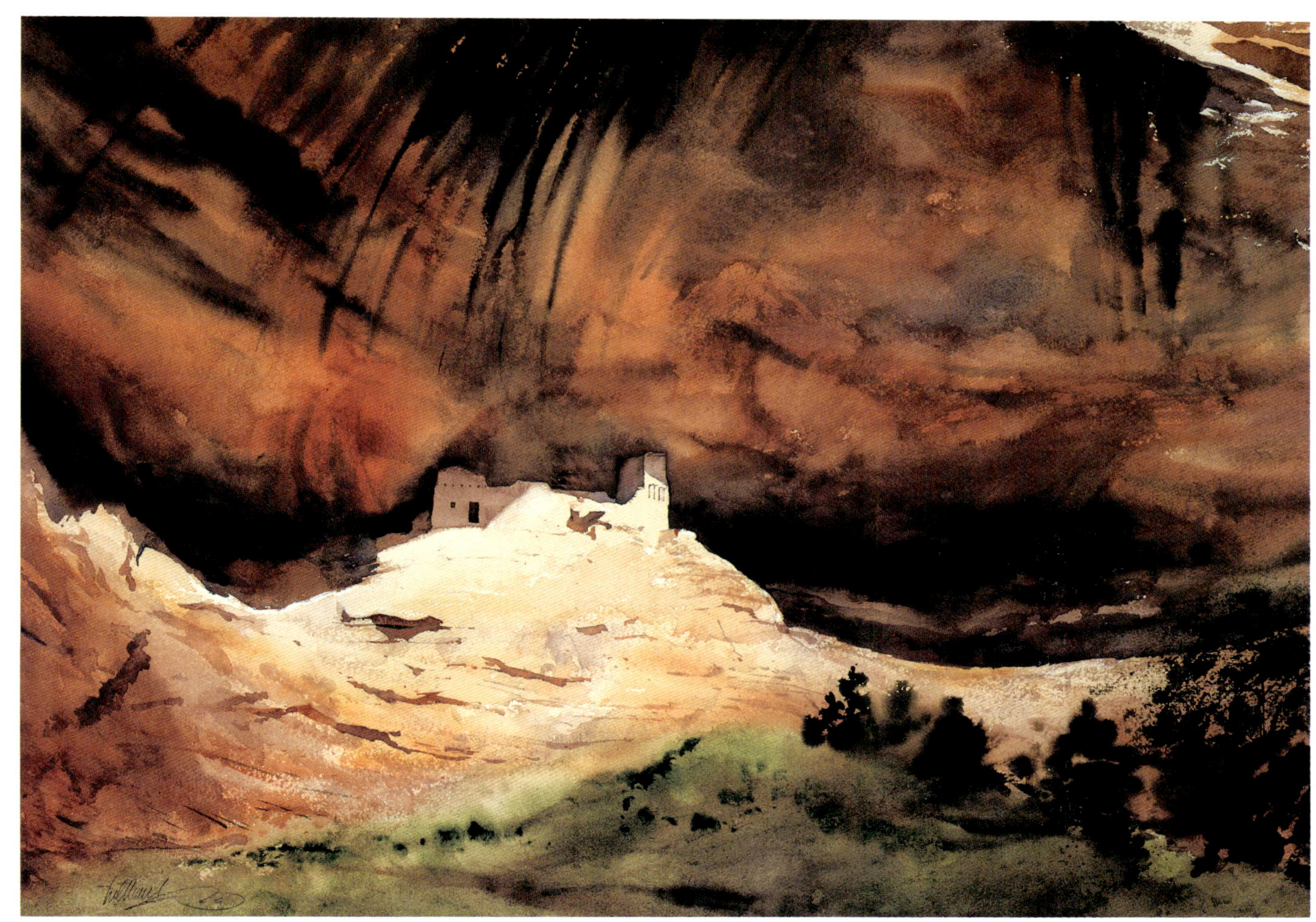

Canyon del Muerto

(OPPOSITE)

Coils

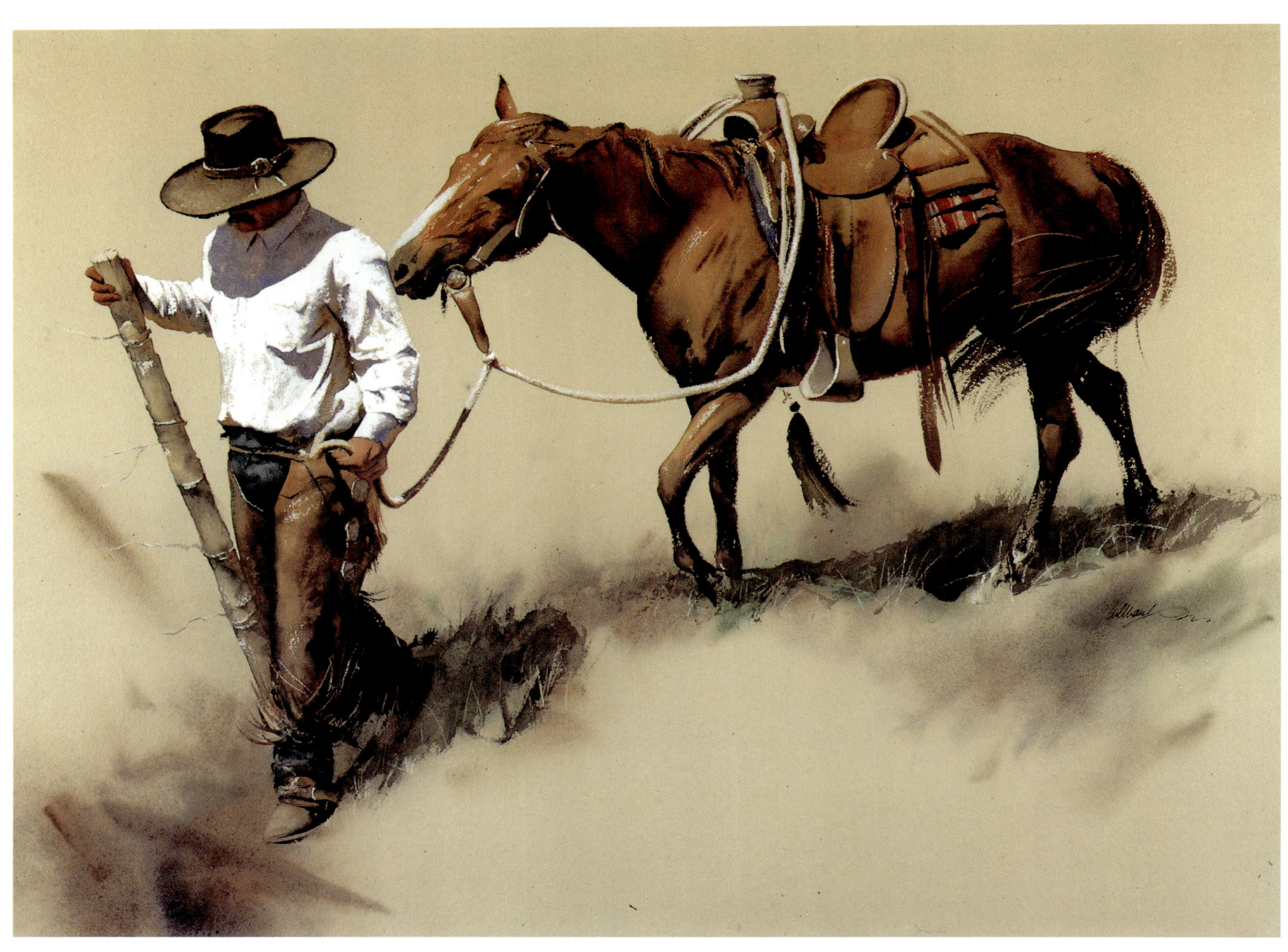

Jingle Bob, Geyser

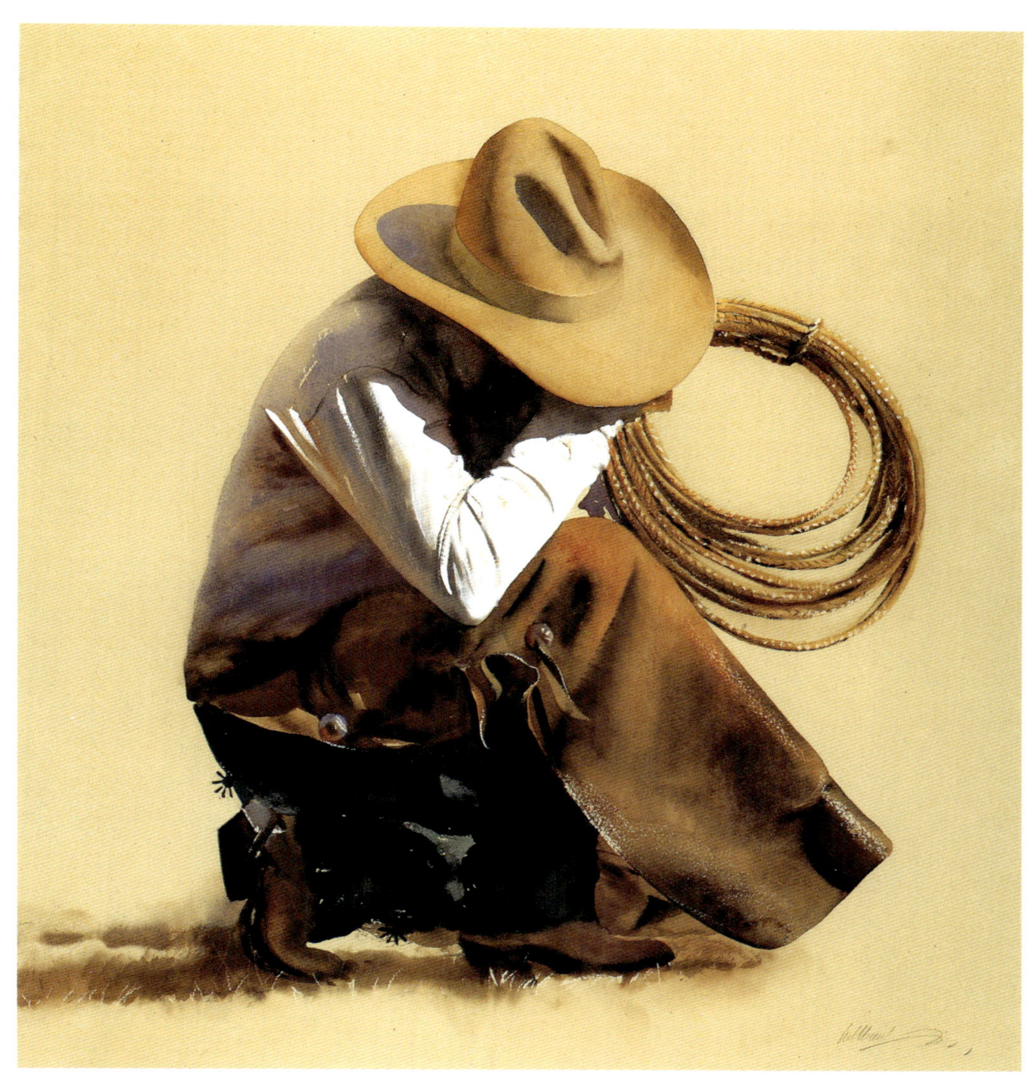

The Visitant

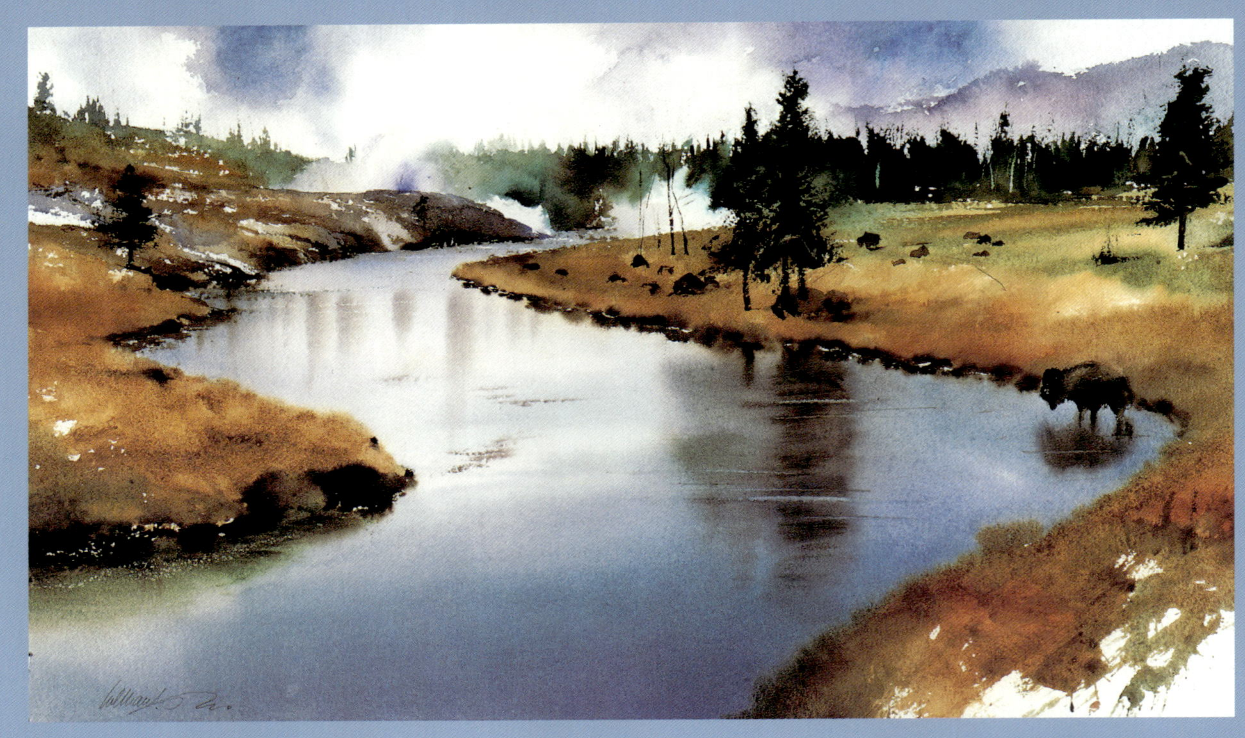

Yellowstone Buffalo Herd

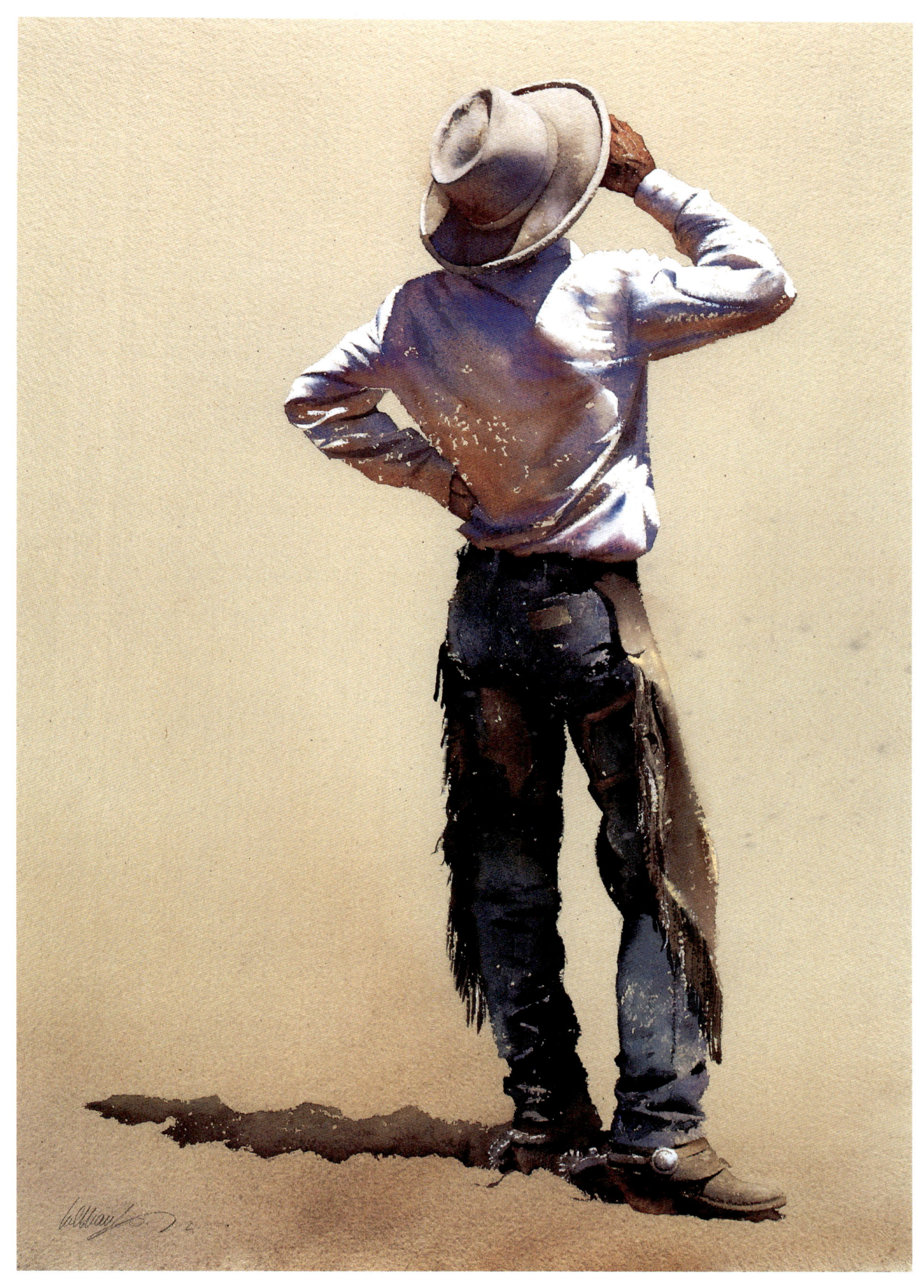

Tall Cool One

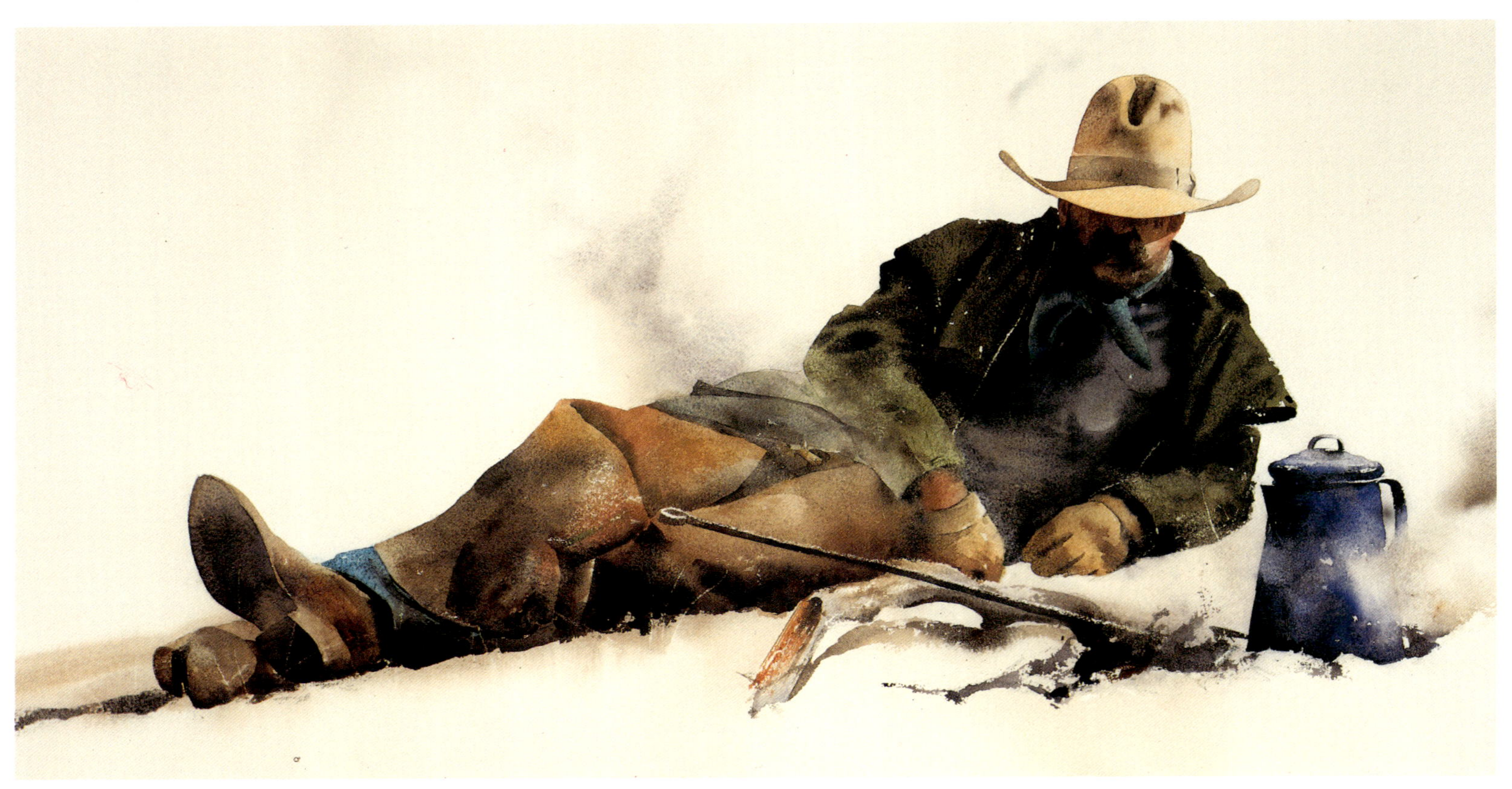

Watched Pot

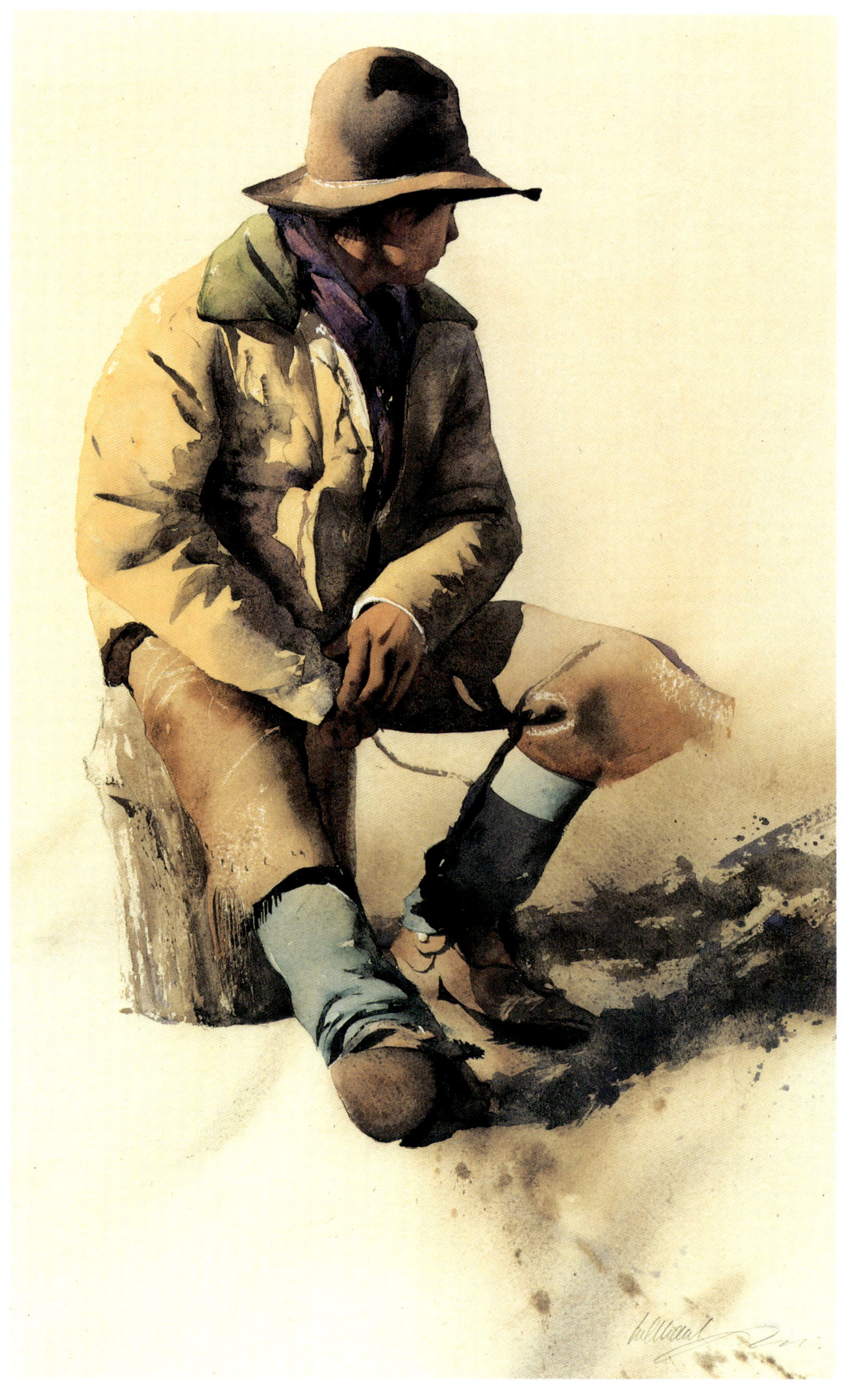

Campfire

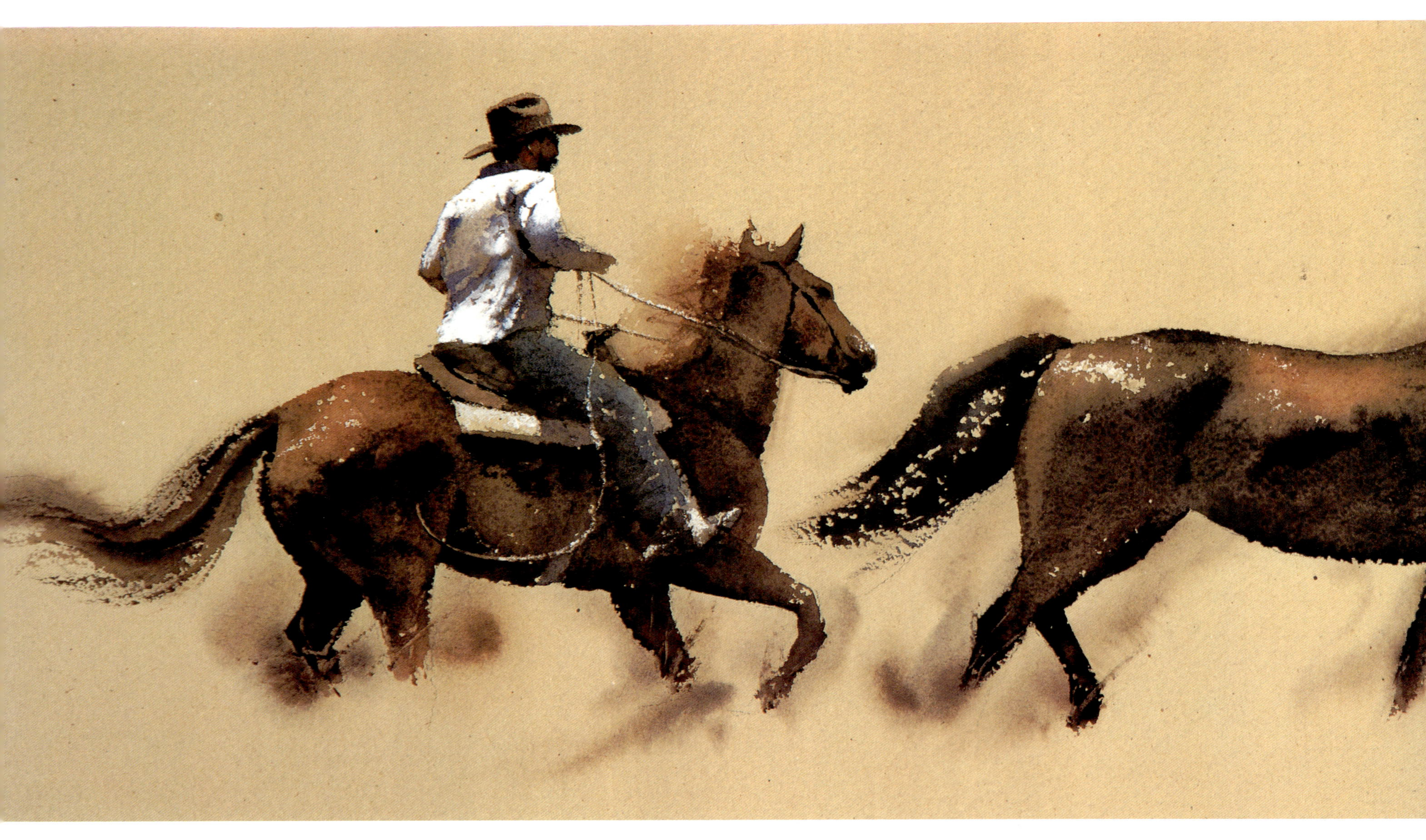

Bringing in the Cavvy

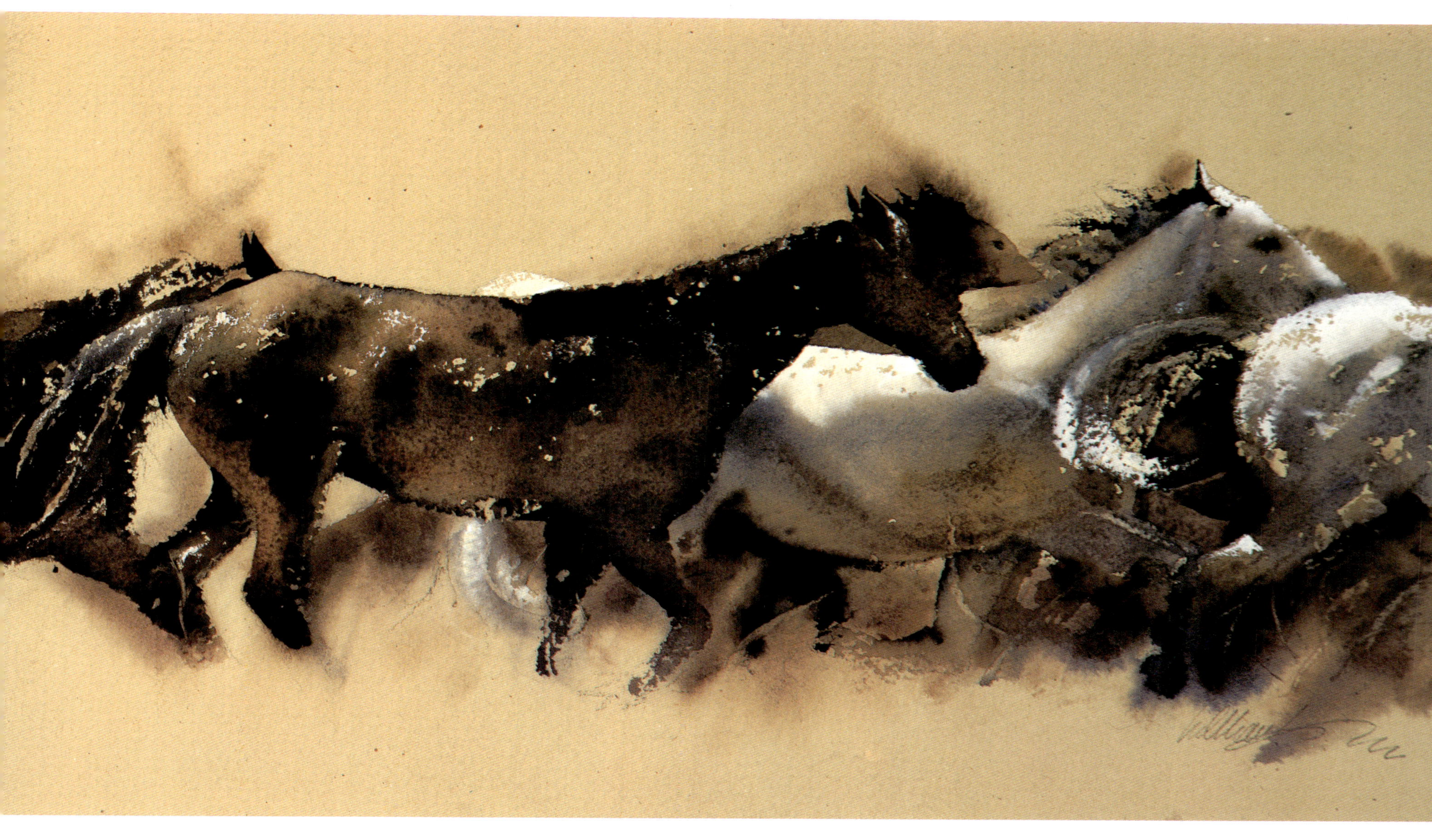

A caviada, or remuda, is a band of saddle horses ranches raise for their cowboys. It's not uncommon for ranches to have a cavvy of one hundred and twenty horses. Each man is responsible for his string of five to twelve mounts. Ranches are evaluated by the quality of their horses, and to many cowboys good horses and a fine cowboss are more important than pay.

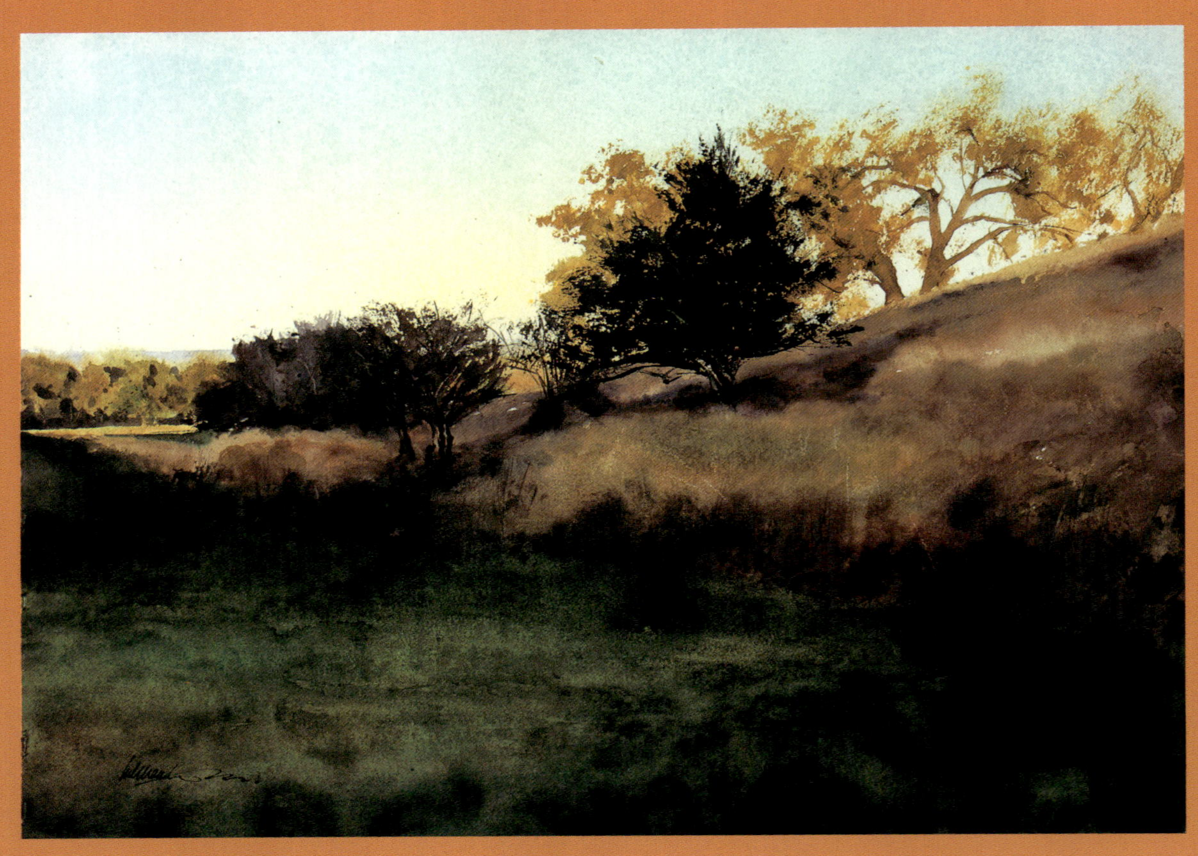

Hogback Orchard

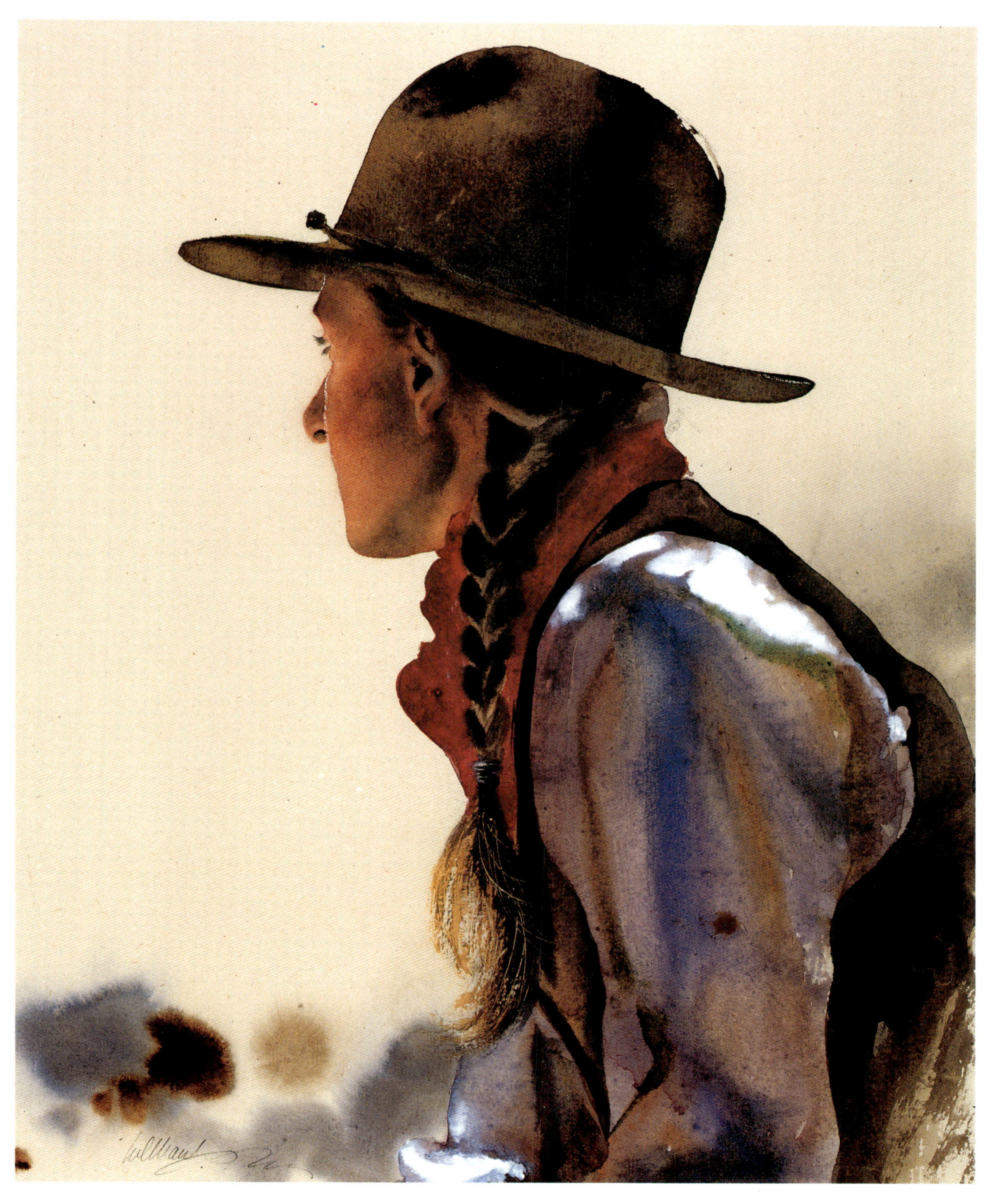

Colleen Watt

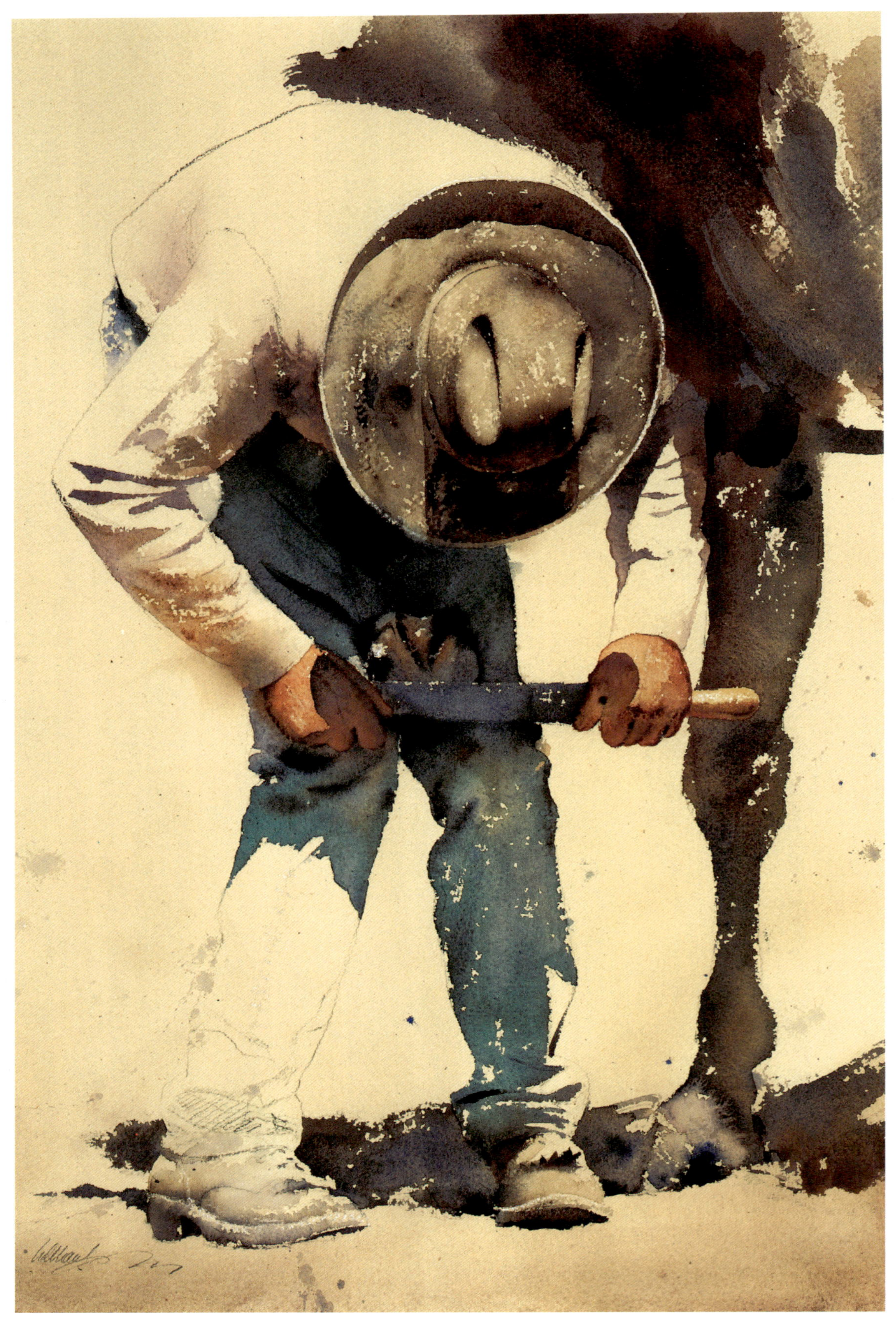

The Rasp

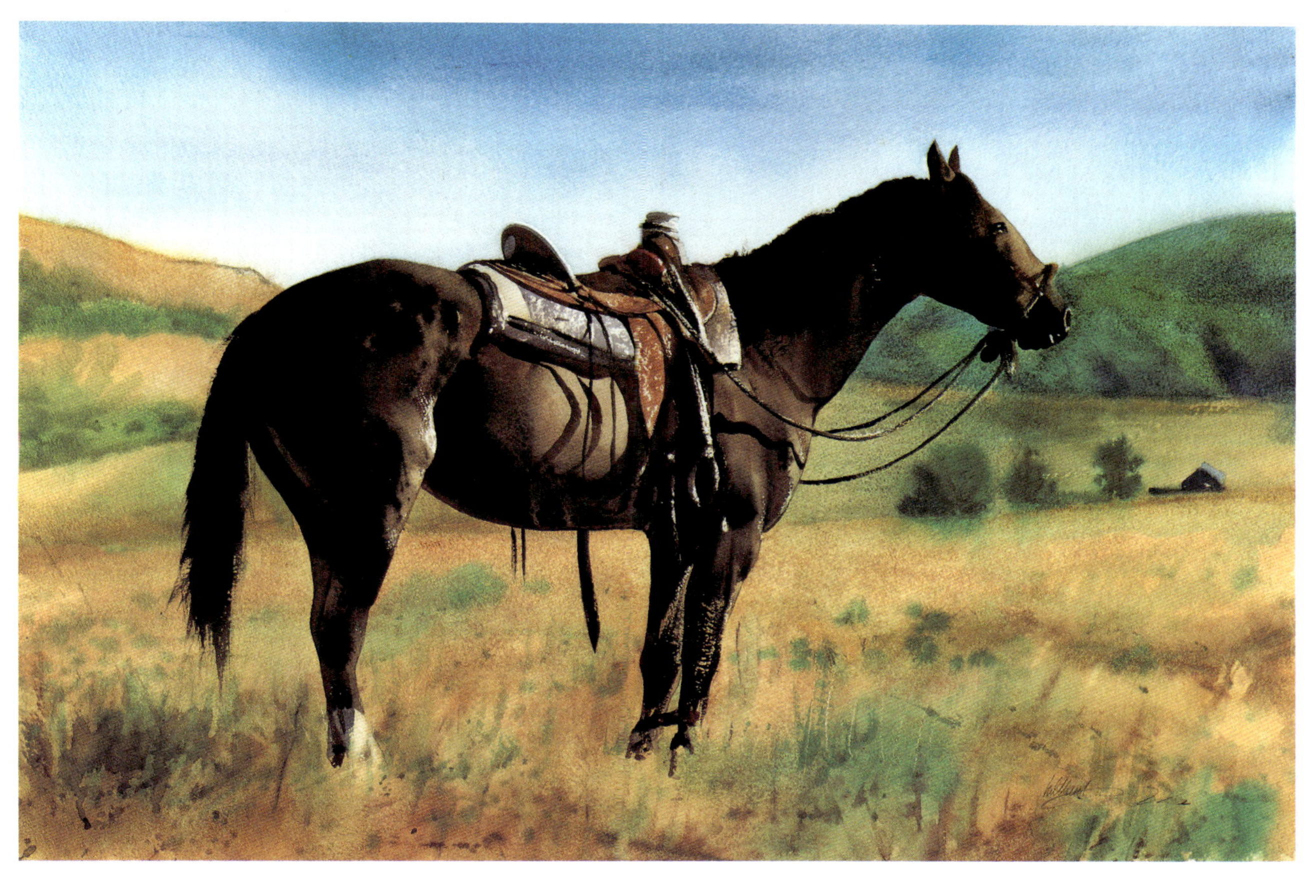

Hobbled

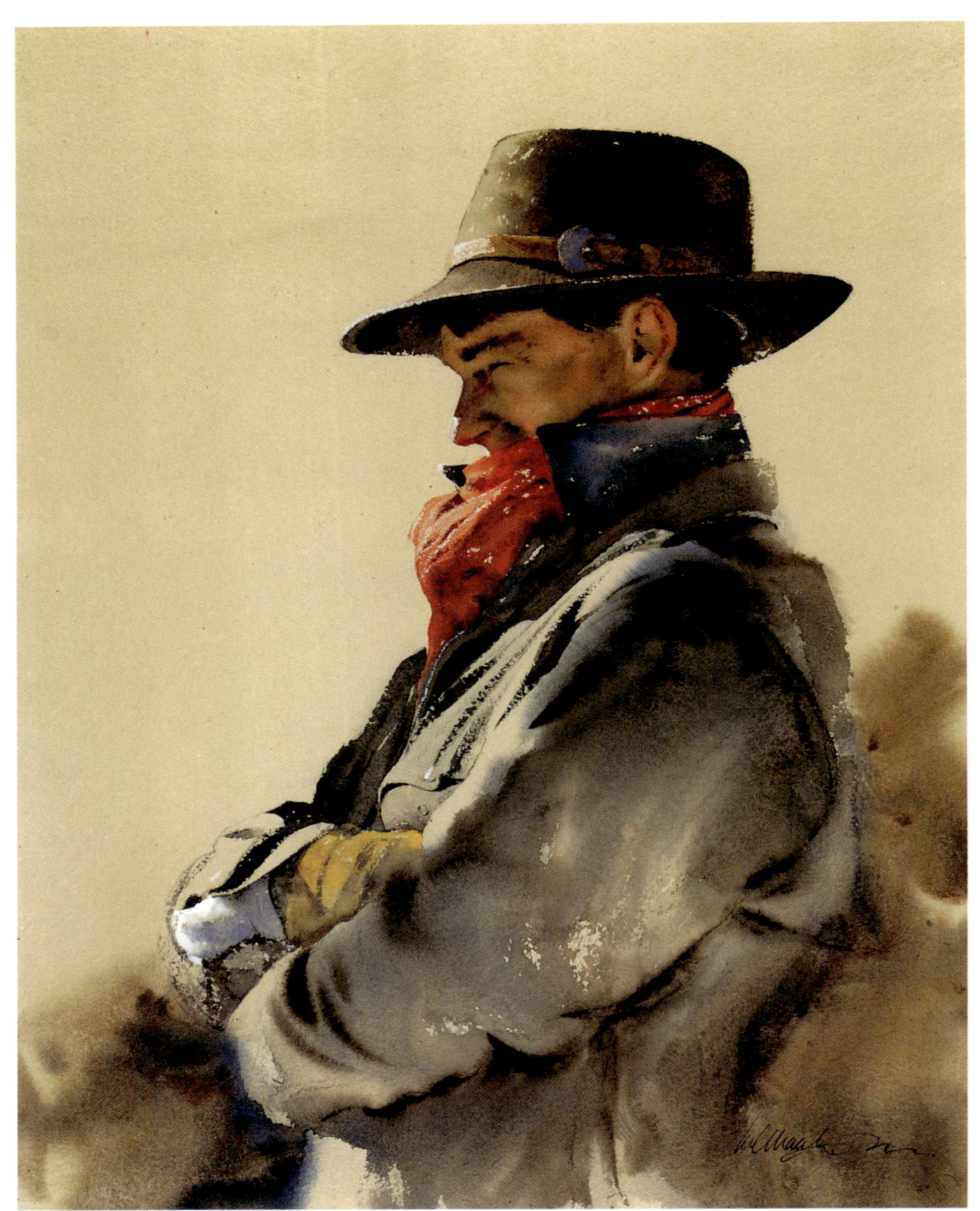

Louie Hawkins

(OPPOSITE)

Bunkhouse

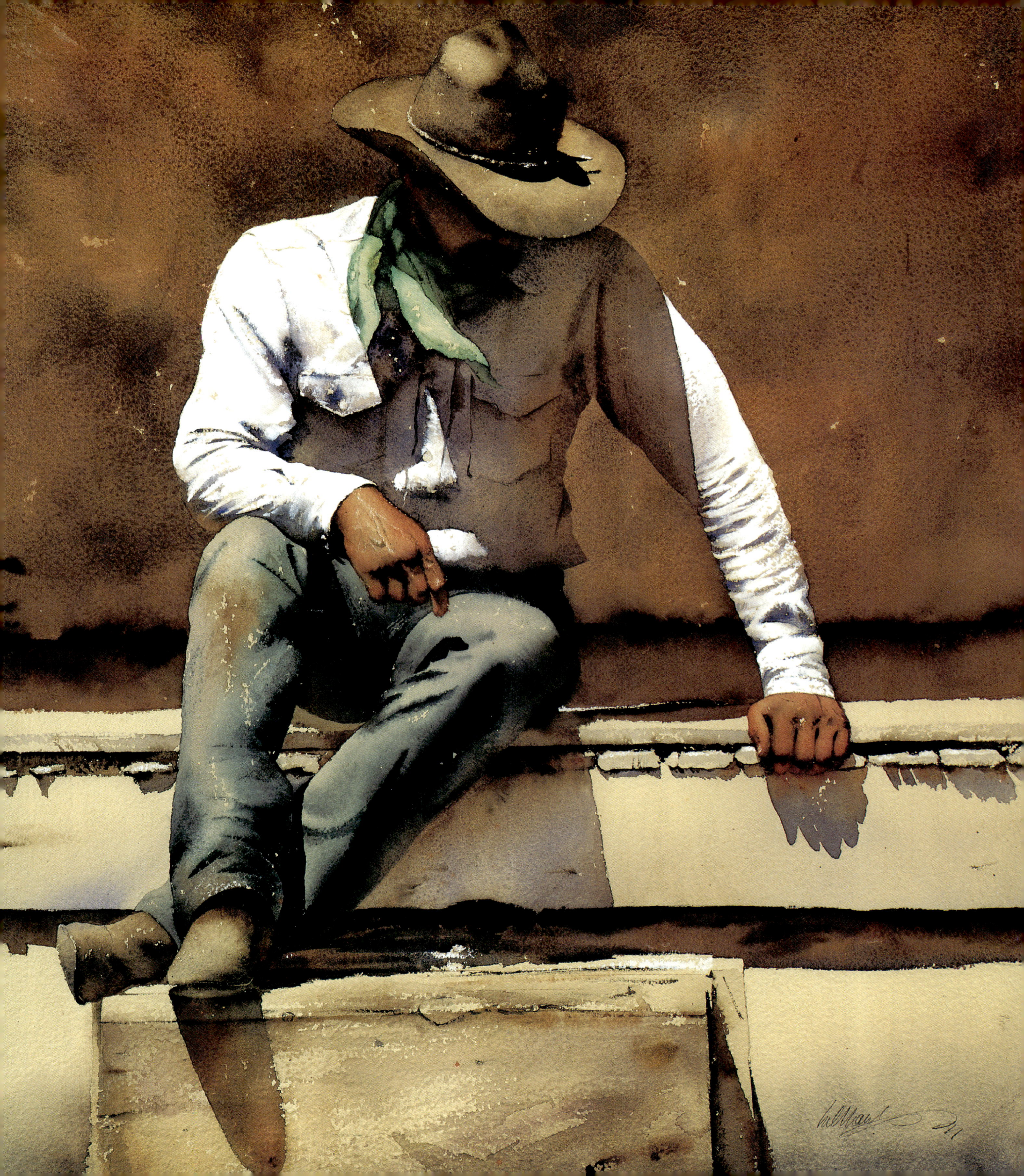

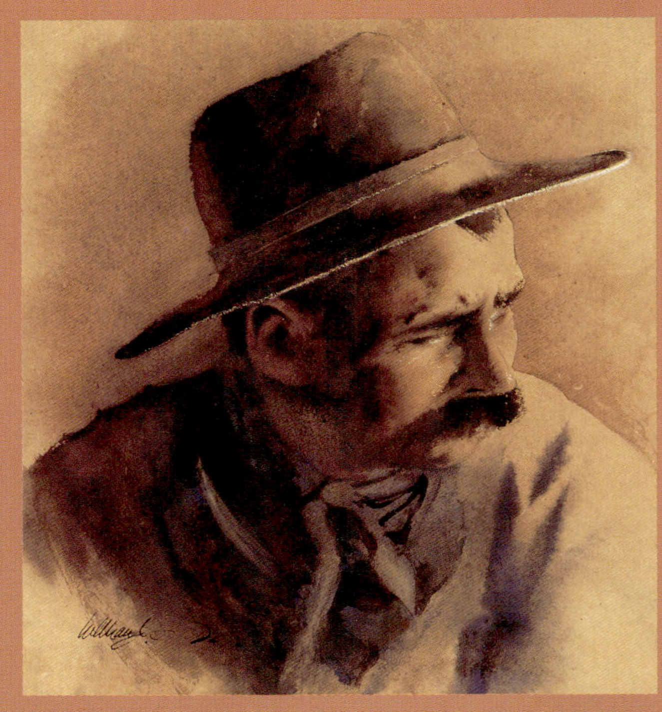

Scott McKay

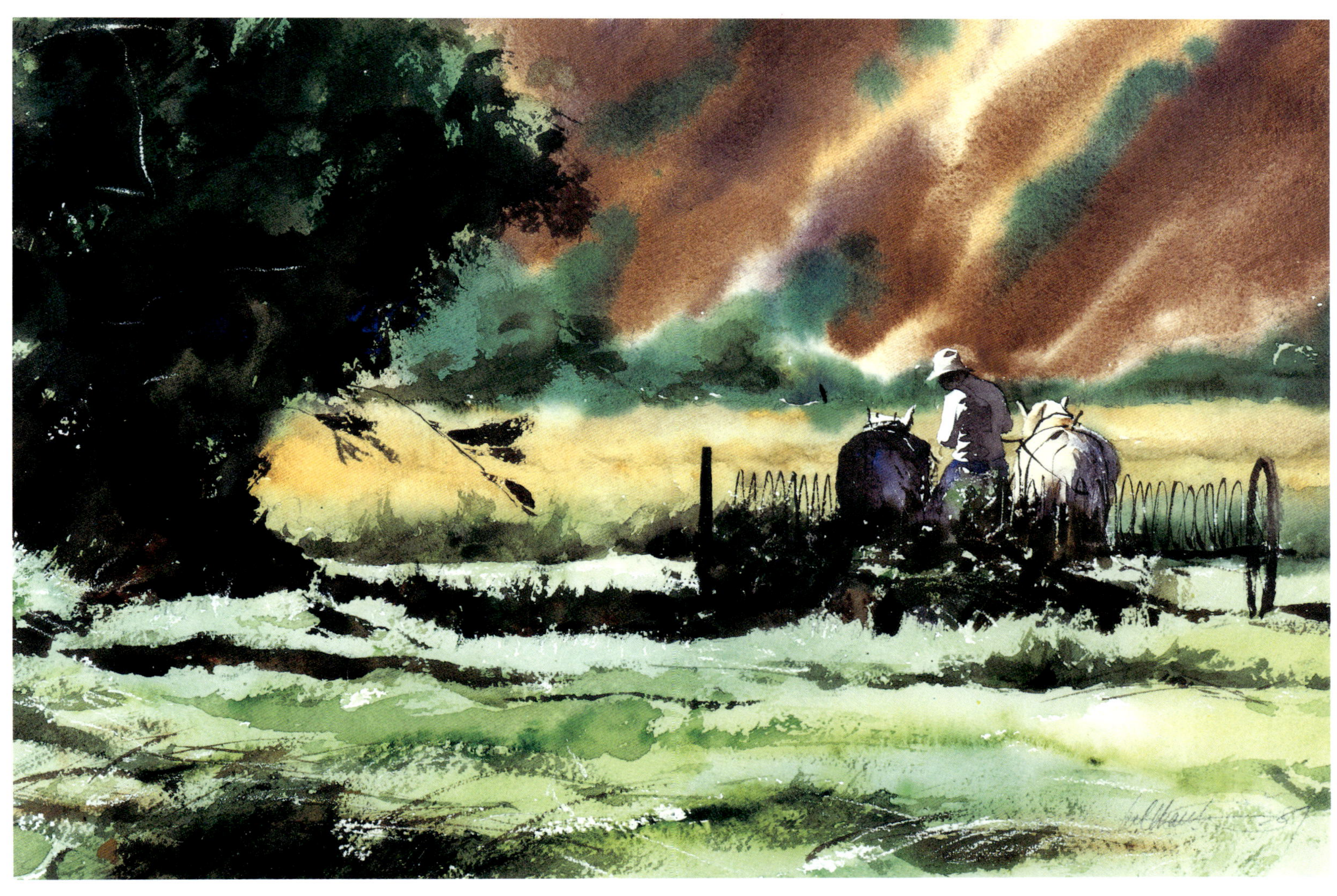

The Hay Rake

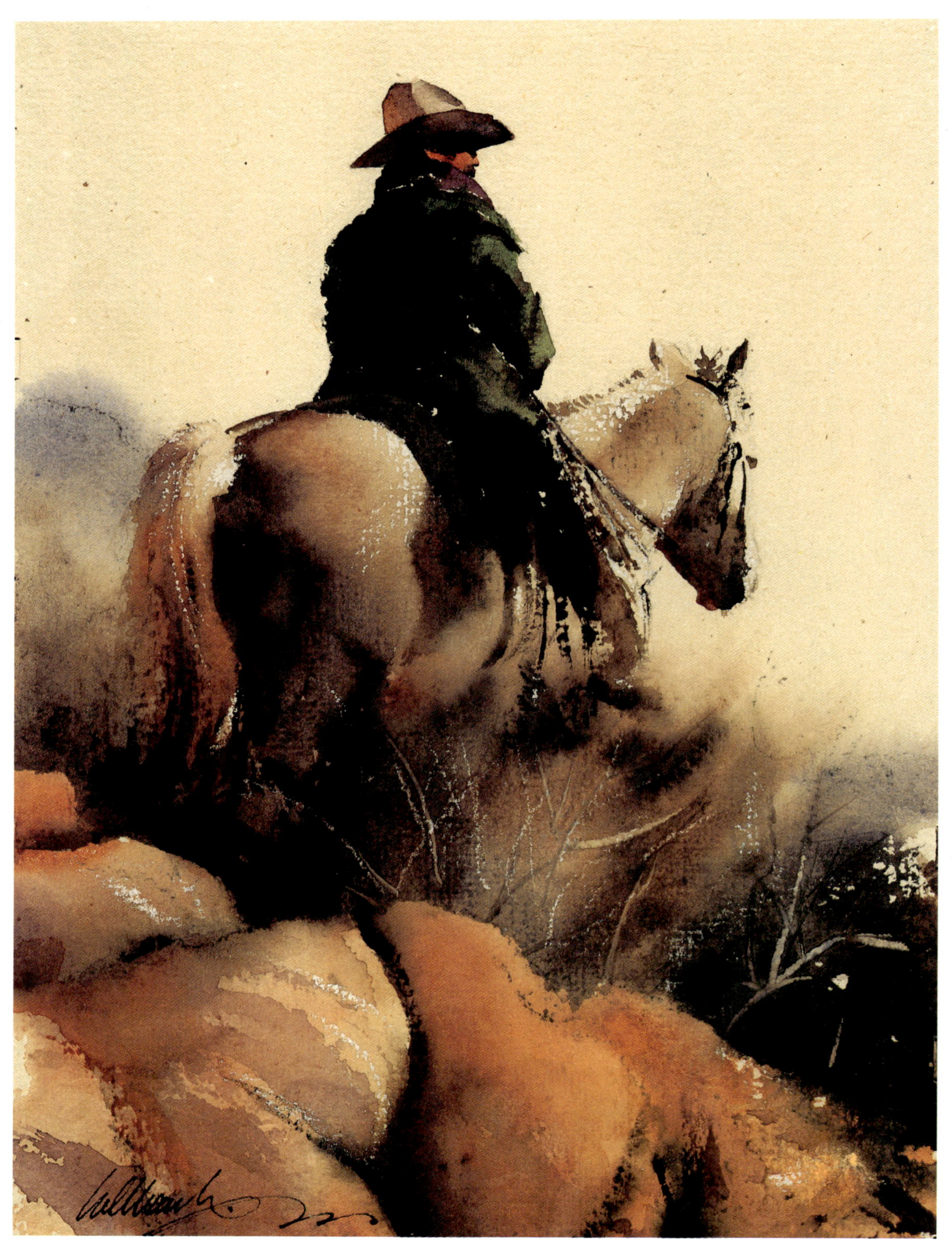

The Big Valley

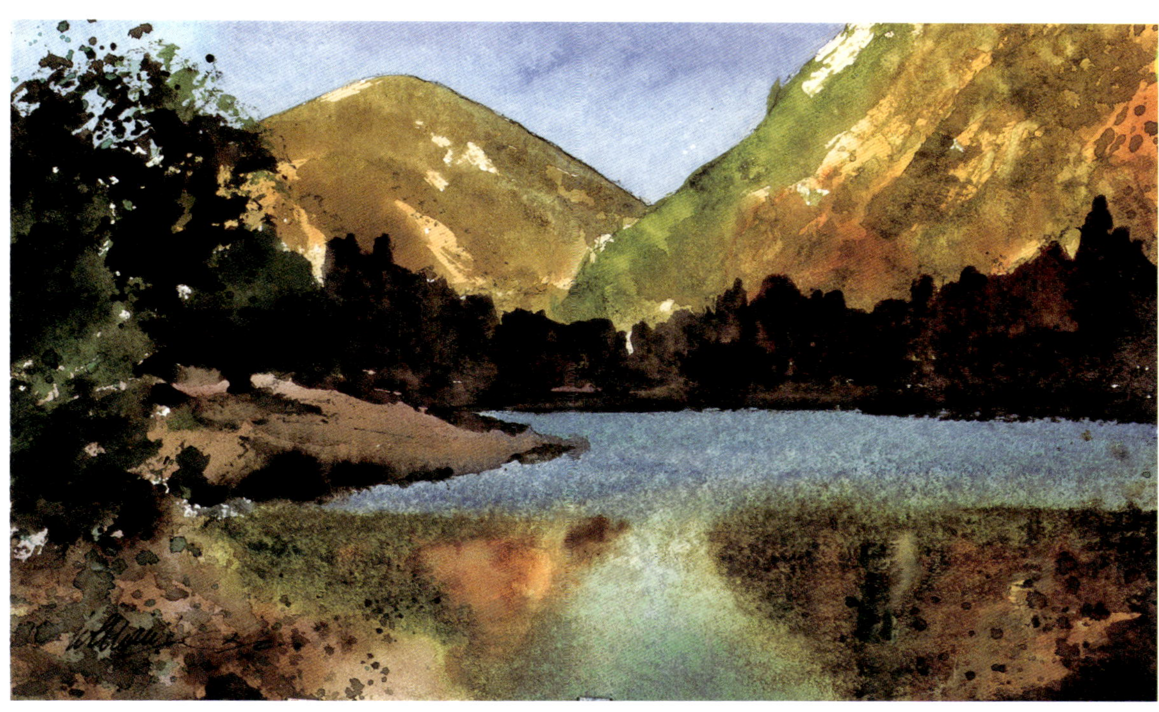

Questa Reservoir

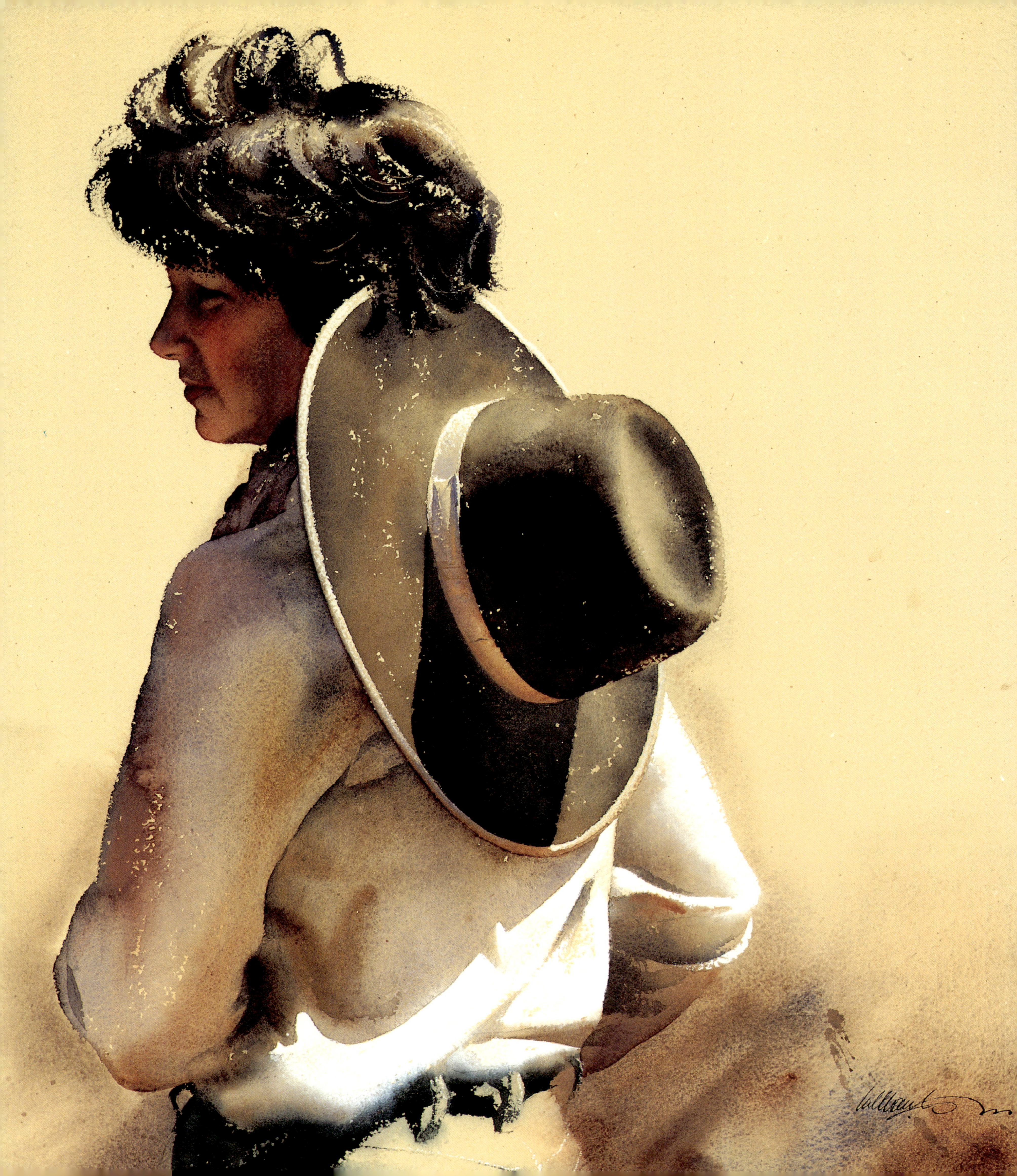

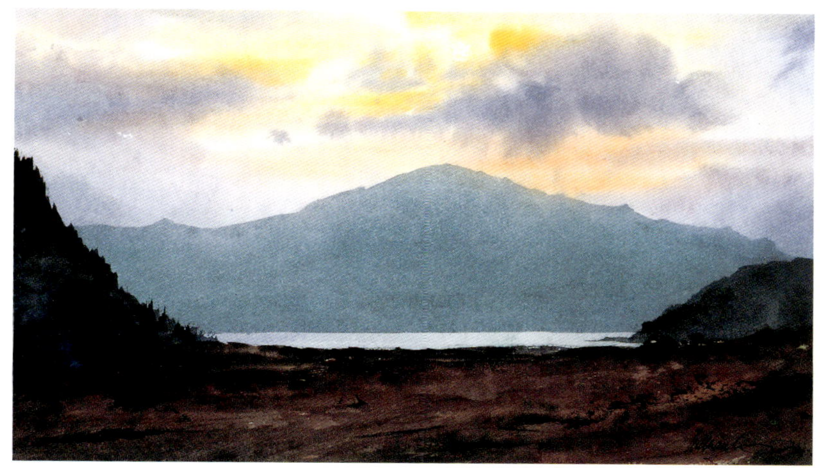

RANCH WOMEN have a staggering array of responsibilities. Some run ranches by themselves. Besides having breakfast on the table before sunup, they must be able to assist in difficult stock births, shoe horses, and even buy bulls. Toni Schutte is a wife, the mother of two, a fine horsewoman, a hairdresser, and a gifted artist.

(OPPOSITE)
Mrs. Schutte

(ABOVE)
Caledonia

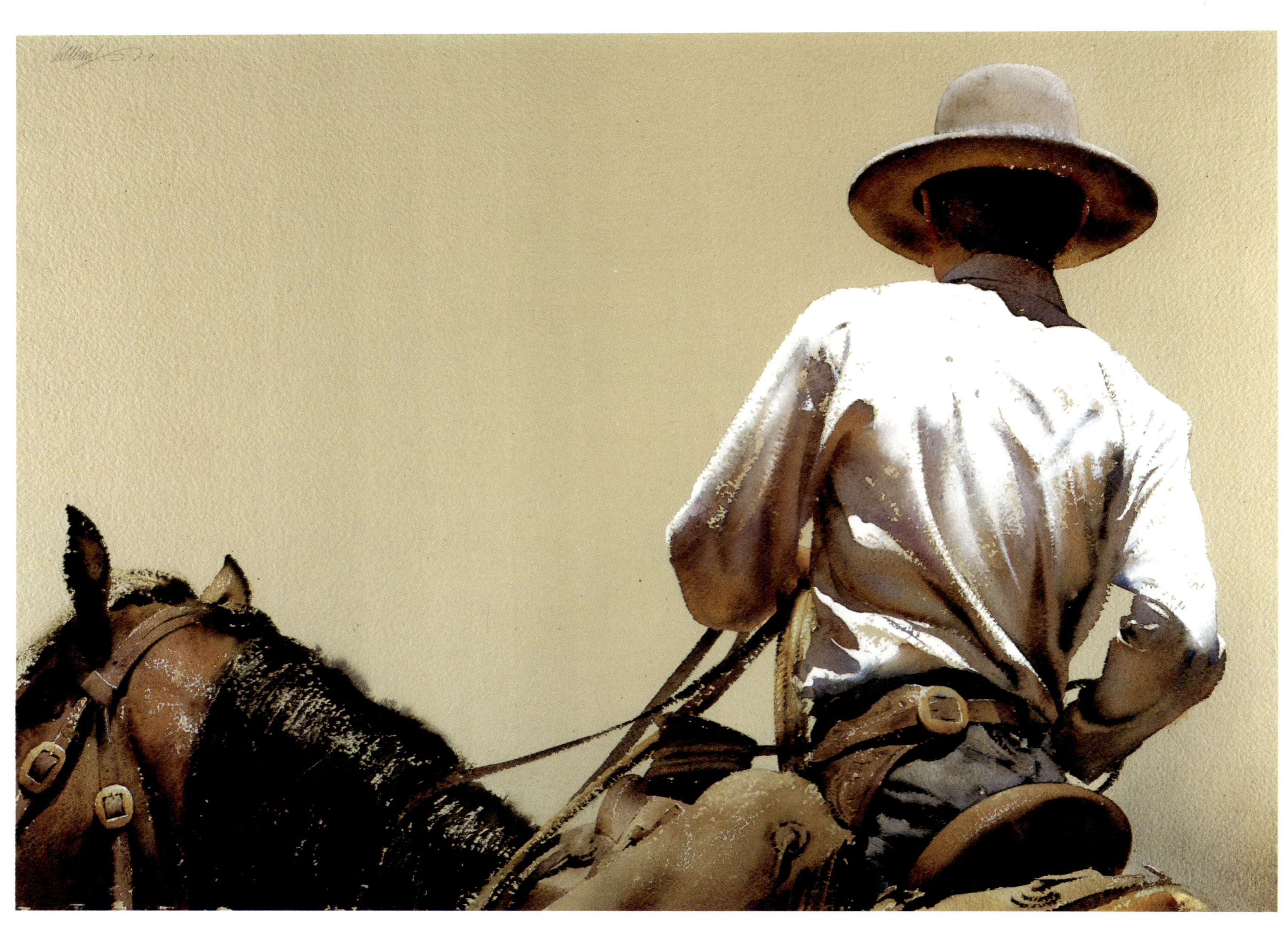

Battle Mountain Branding Trap

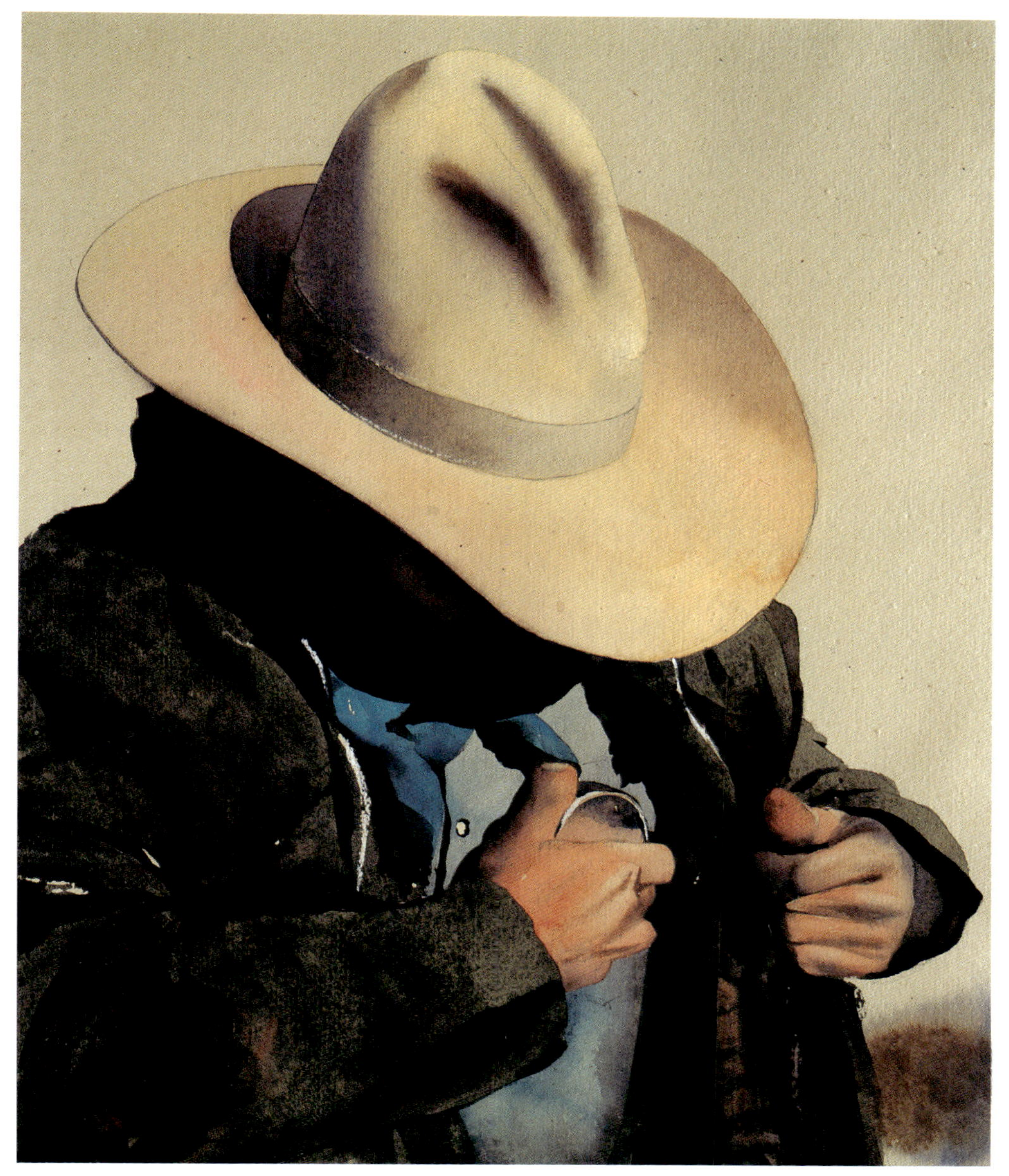

Cowboy Cannister

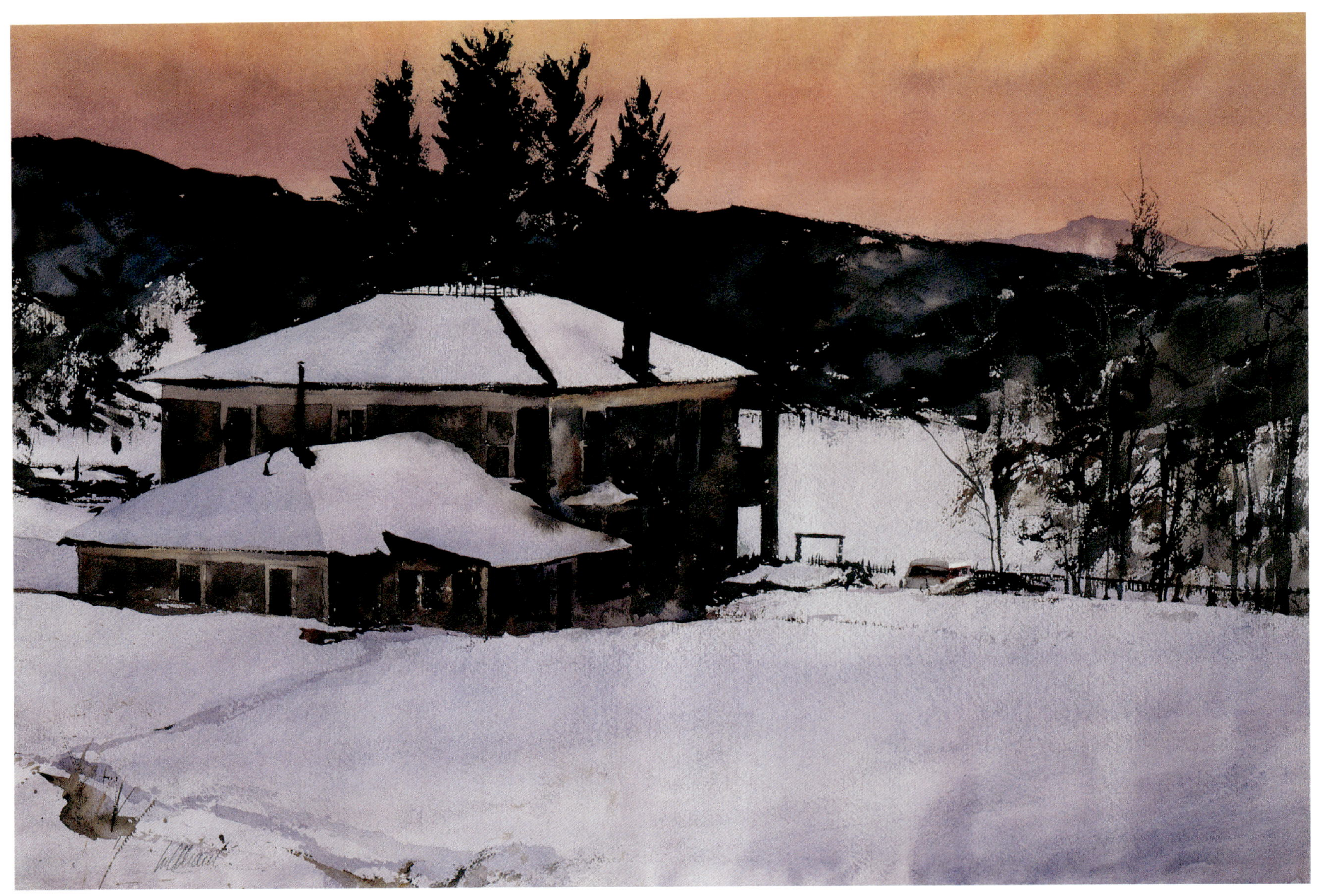

Reverie

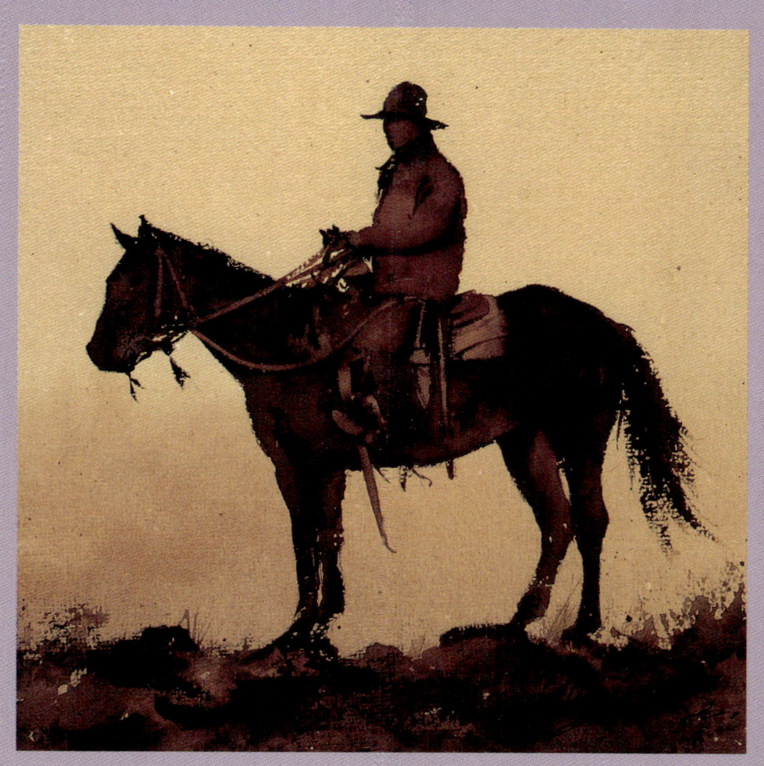

Montana

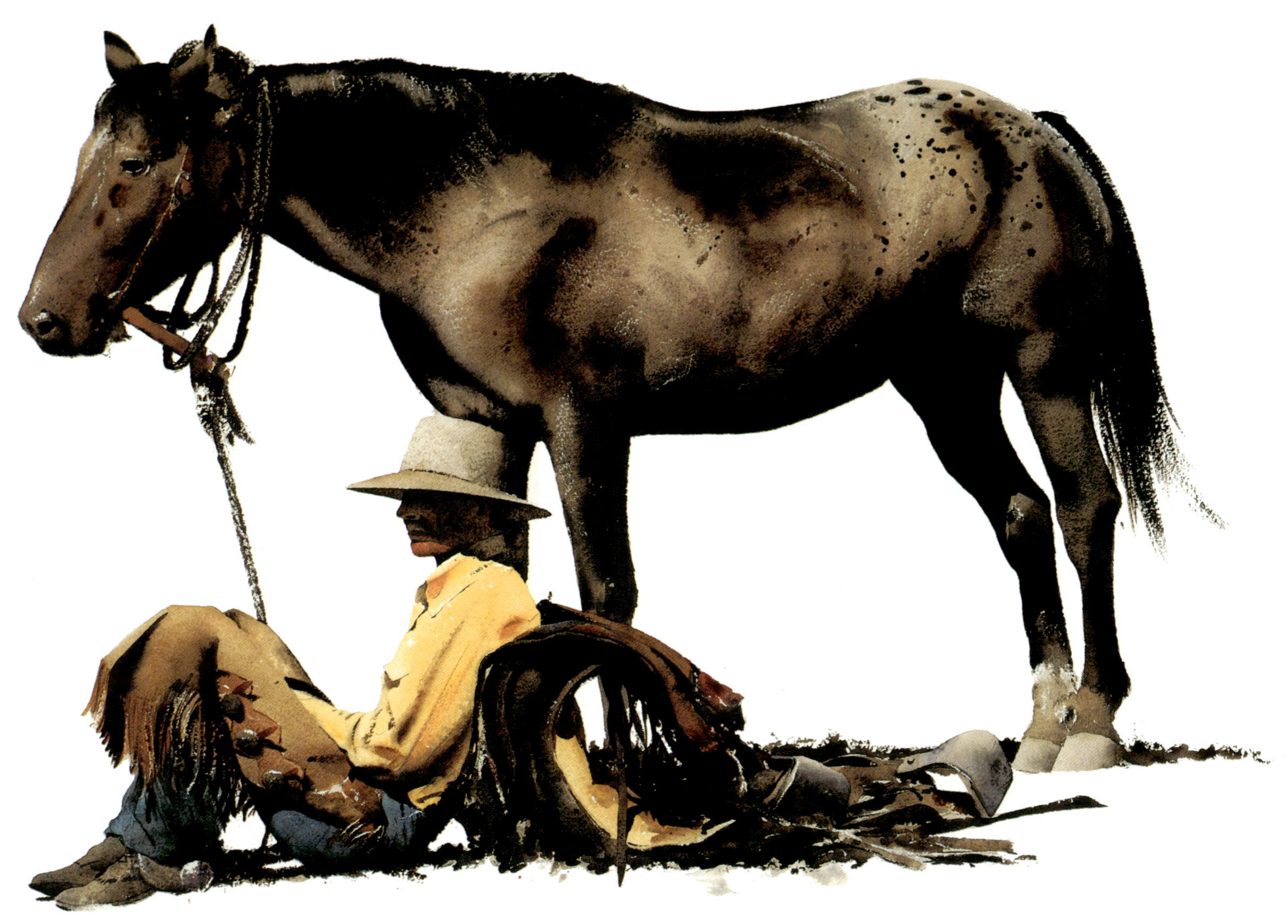

Bill Black

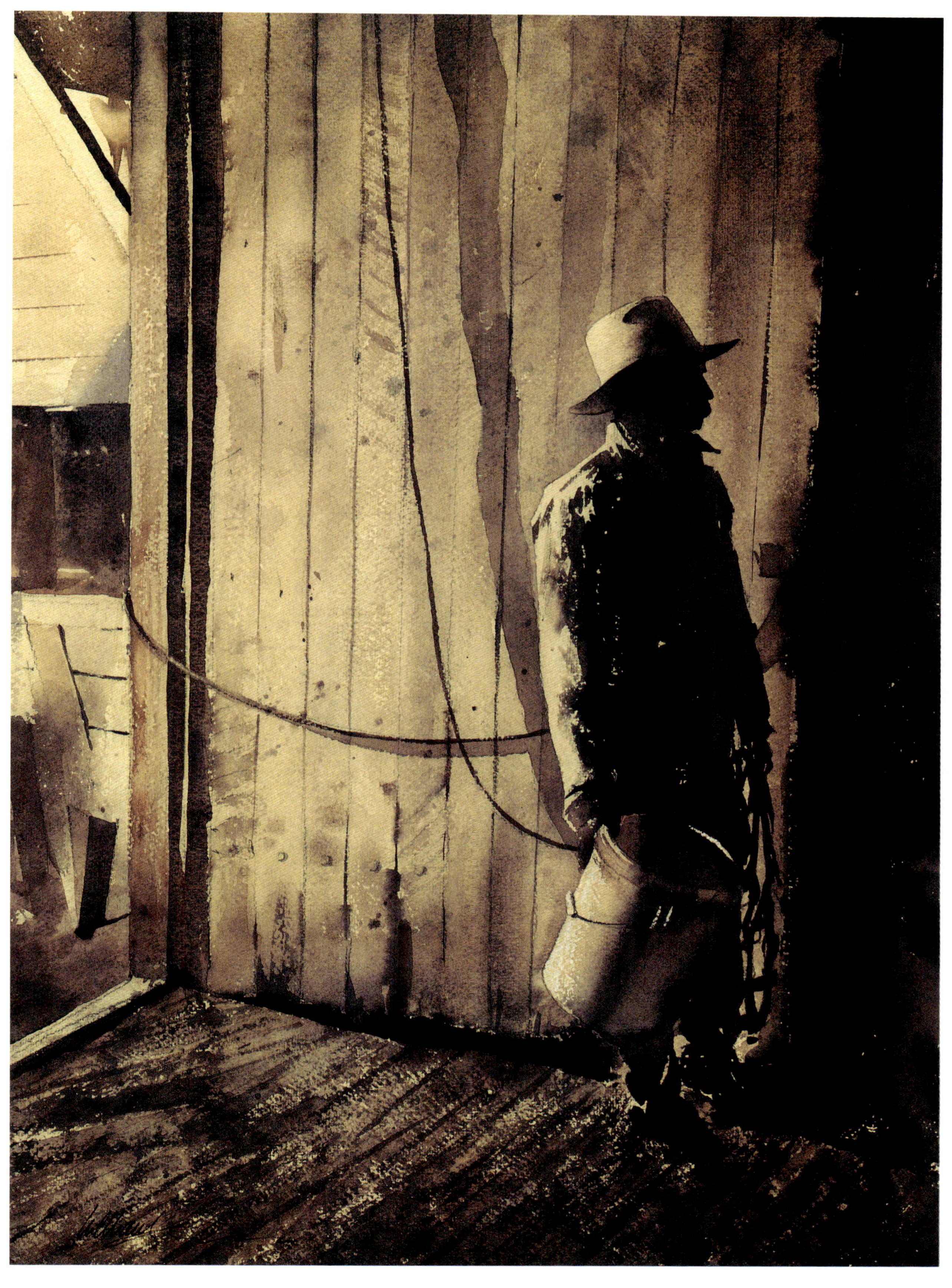

Morning Yodel

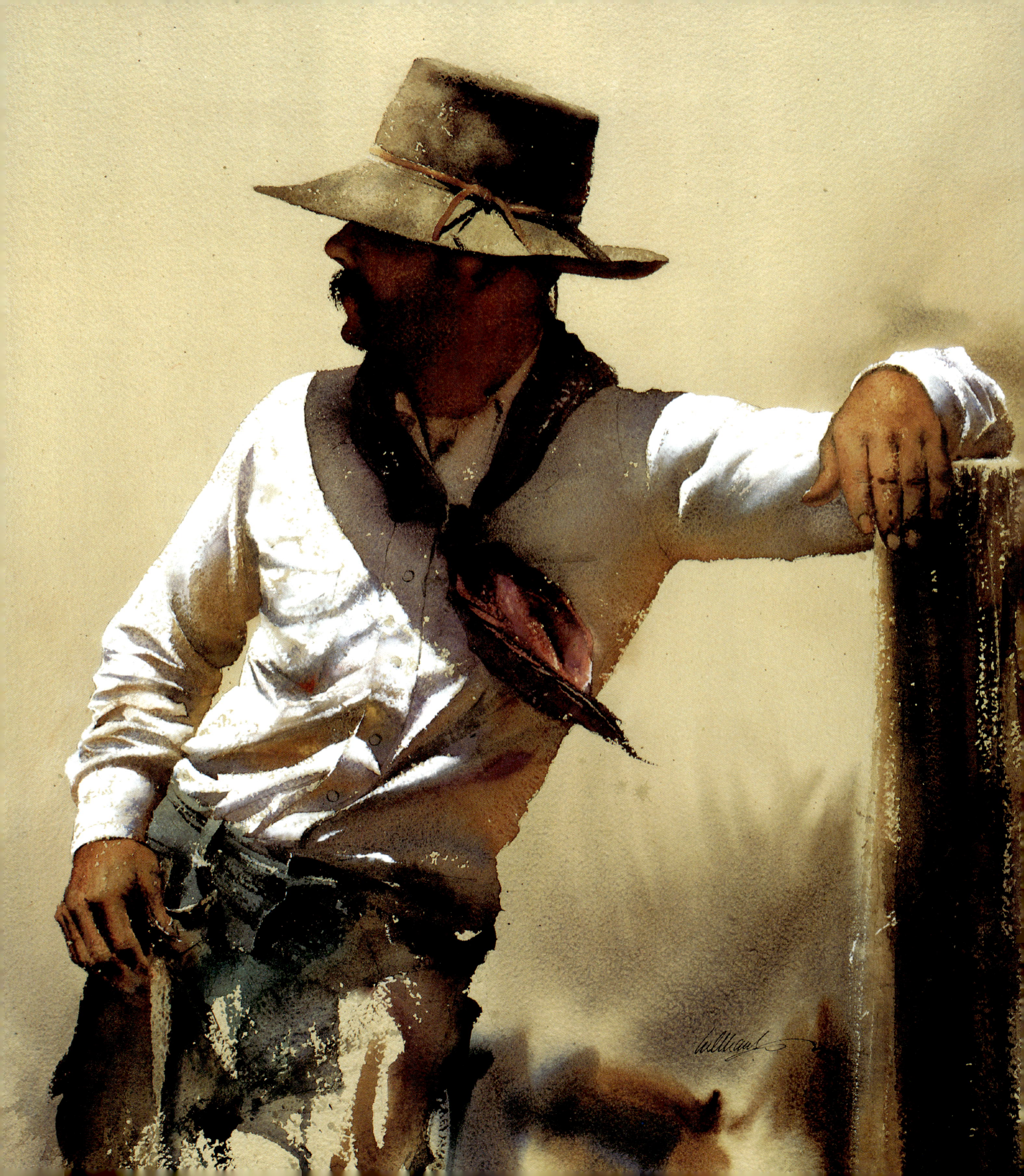

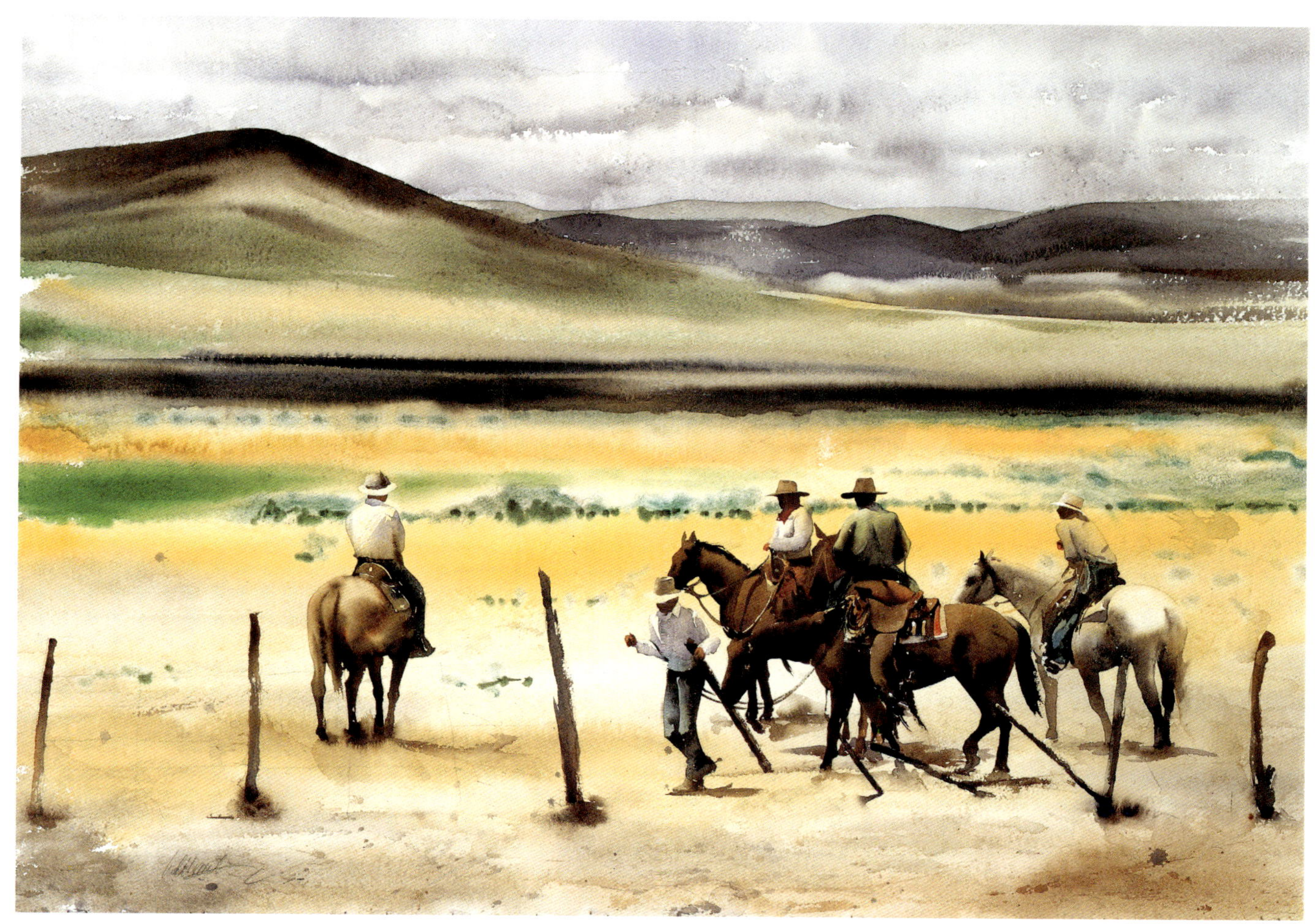

Closing the Gate

(OPPOSITE)

Bountiful

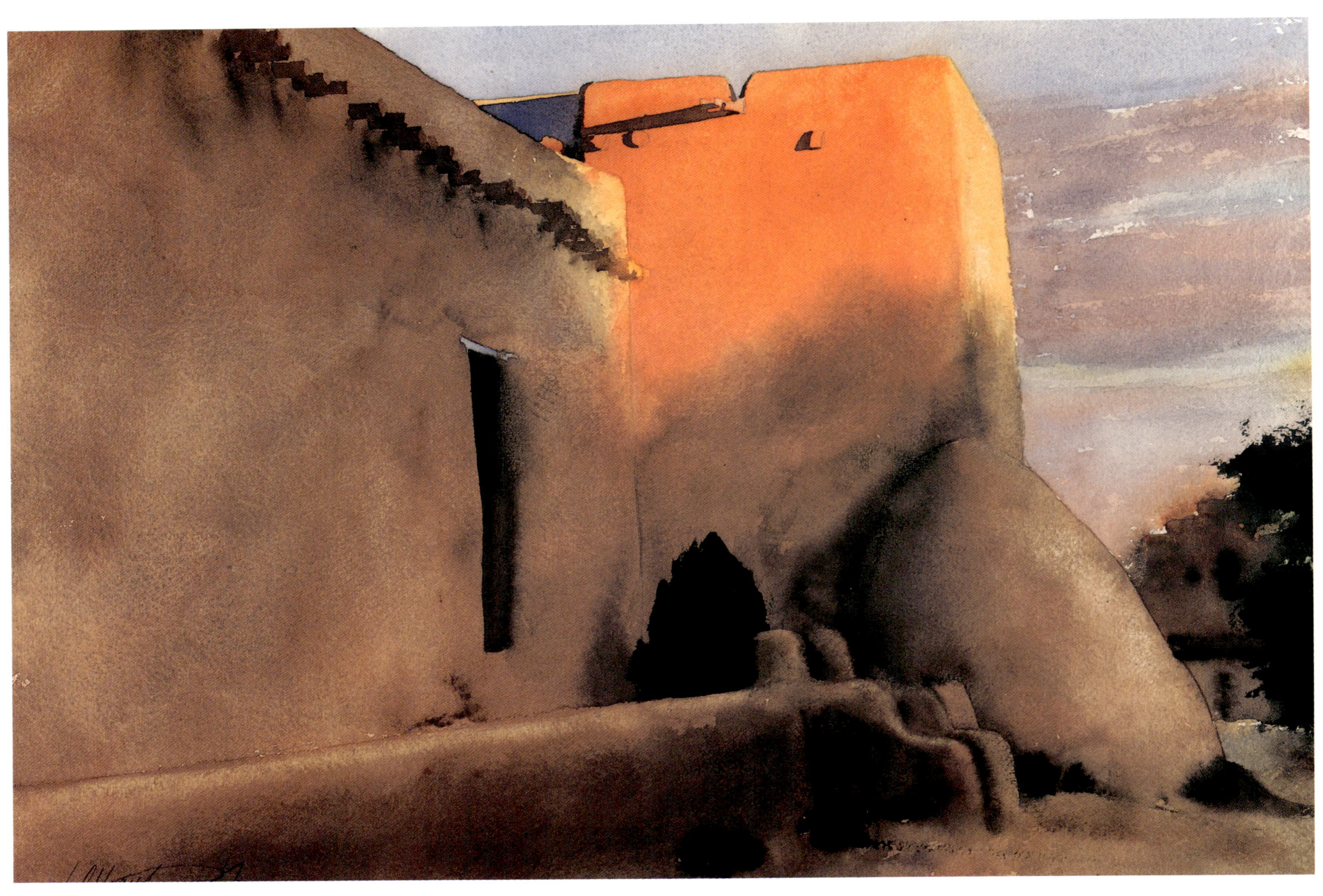

Dawn, Ranchos de Taos

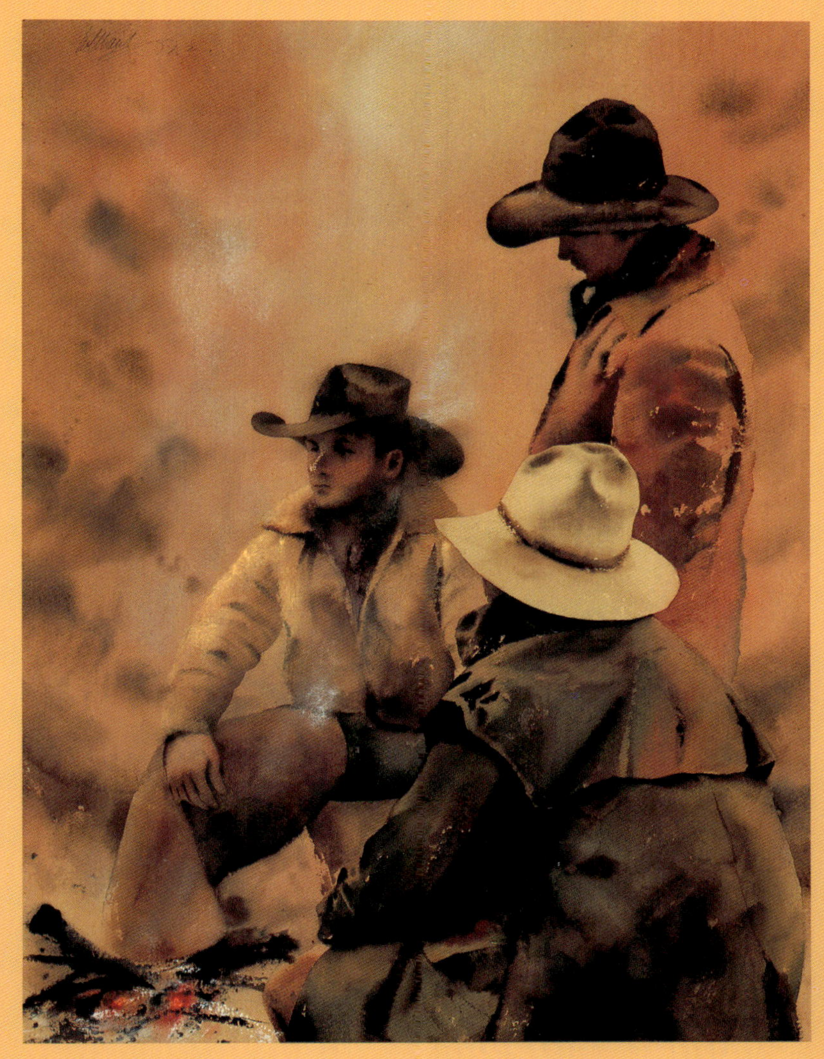

Before Breakfast

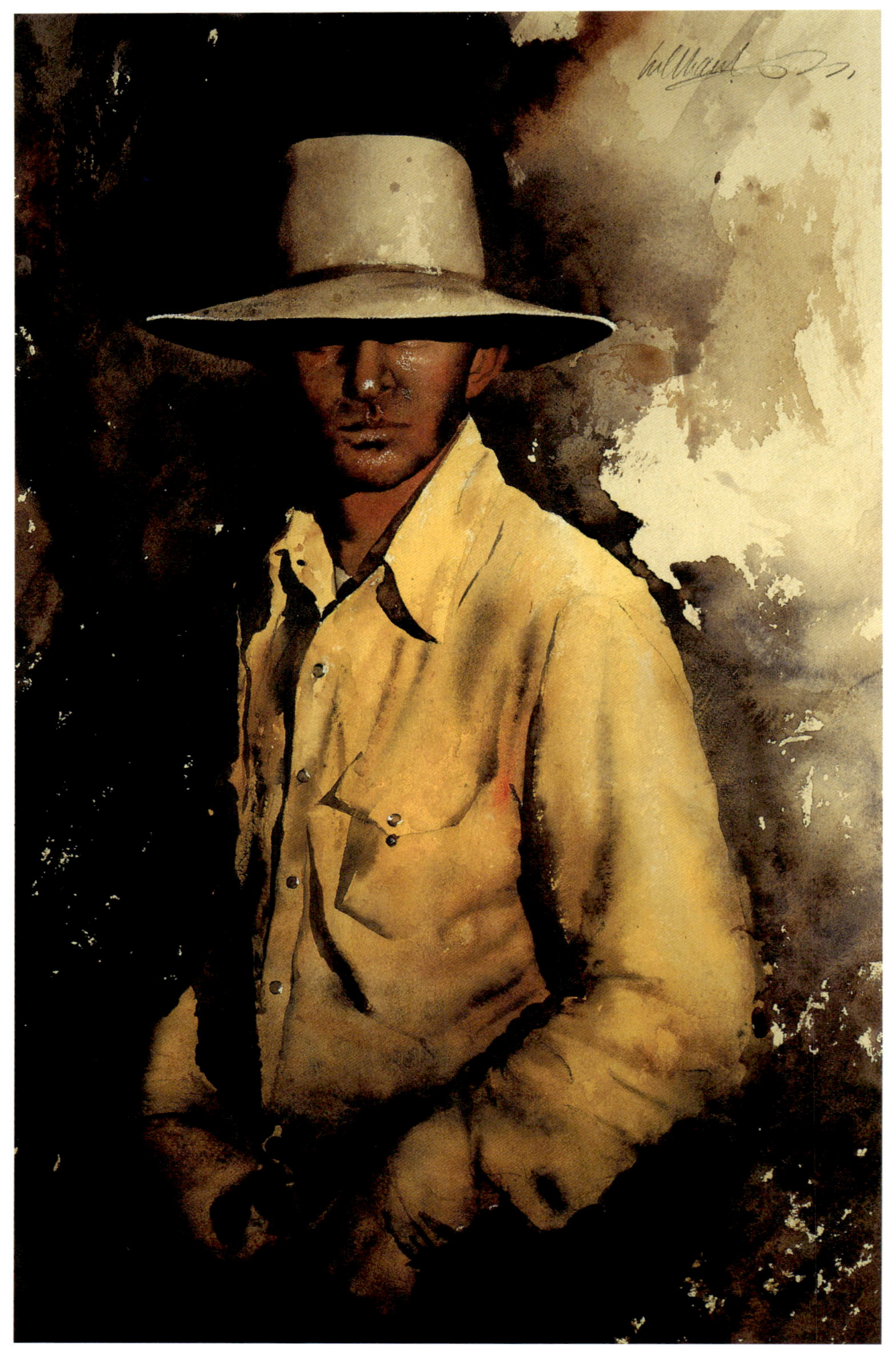

Blackie

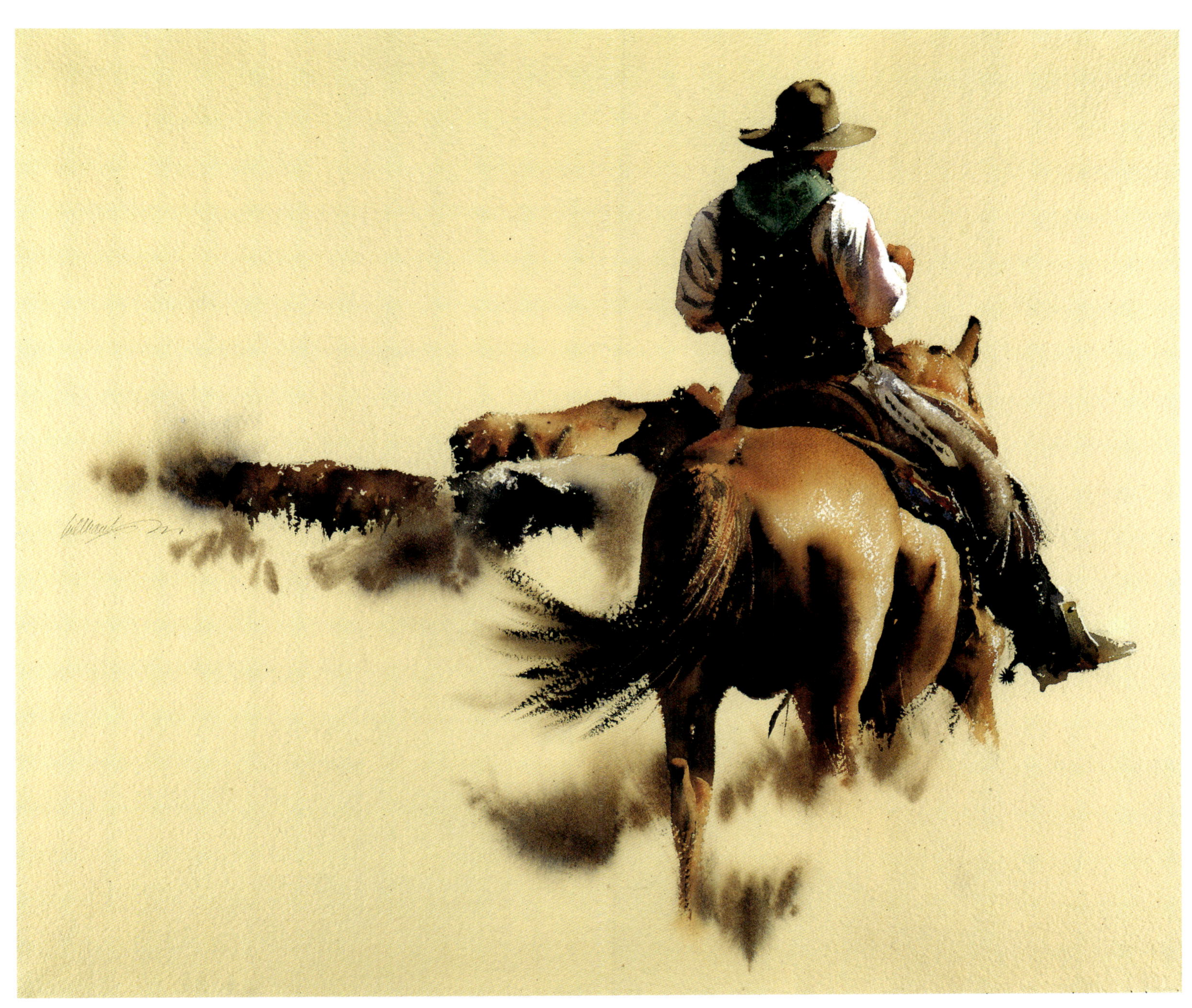

Hoot's Cut-off

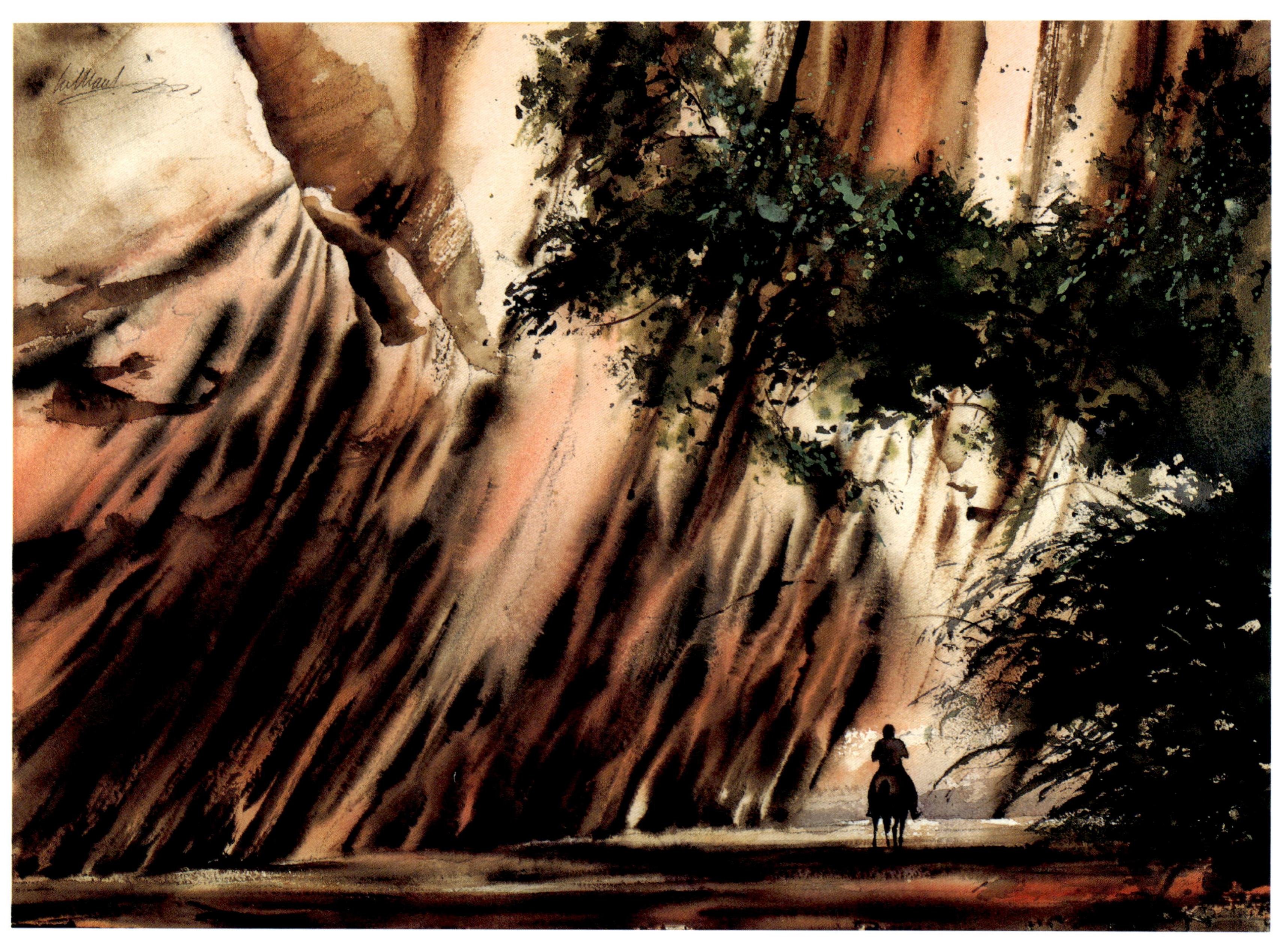

Canyon Shadows

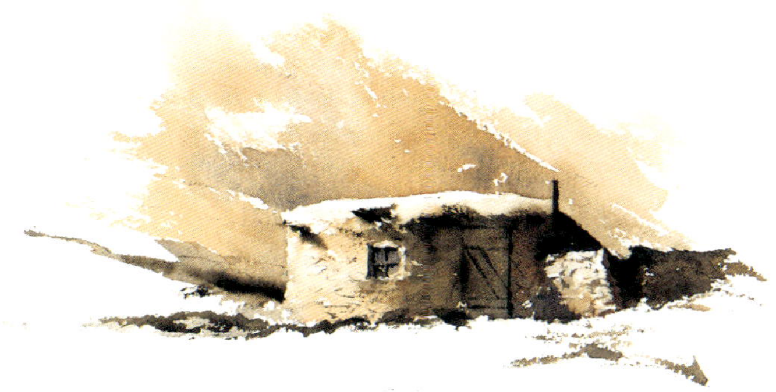

Canyon de Chelly is situated in the Navajo reservation of northern Arizona. It is full of Anasazi ruins, petroglyphs, and ancient secrets. The Navajo farm the land and raise sheep on the canyon floor. The only way to get down is on horseback, and even then you need to be accompanied by an Indian guide.

(above)

Navajo Hogan

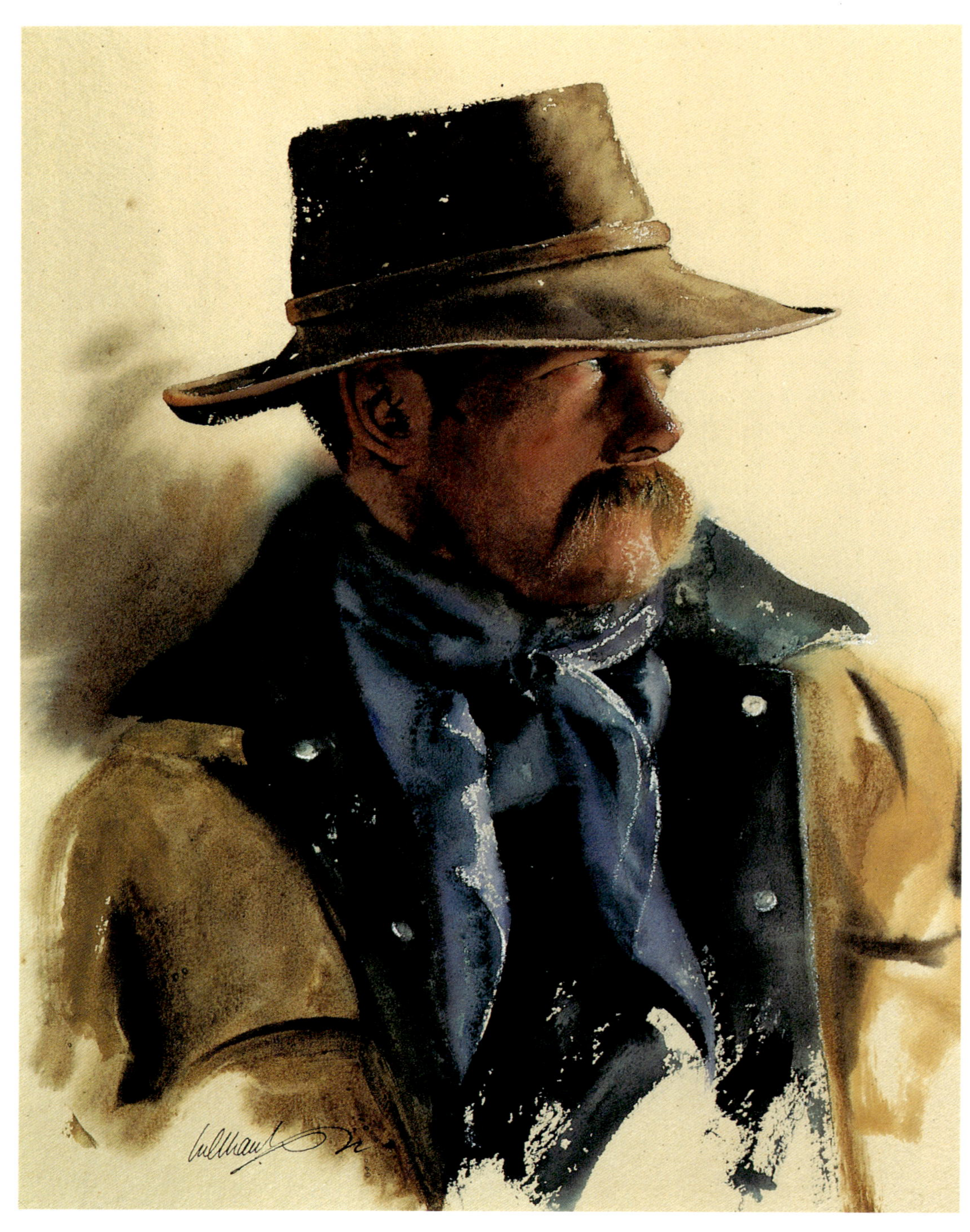

Tom Freeman

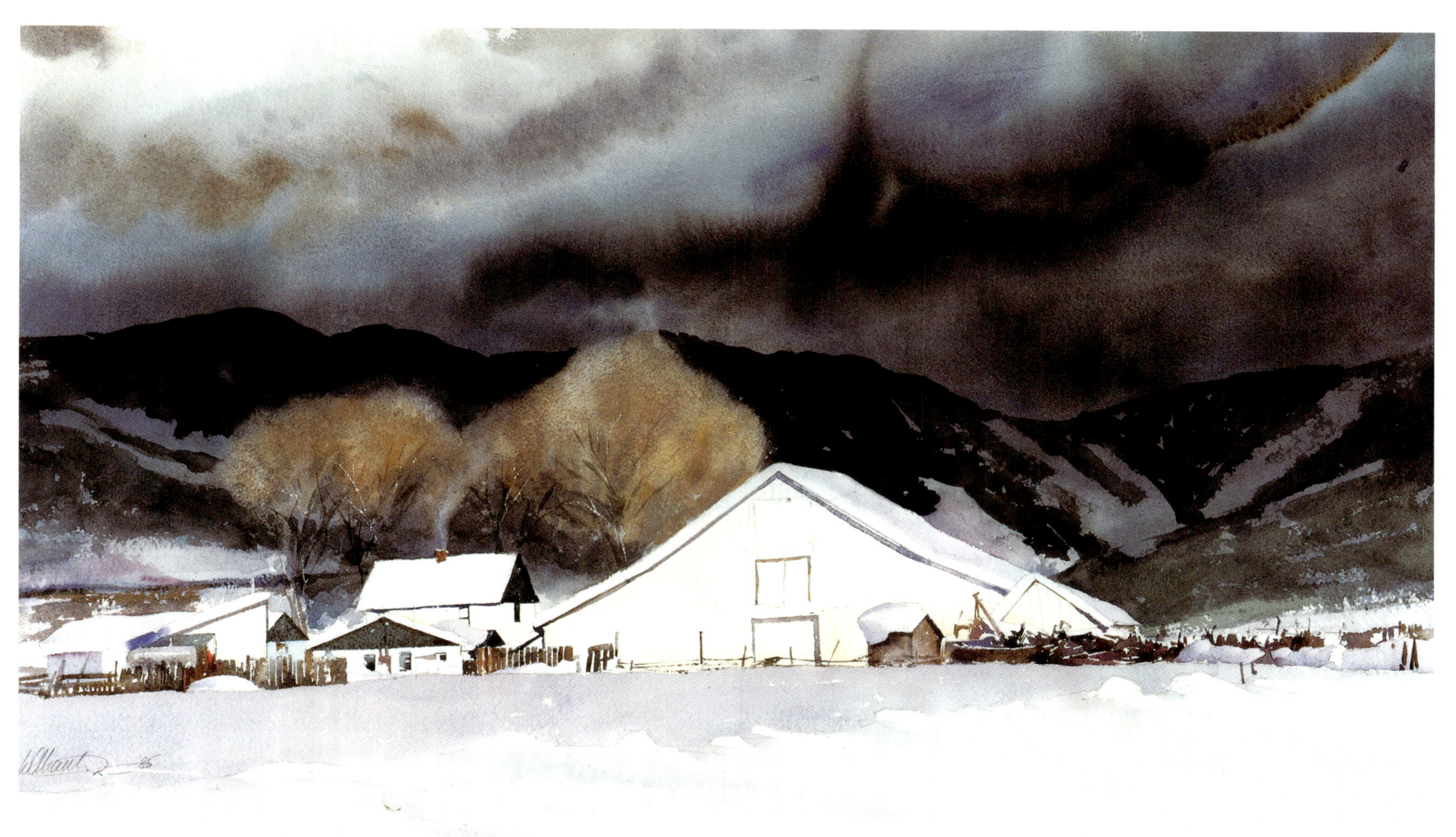

Impending Storm

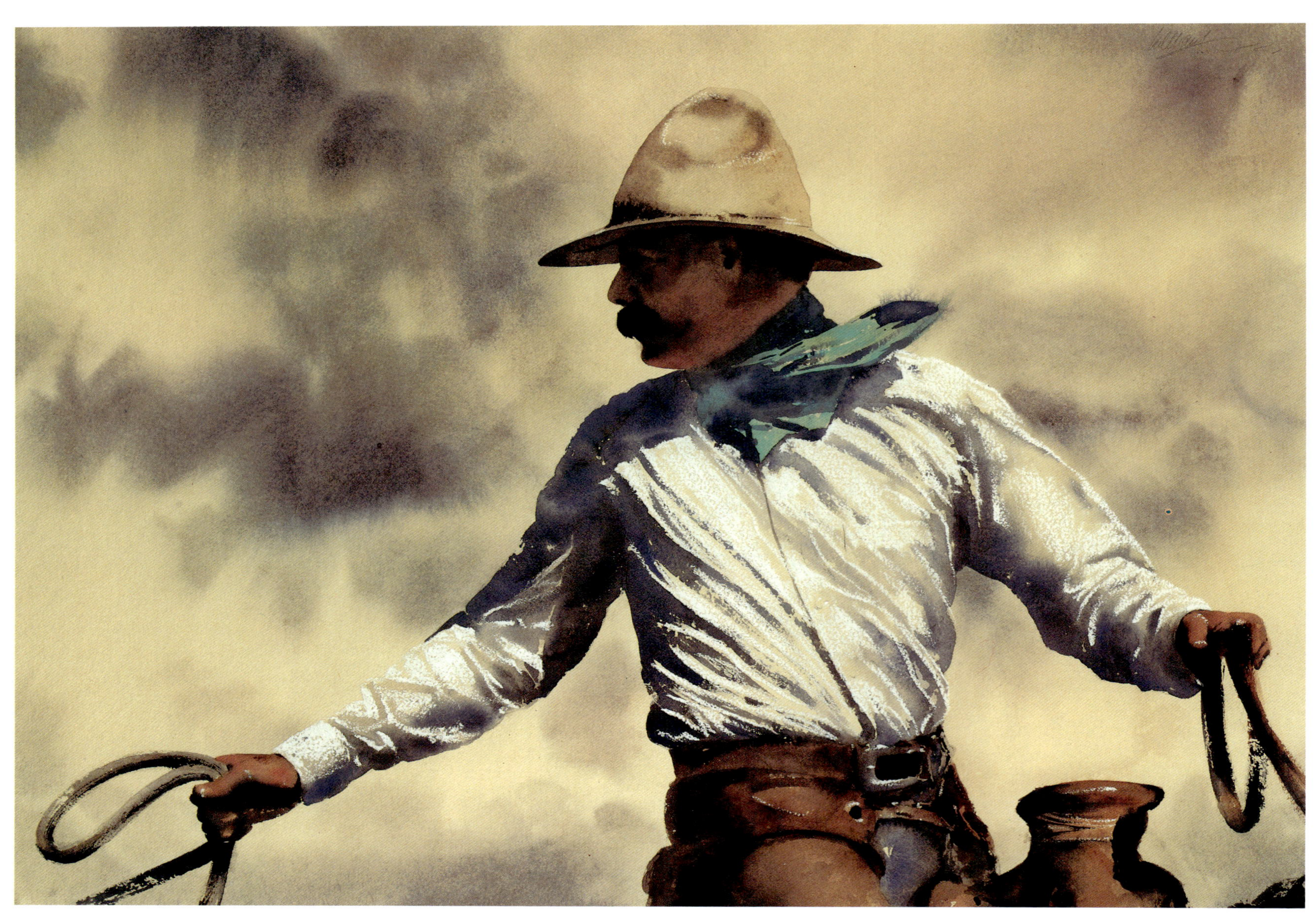

The Packer

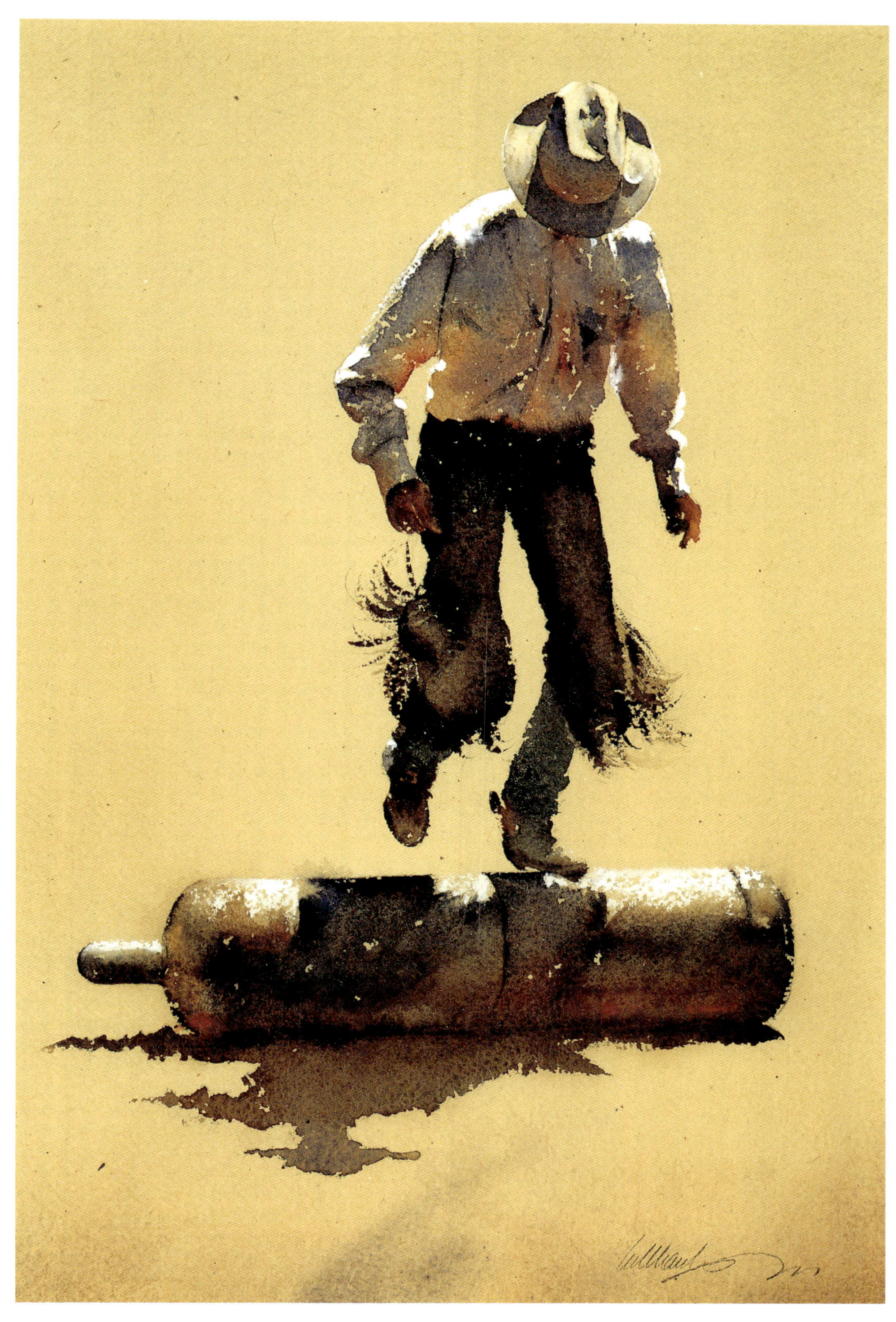

Moving Gas

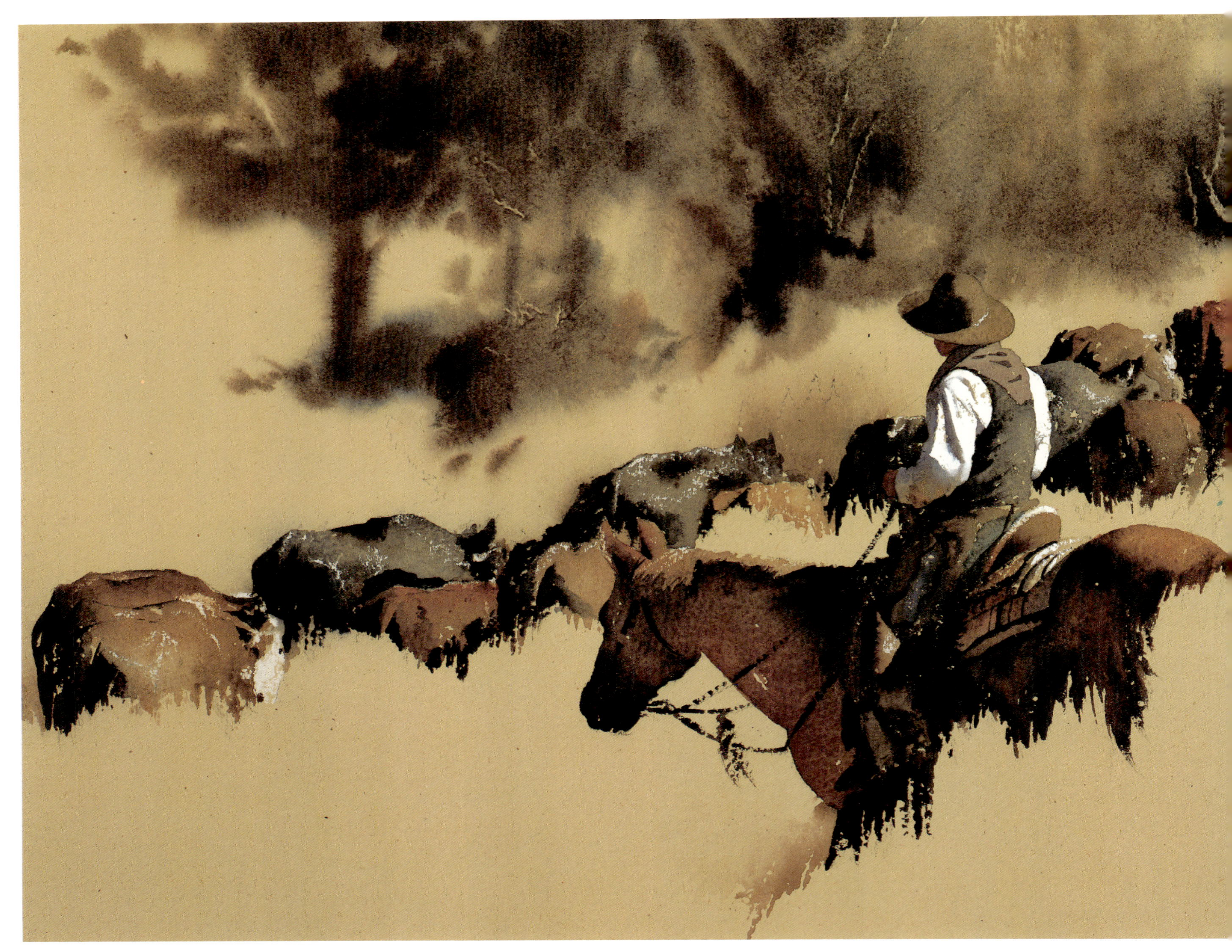

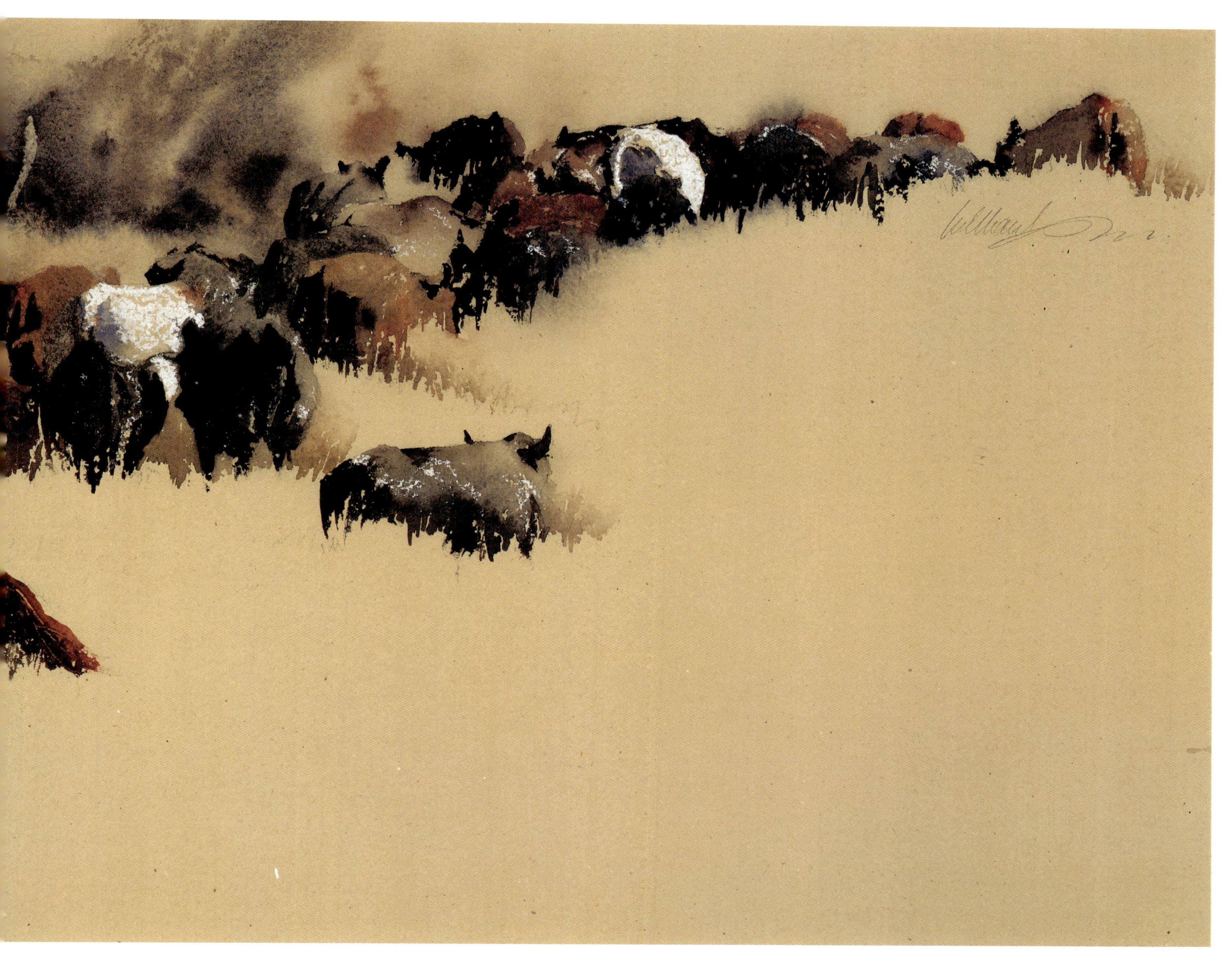

Heading Up to Frenchglen

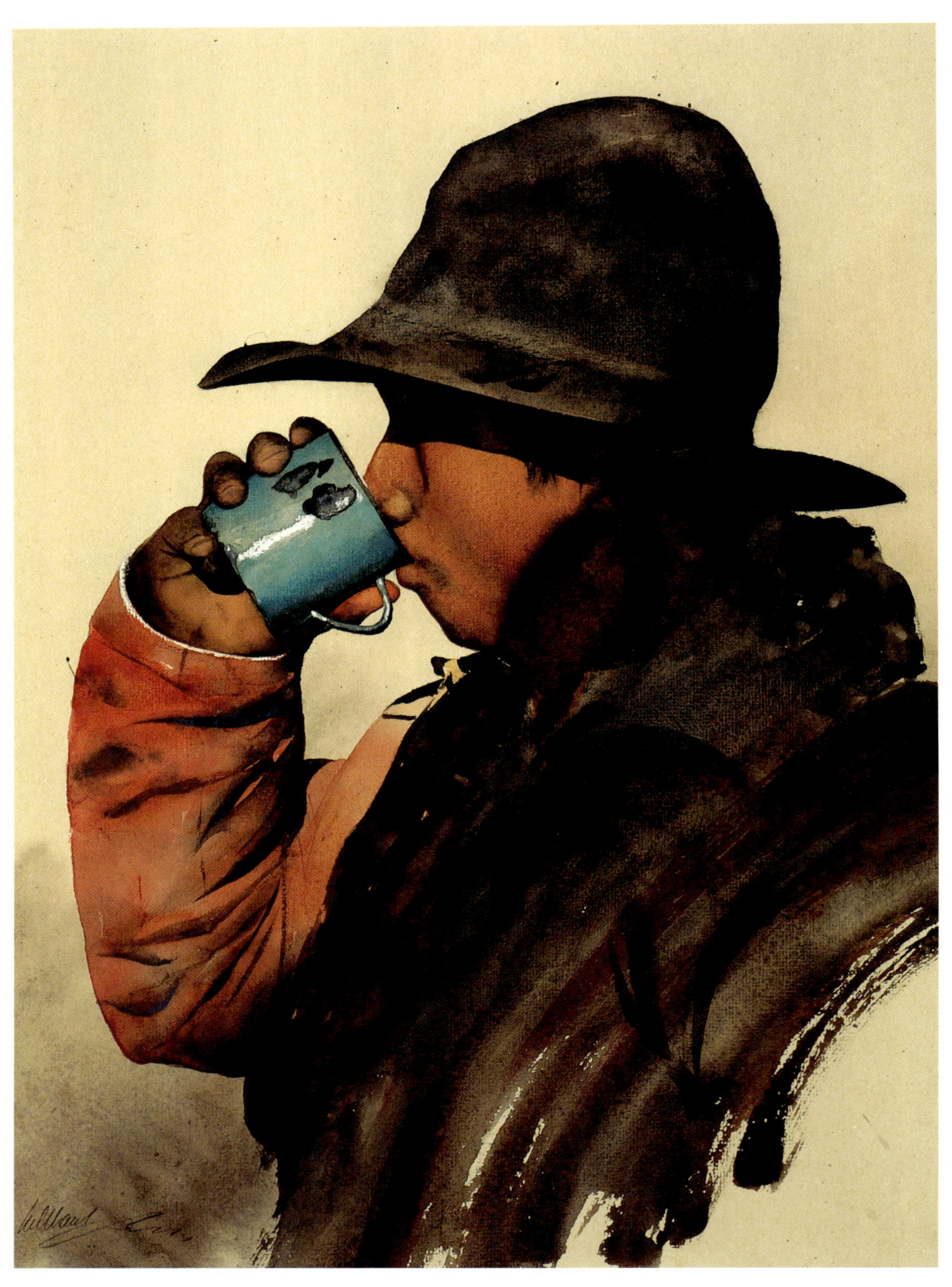

The Chipped Cup

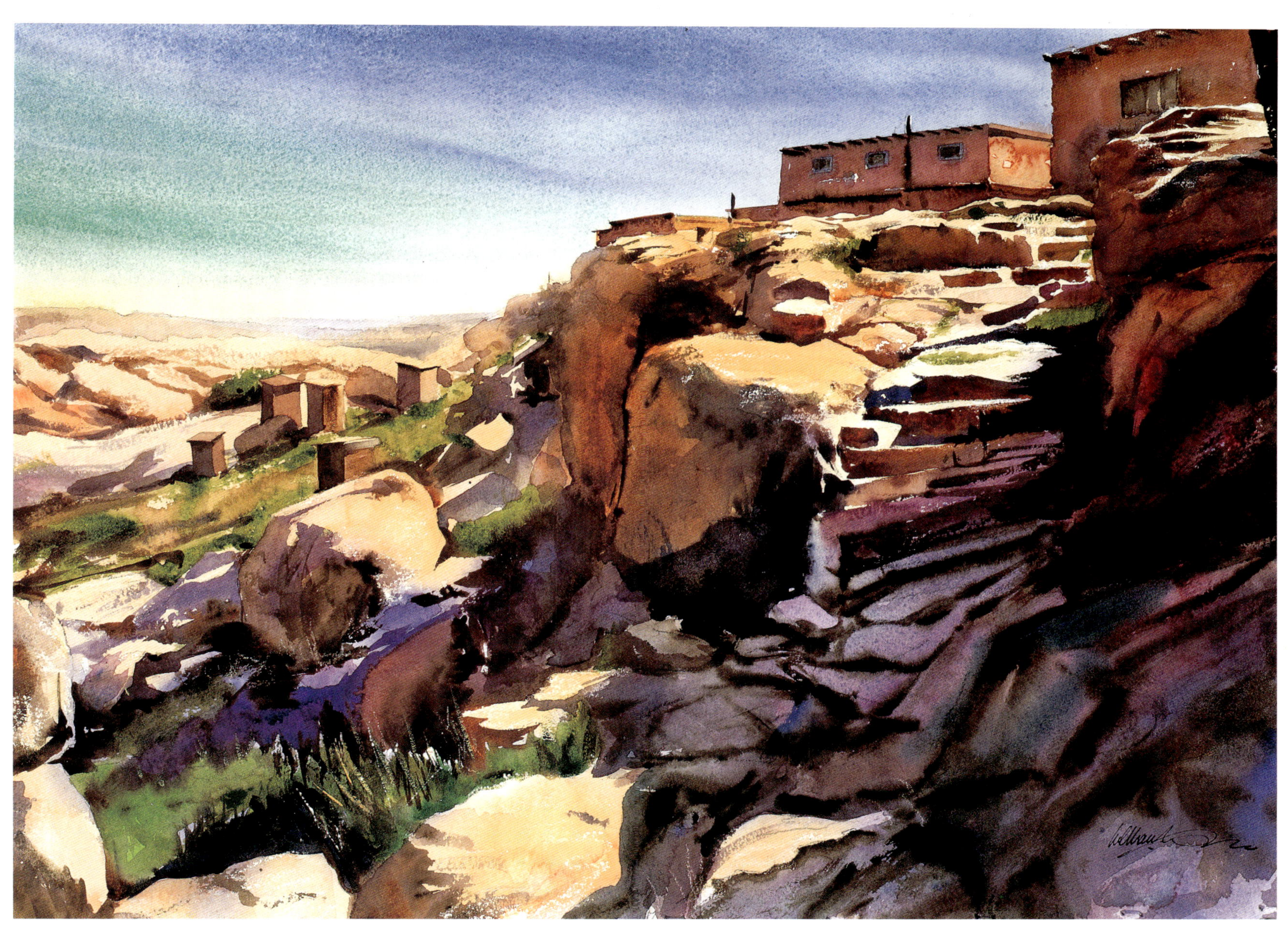

Acoma Steps

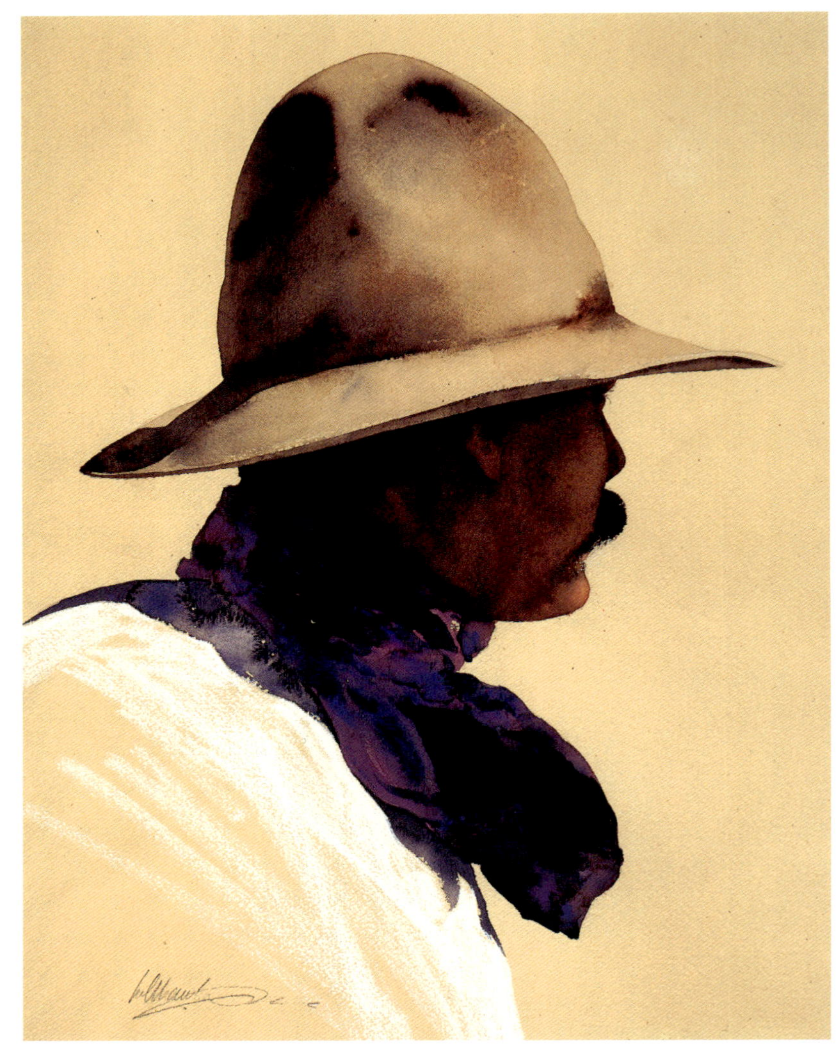

Randy Rieman

(OPPOSITE)

Jeremiah Watt

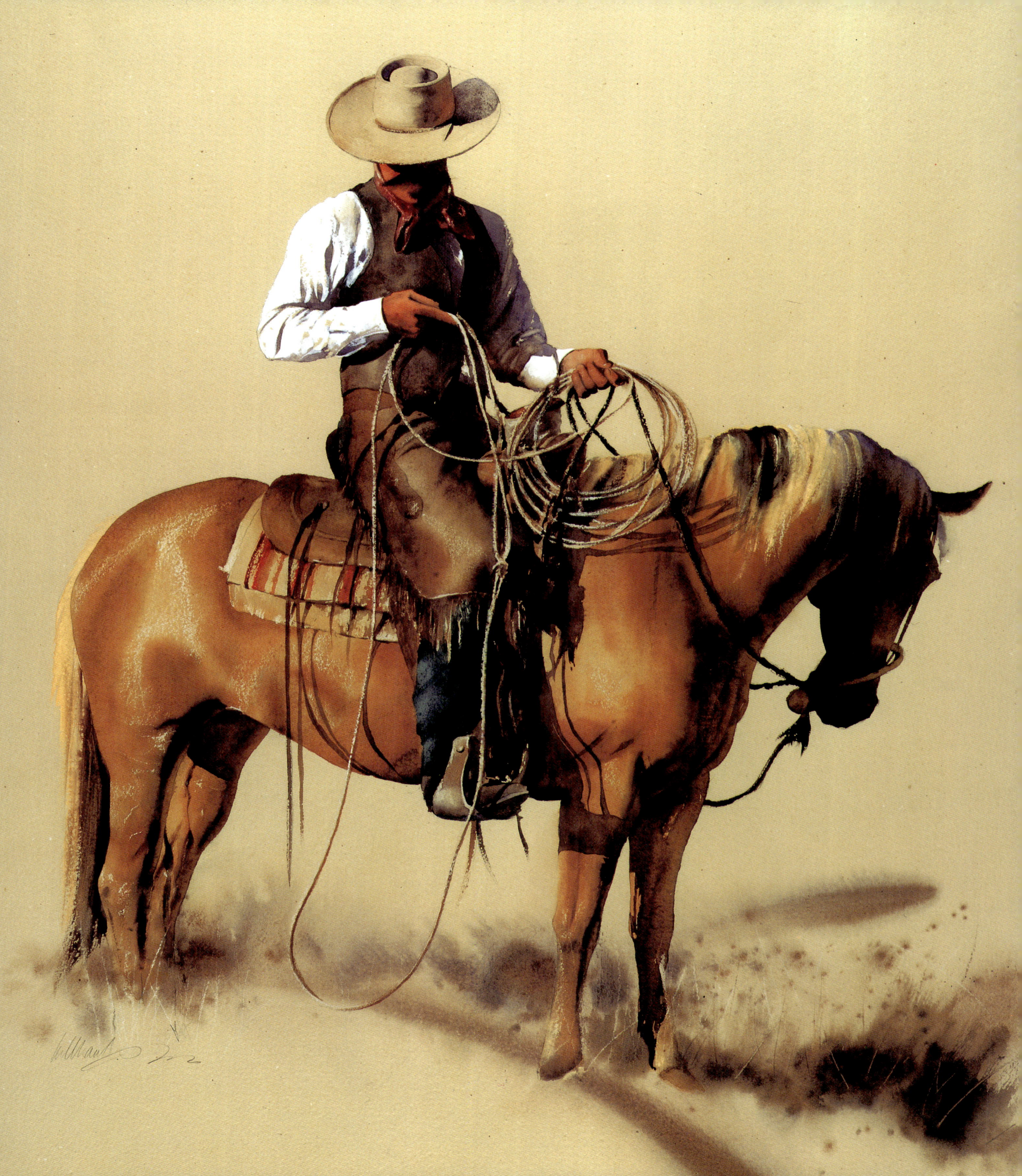

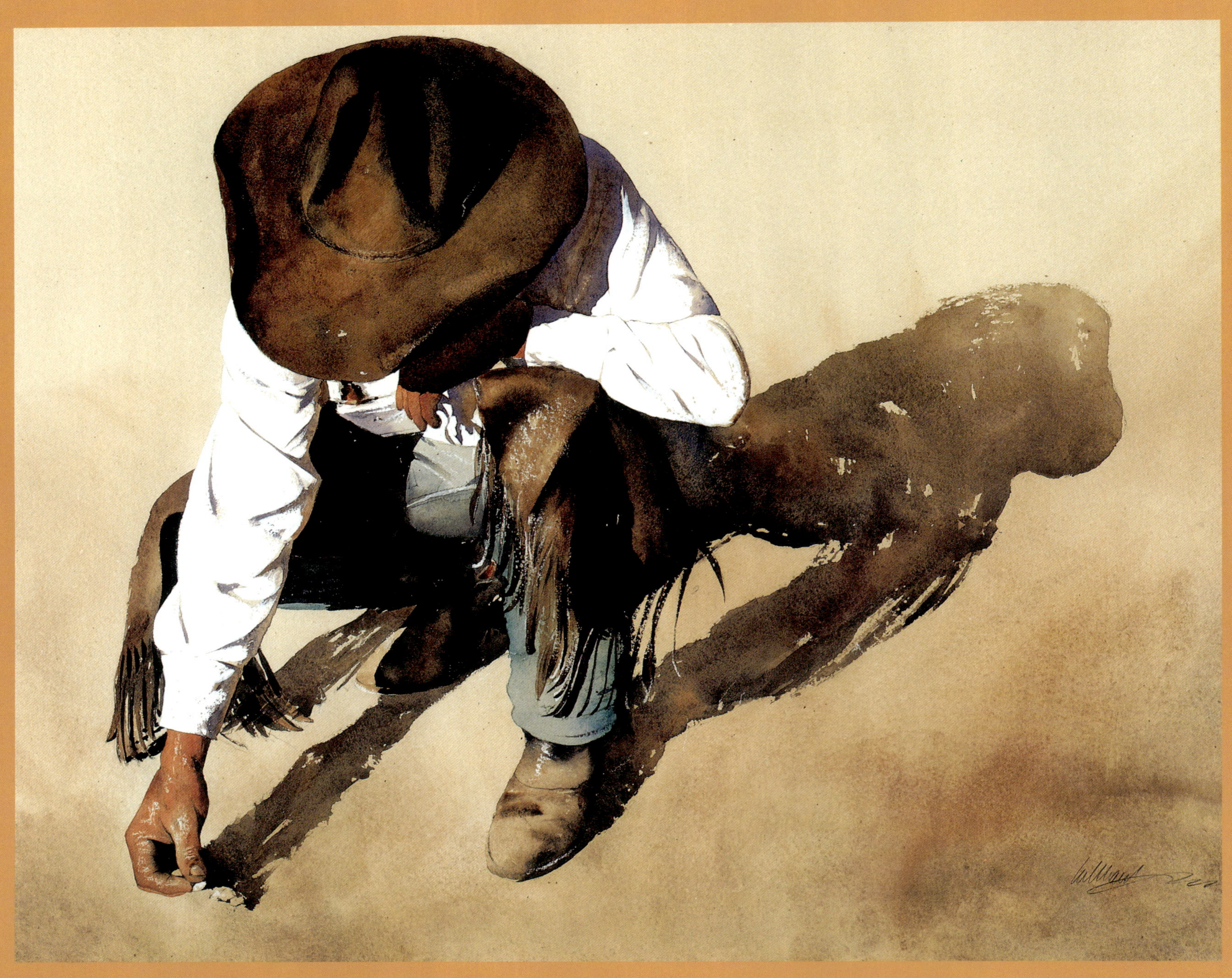

Vital Signs

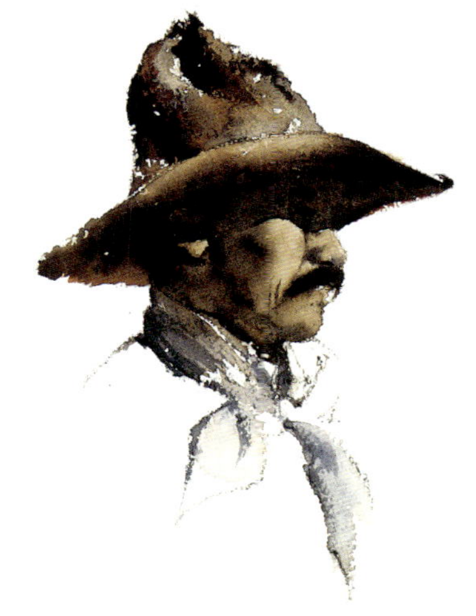

MANUEL PALOMINO is a vaquero. He is carrying on a tradition of horsemanship and cowboying like that of his American cousins, the buckaroos of the Great Basin area. Manuel is well known for the big, pretty loop he throws and, like most vaqueros, prefers a maguey, or Mexican grass rope. He lives in central California on the eastern edge of the Diablo Range.

(ABOVE)
Manuel Palomino

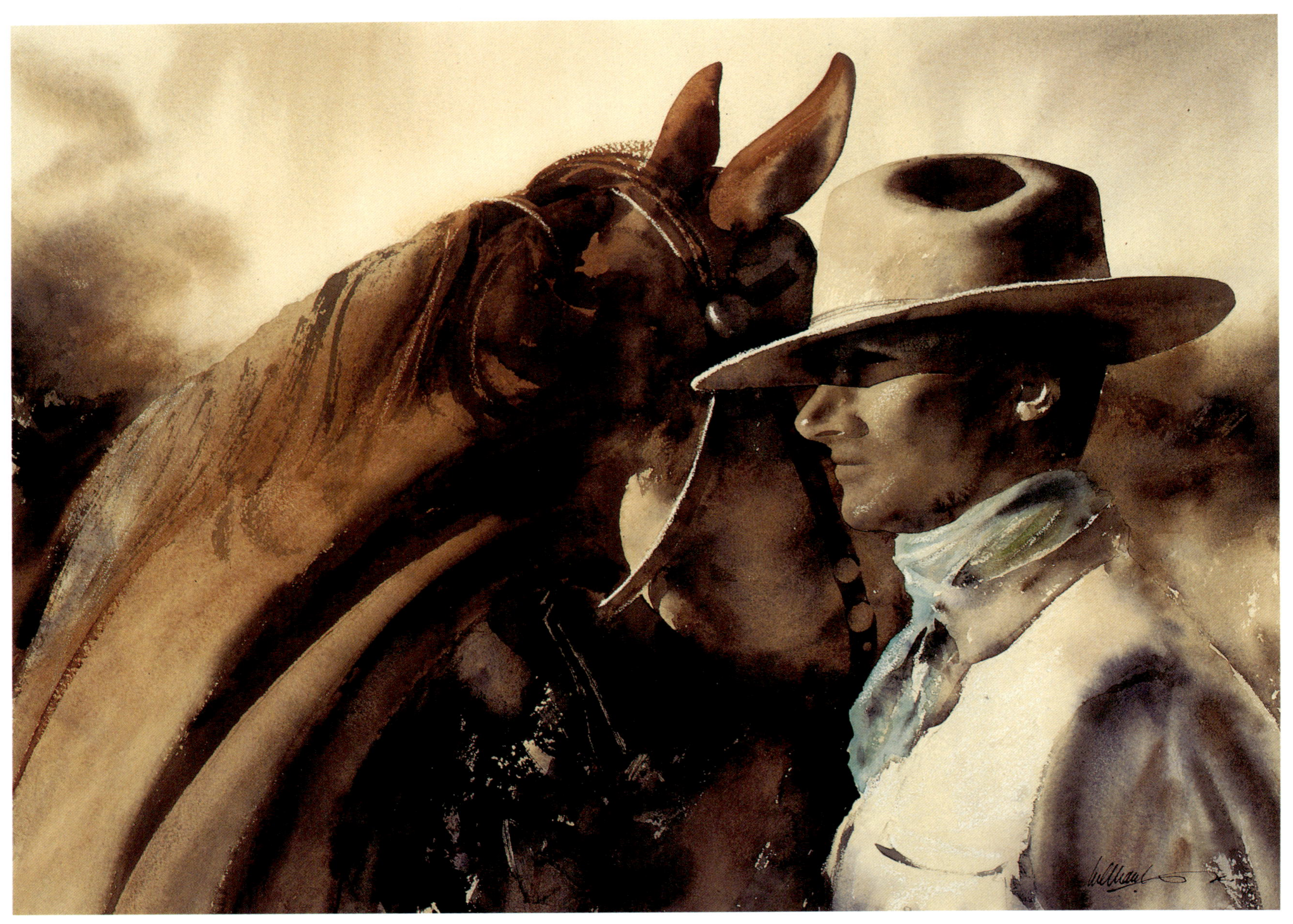

Buckaroo Team

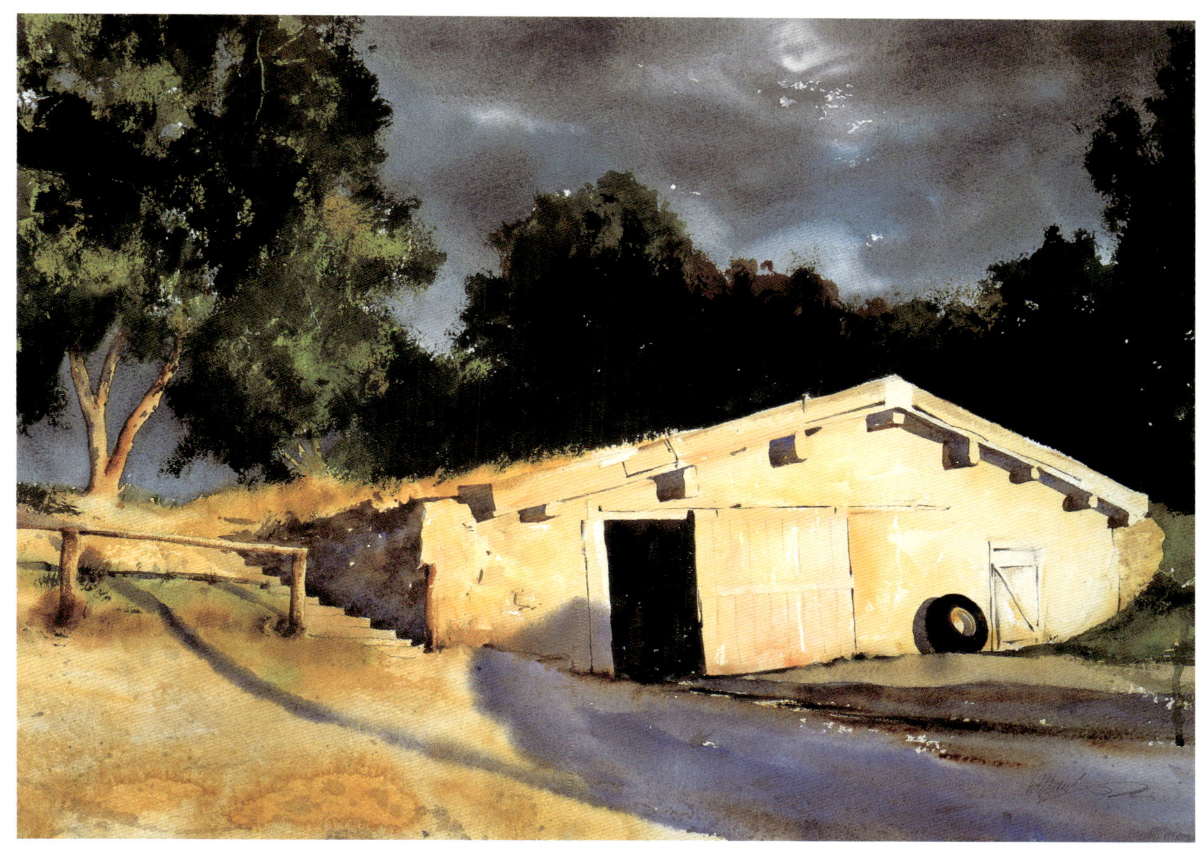

The Potato Cellar

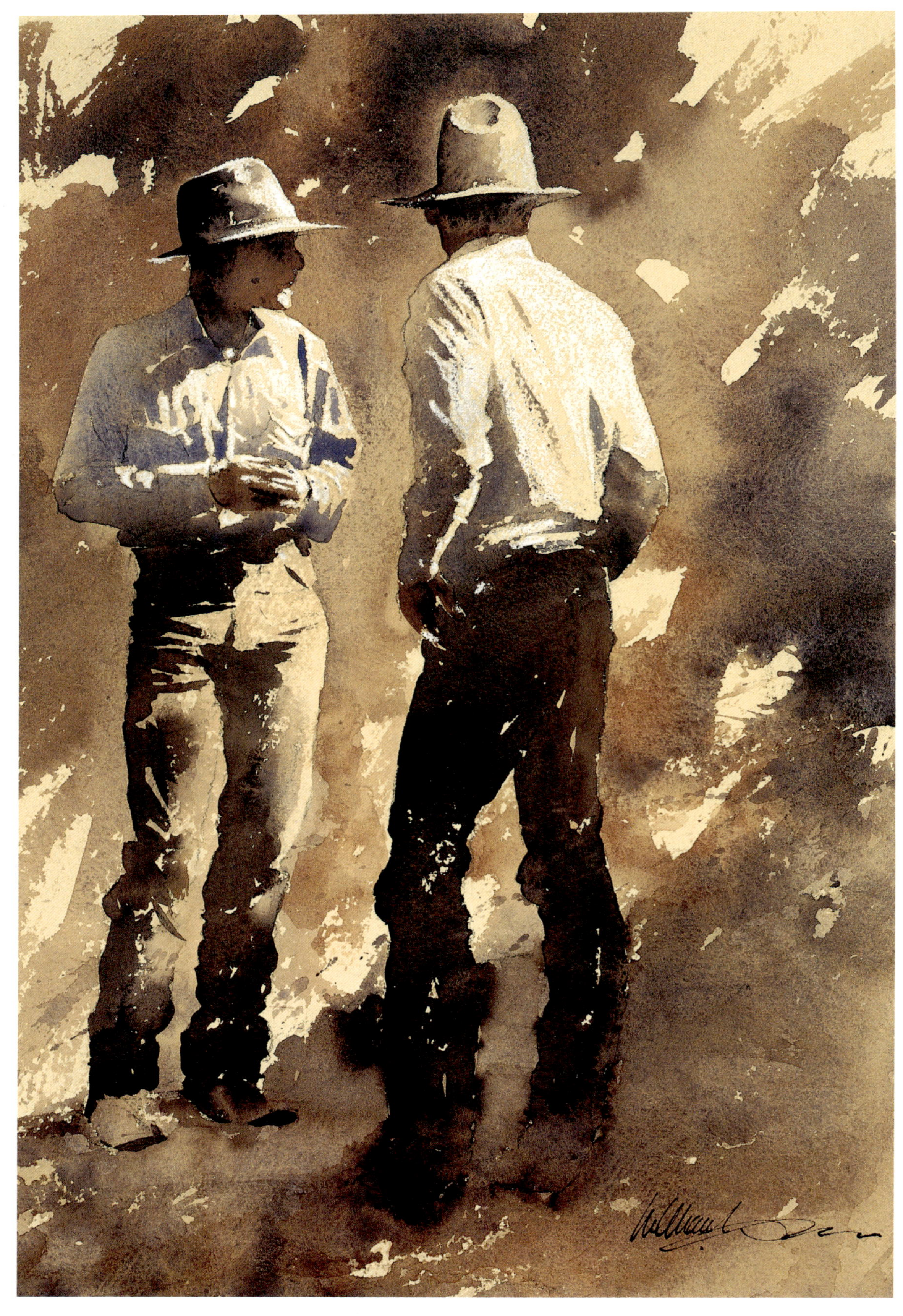

Conversation

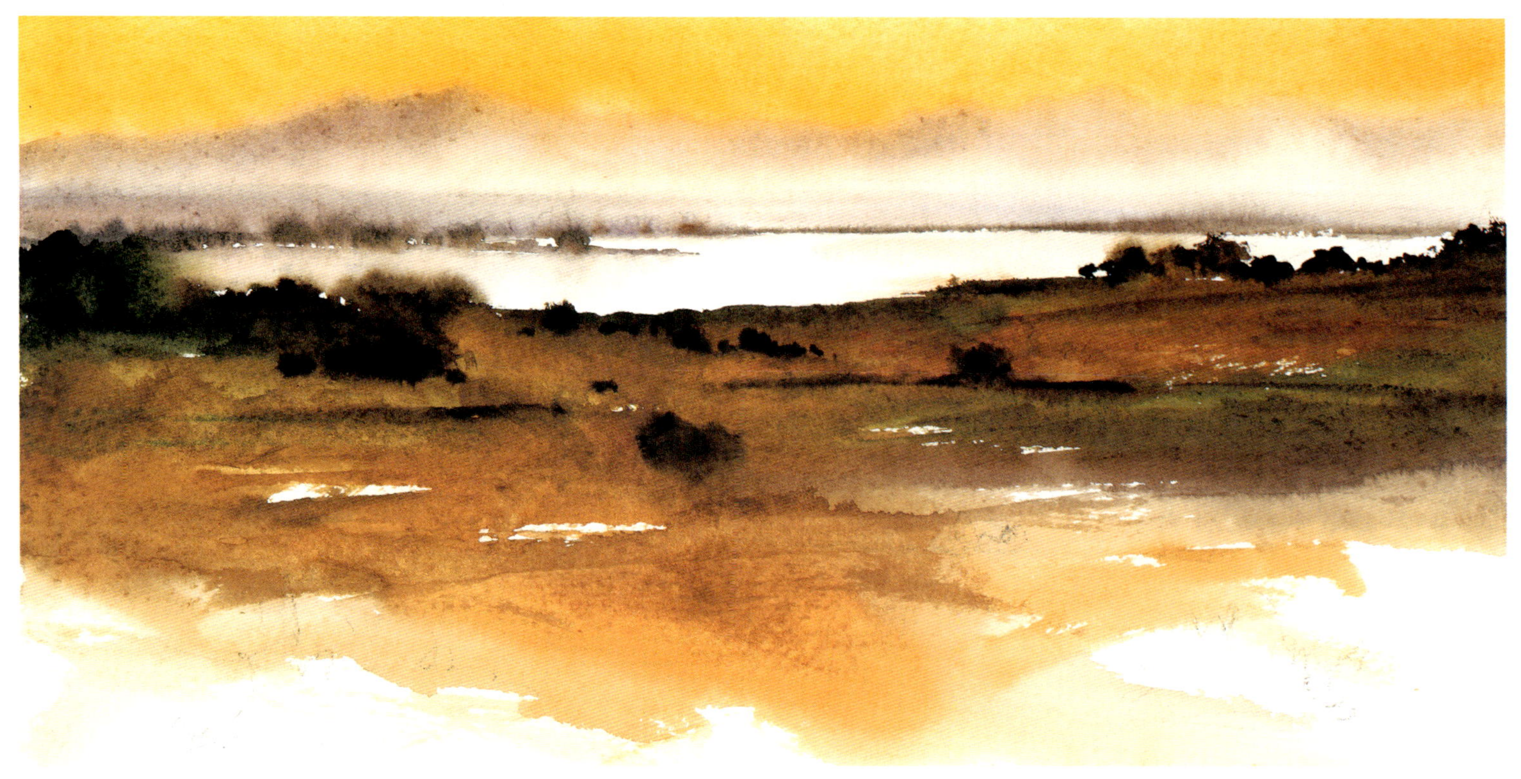

Cimarron

Cowboys say that a fine cowdog is worth two good men. In Texas and Arizona they're called "sic-em" dogs. In the Great Basin region and California, border collies are used for gathering and herding cattle. This dog belonged to Martin Black, superintendent on the Gamble and Winecup Ranches in Nevada. He is a great horseman and dog breeder.

Stock Dog

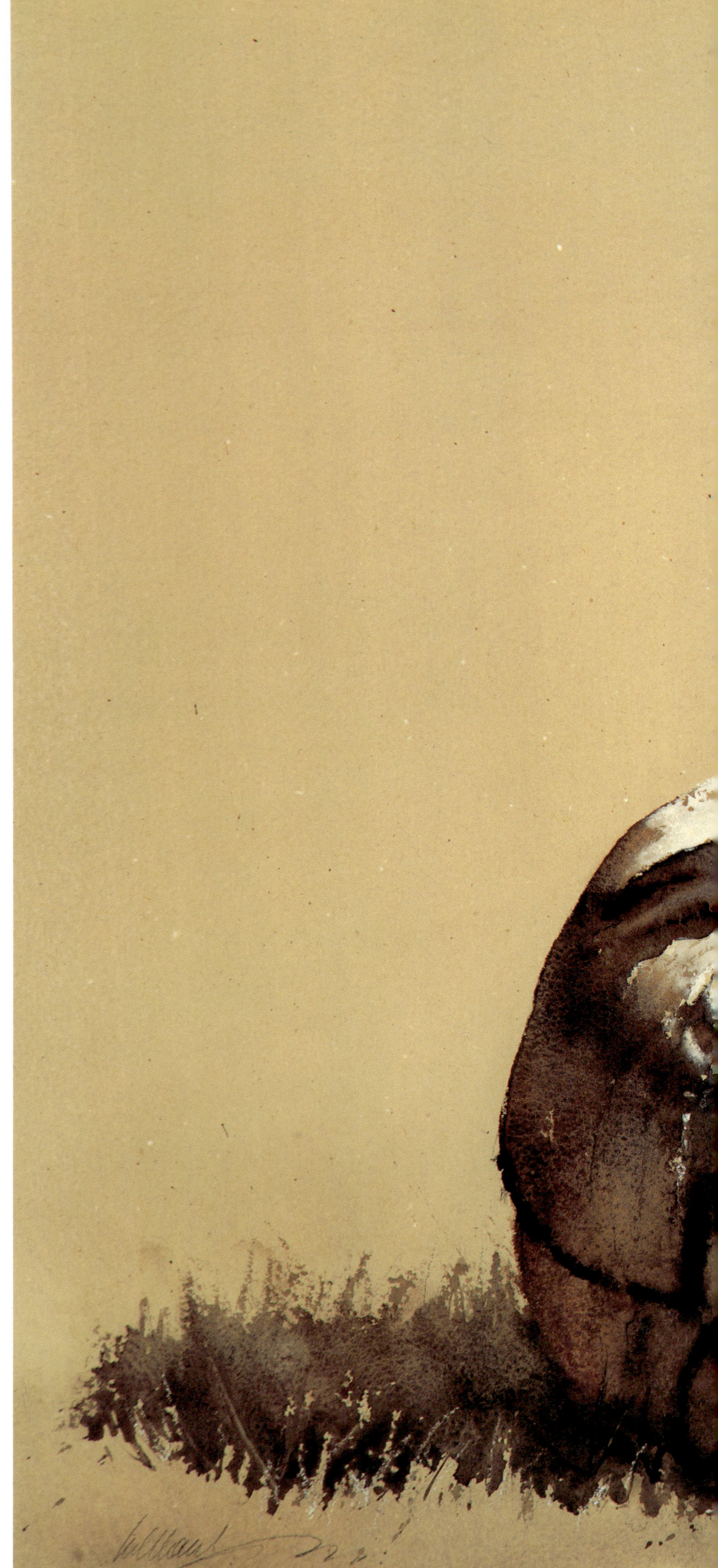

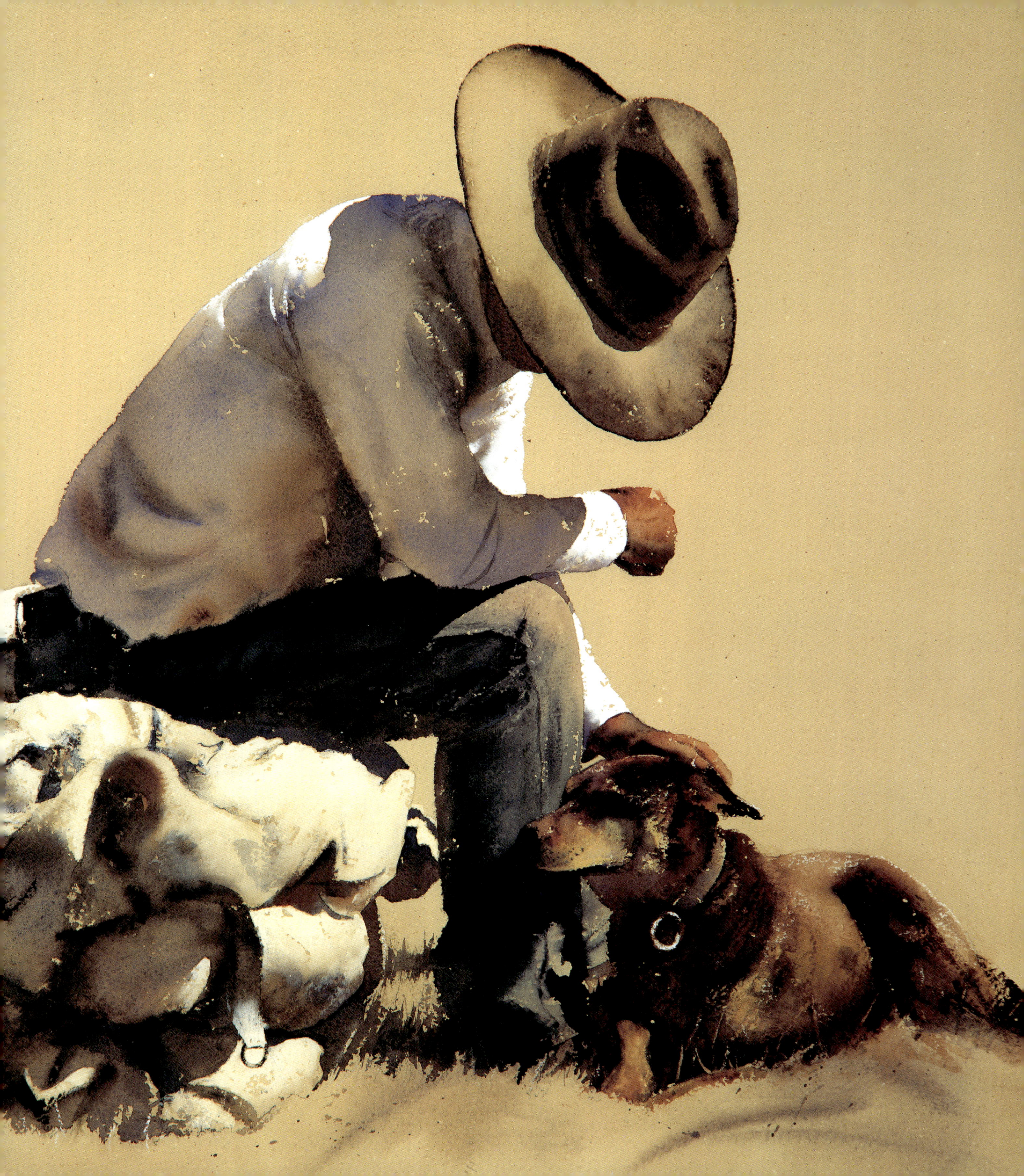

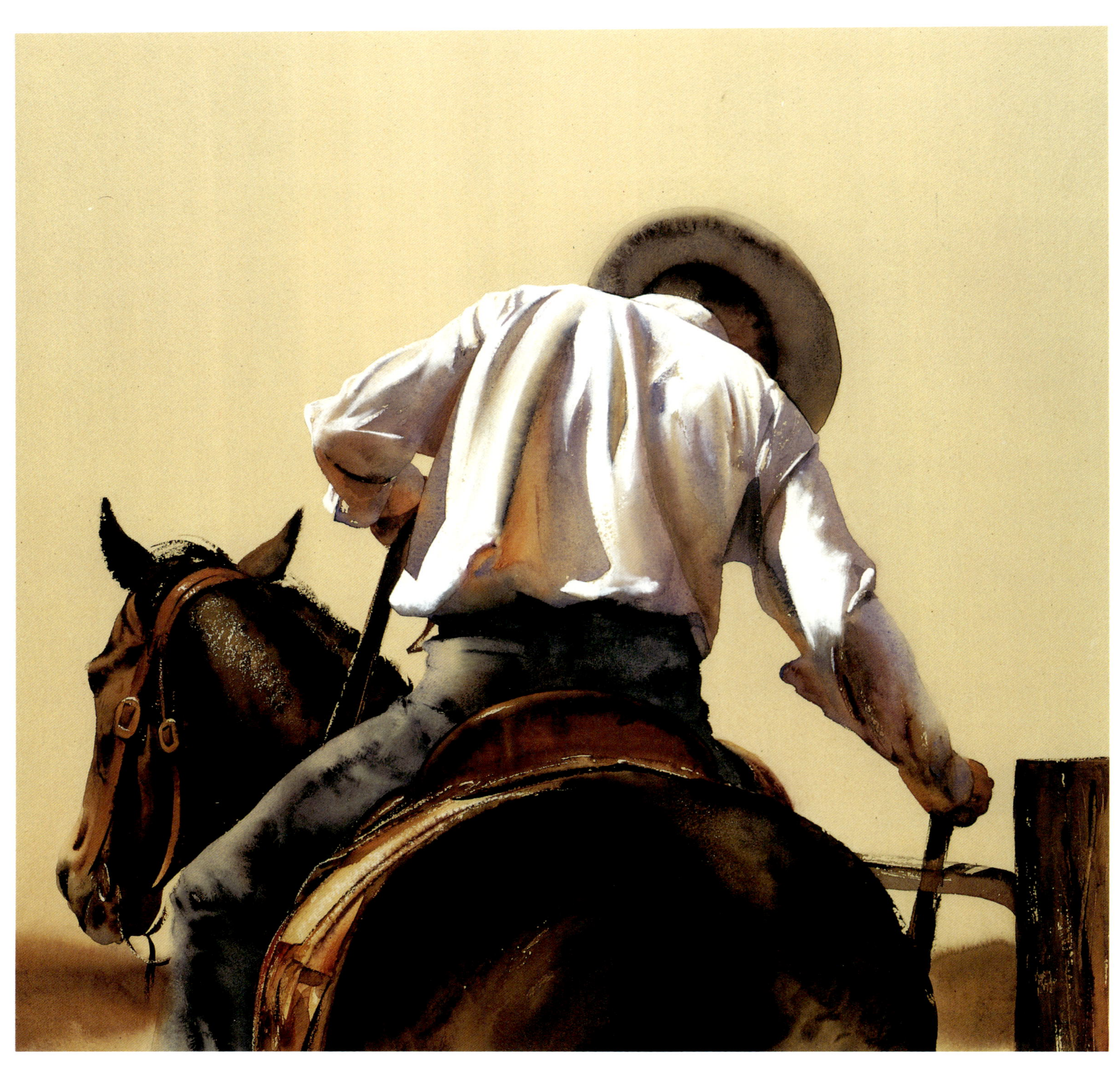

Opening the Gate

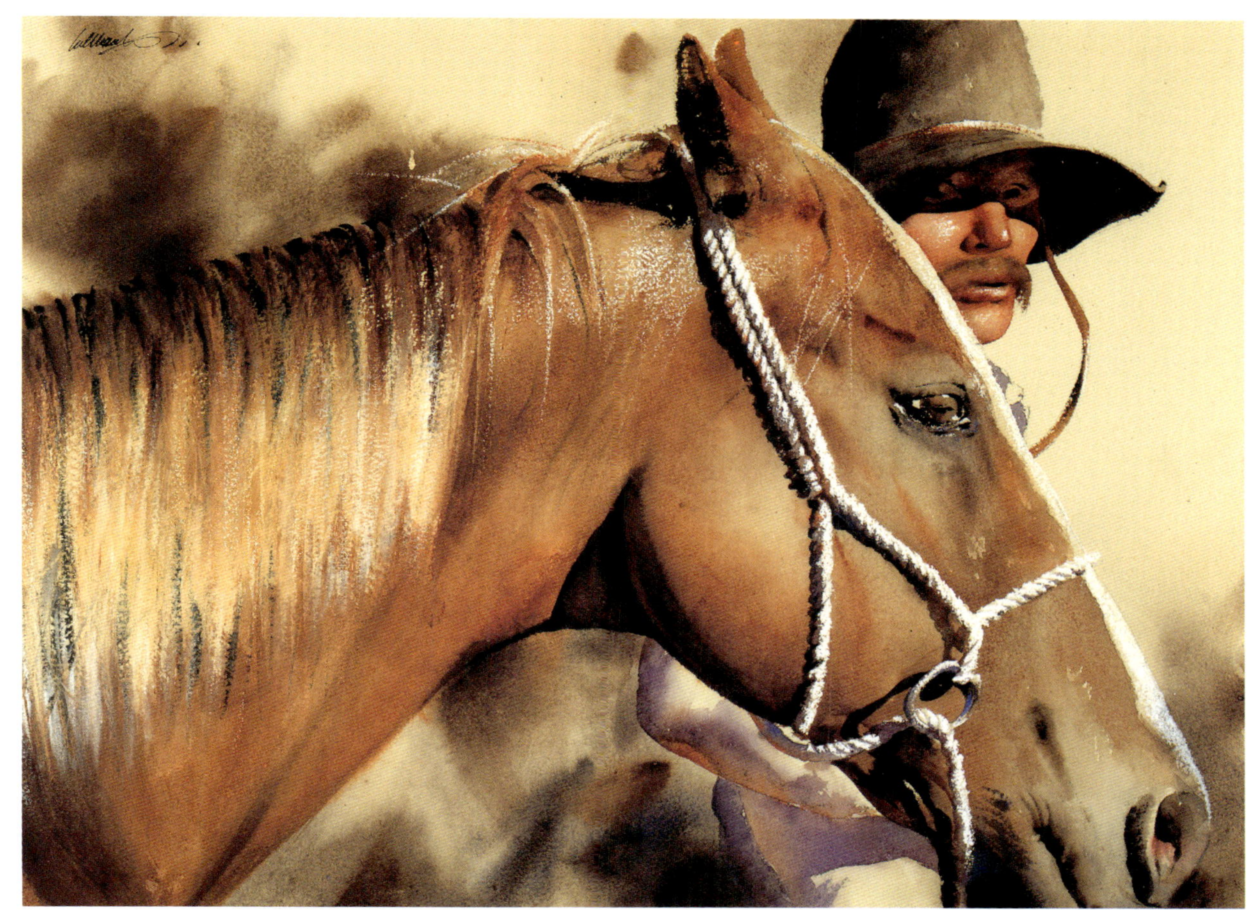

Ichabod

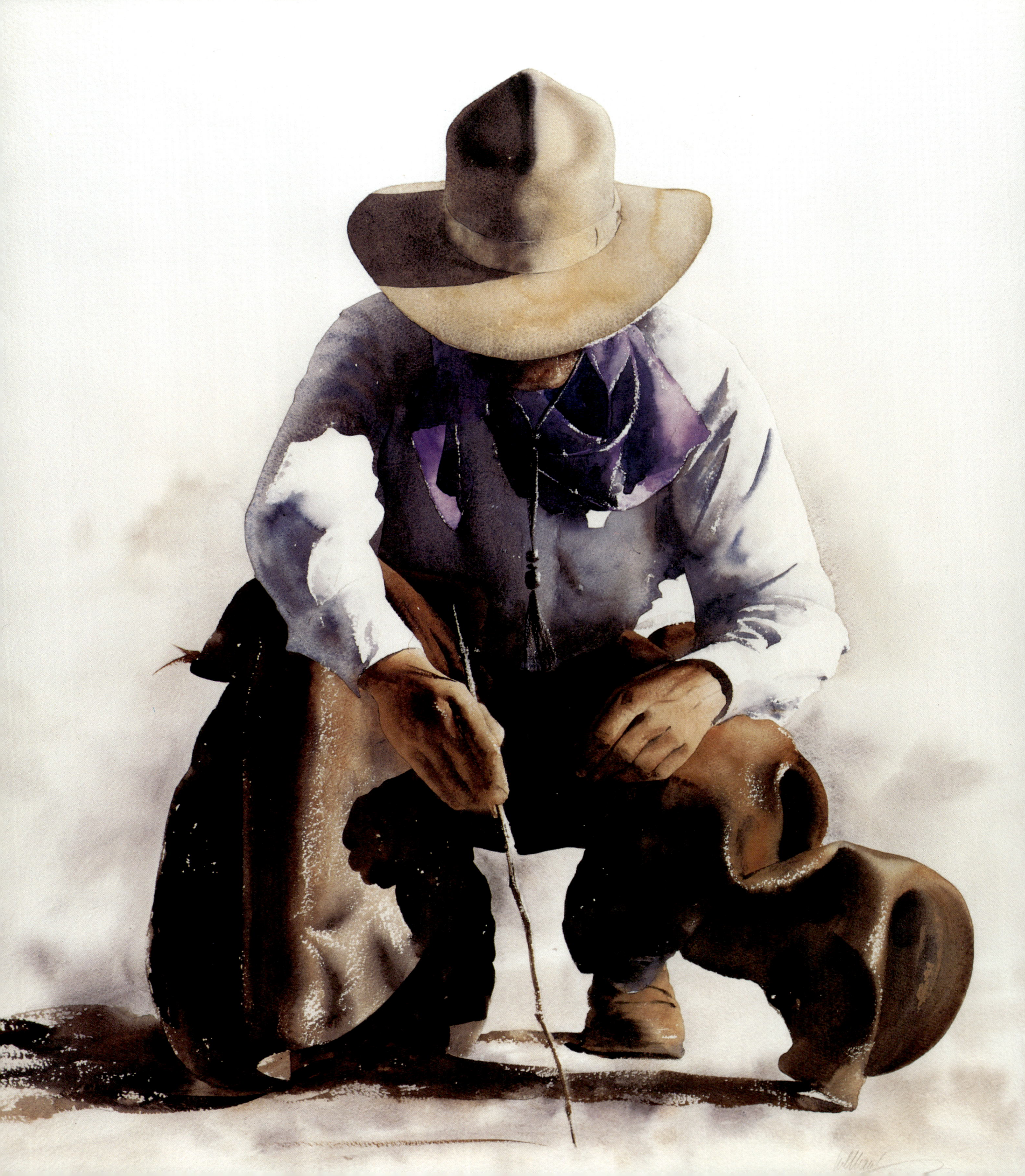

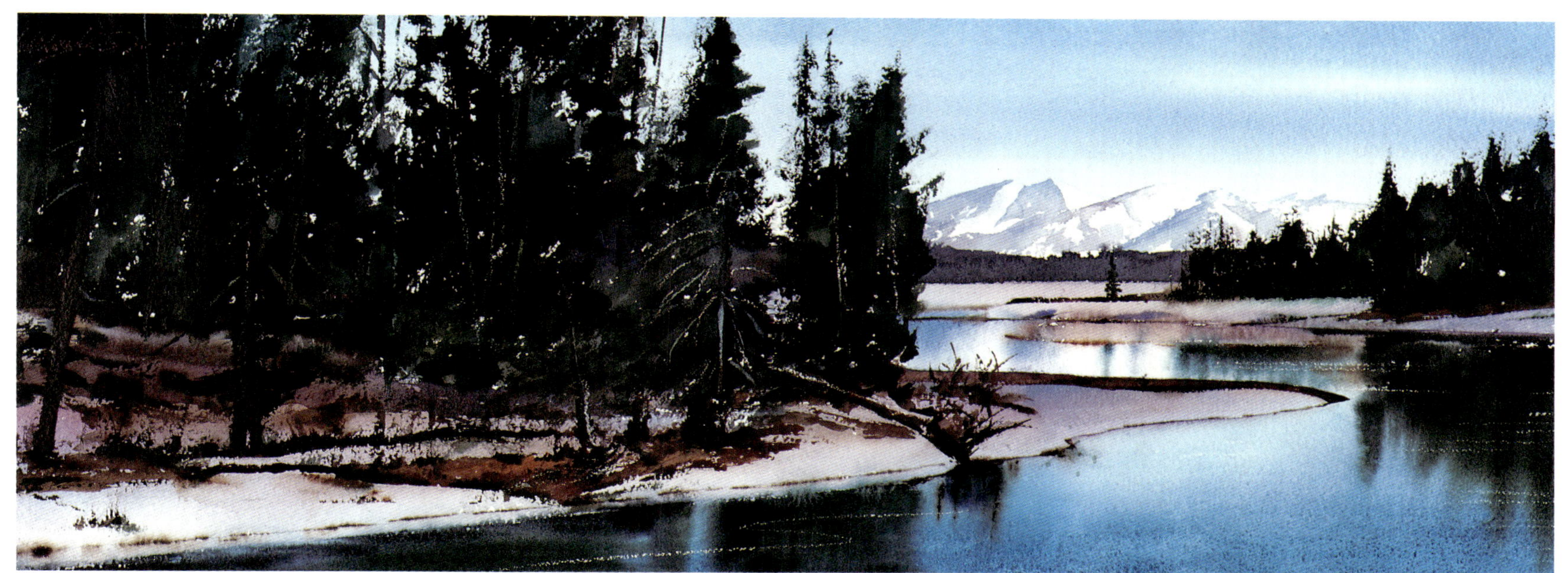

Yellowstone Thaw

(OPPOSITE)

The Cypher

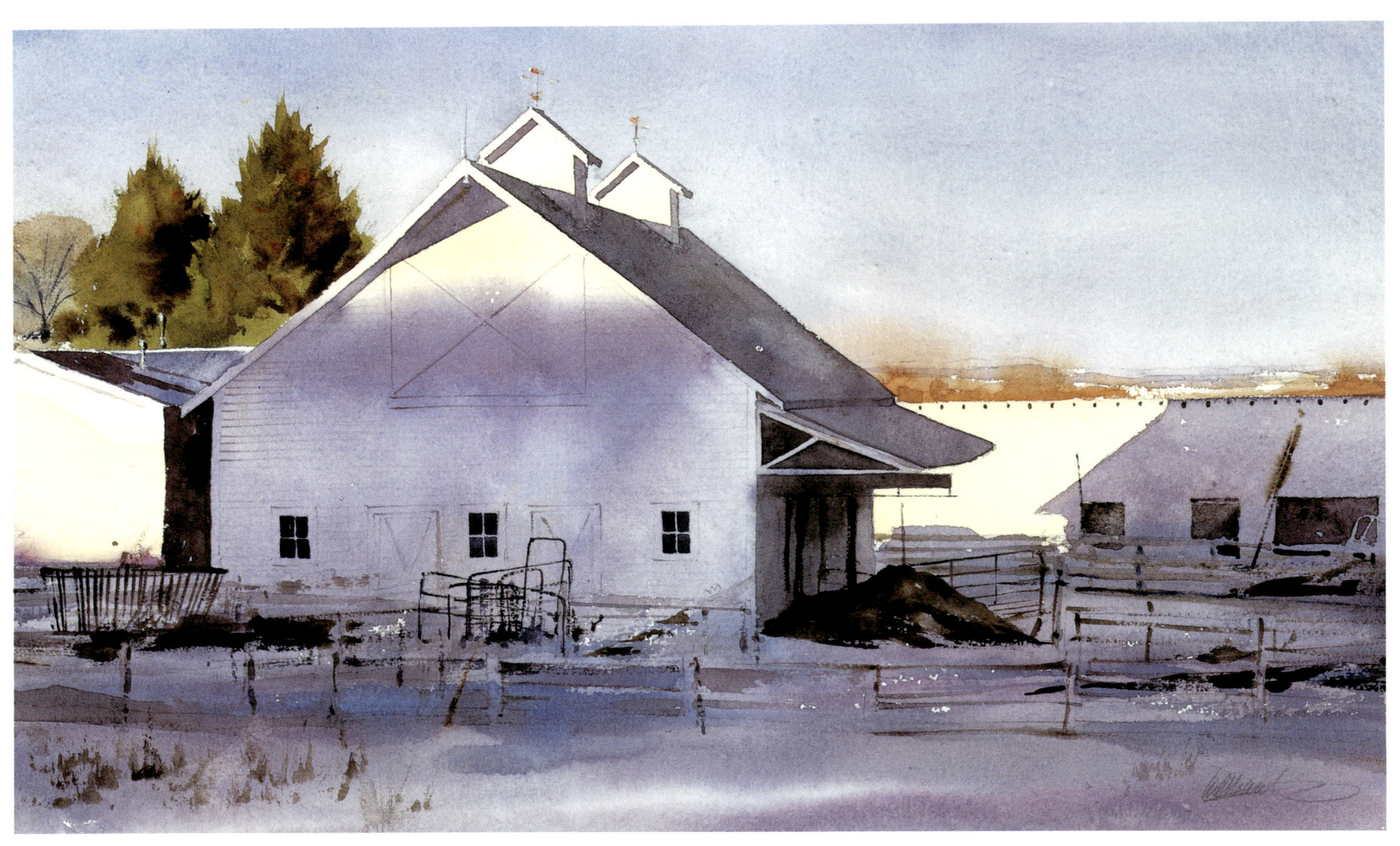

Morning Shadow

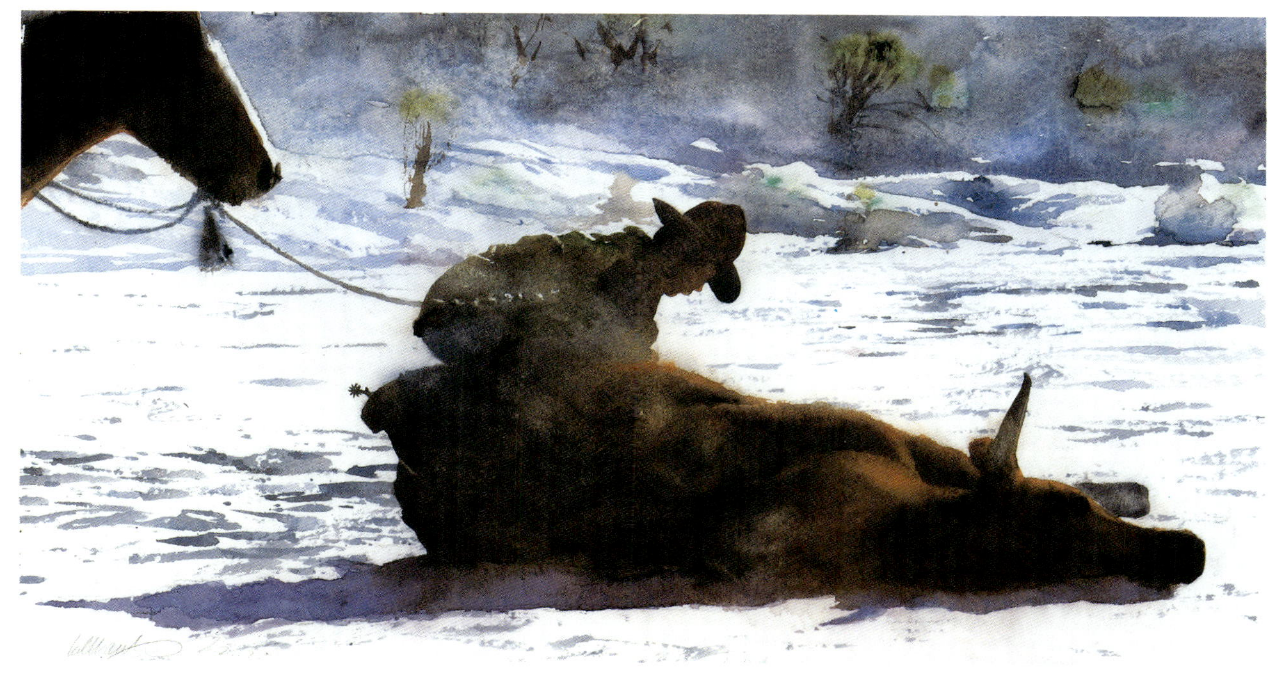

Thirty Below

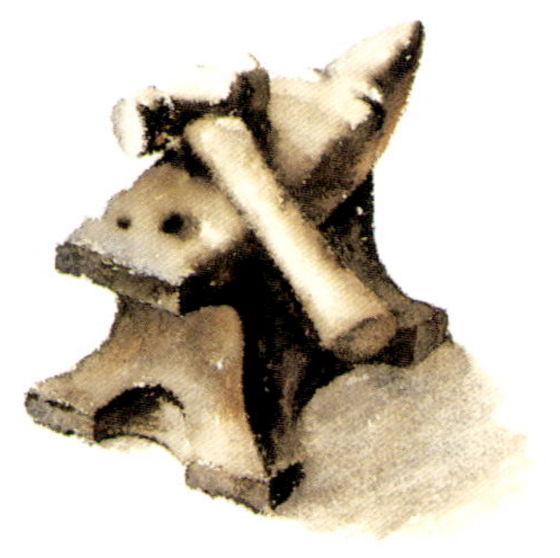

RANDY STOWELL grew up surrounded by handtools. He learned to repair and make them himself, and over the years he has collected and restored countless artifacts of the nineteenth century, including sheep wagons and buck-rakes. He and his brother Gary still use teams of horses to feed and harvest (see *The Hay Rake* on page 51). When there's a breakdown, repairs can usually be done on the ranch. That's important since the nearest gas station is hours away.

(ABOVE)
Anvil

(OPPOSITE)
Randy Stowell

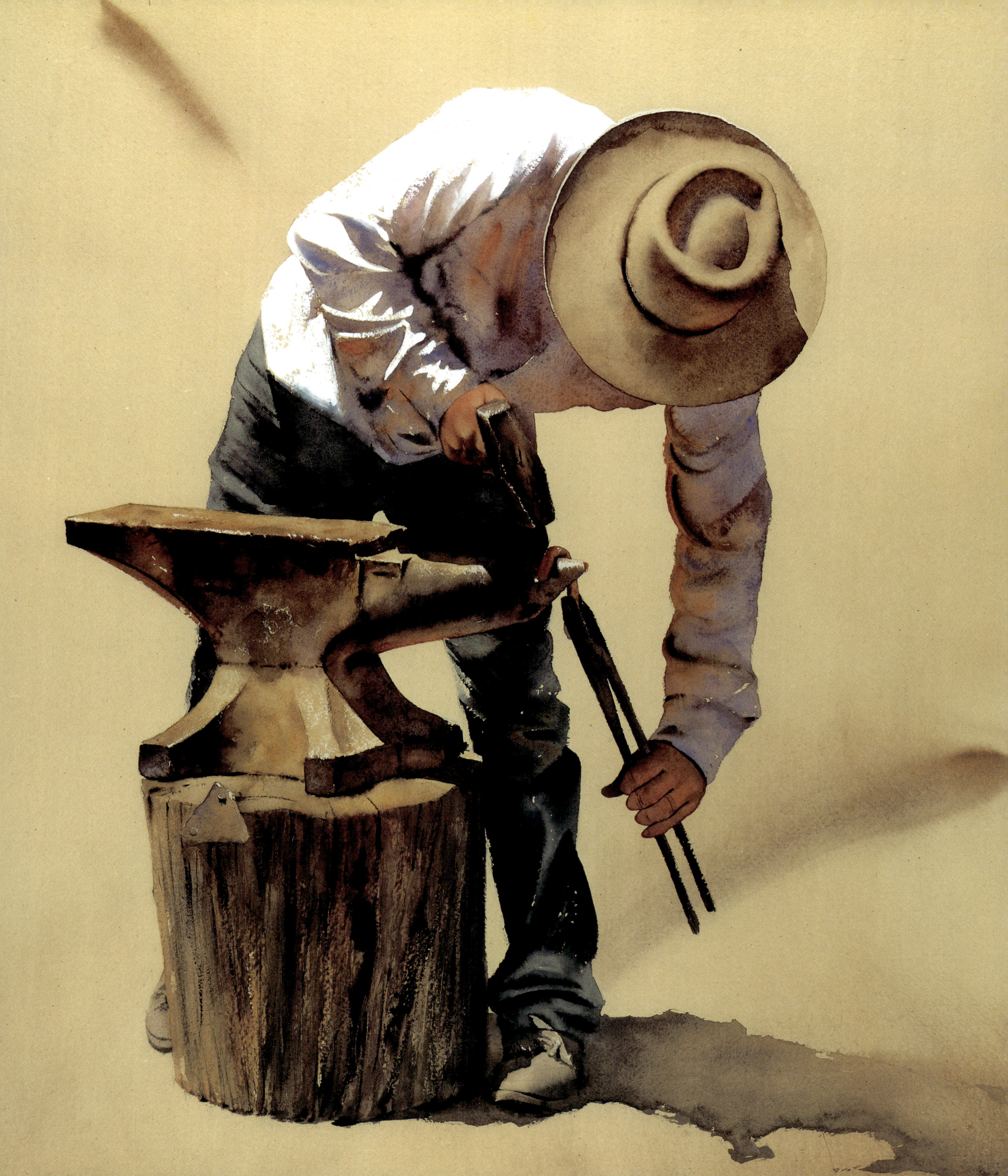

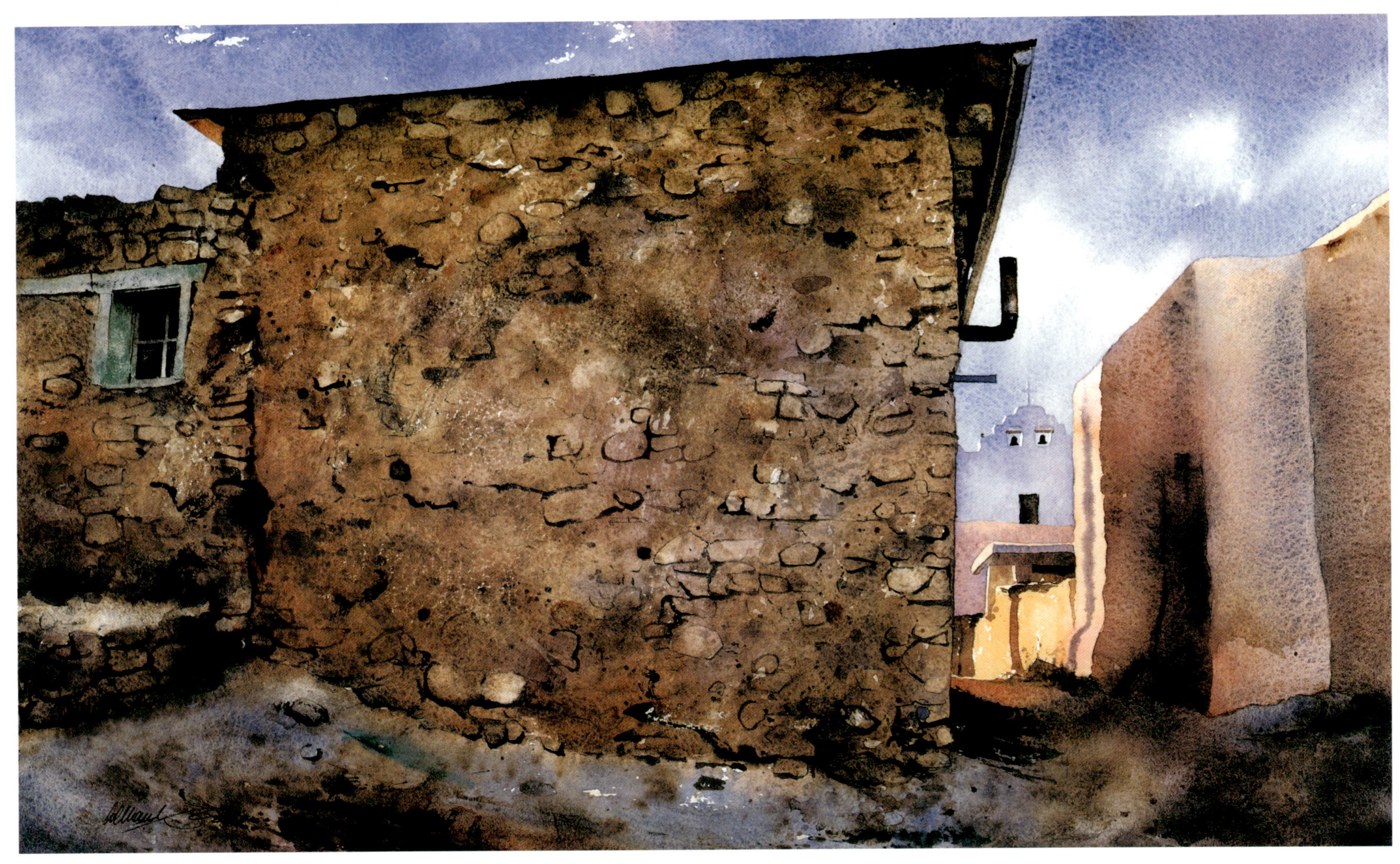

Laguna Passage

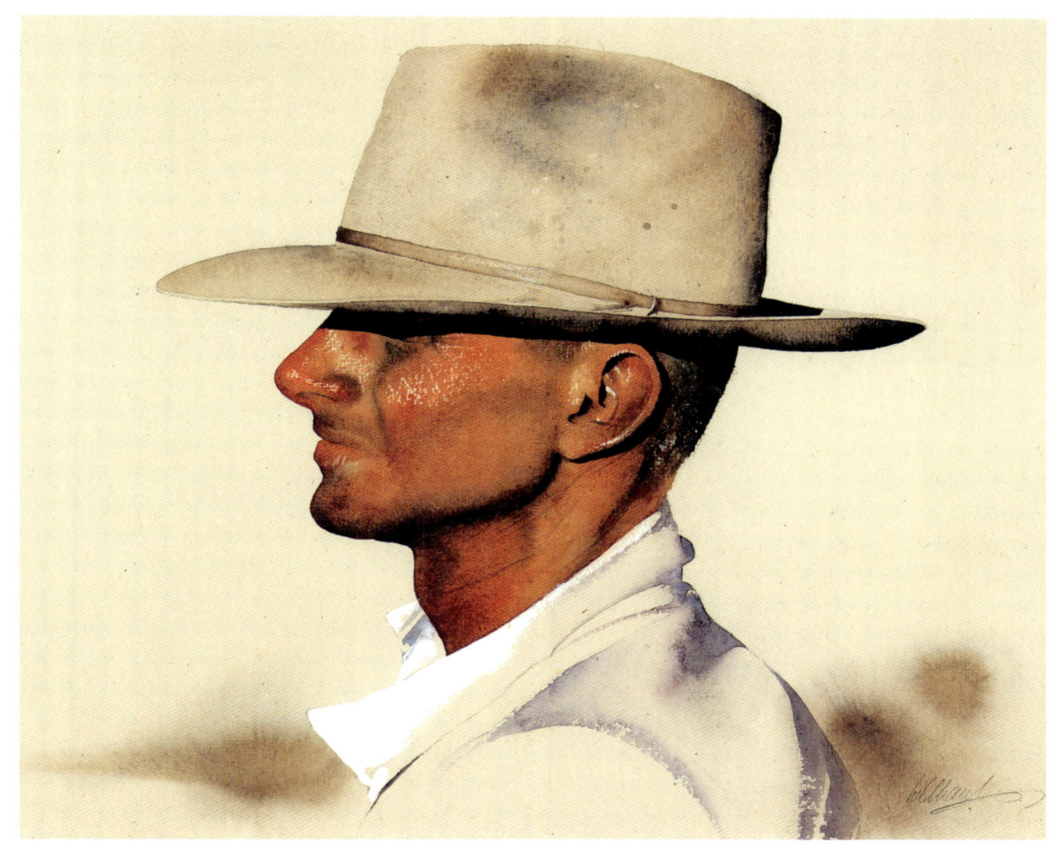

Mr. Schutte

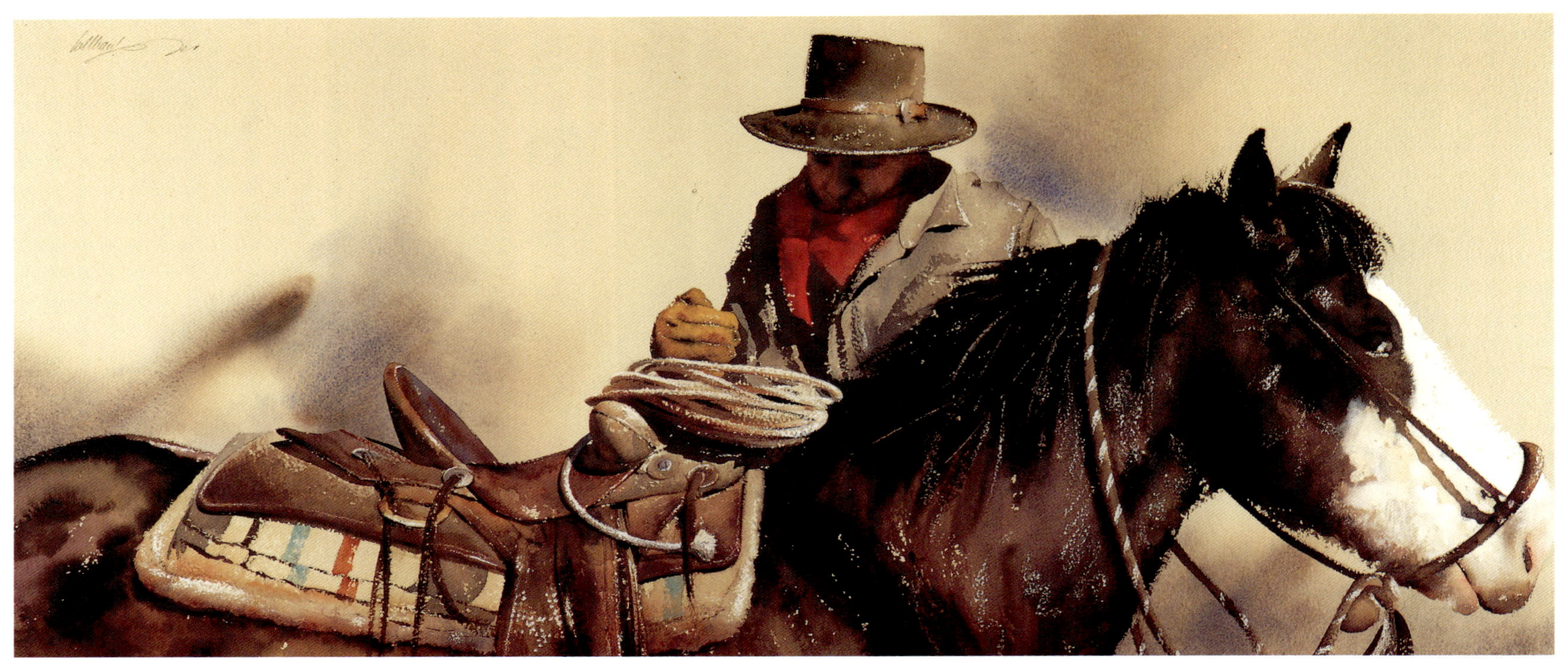

Mounting Paleface

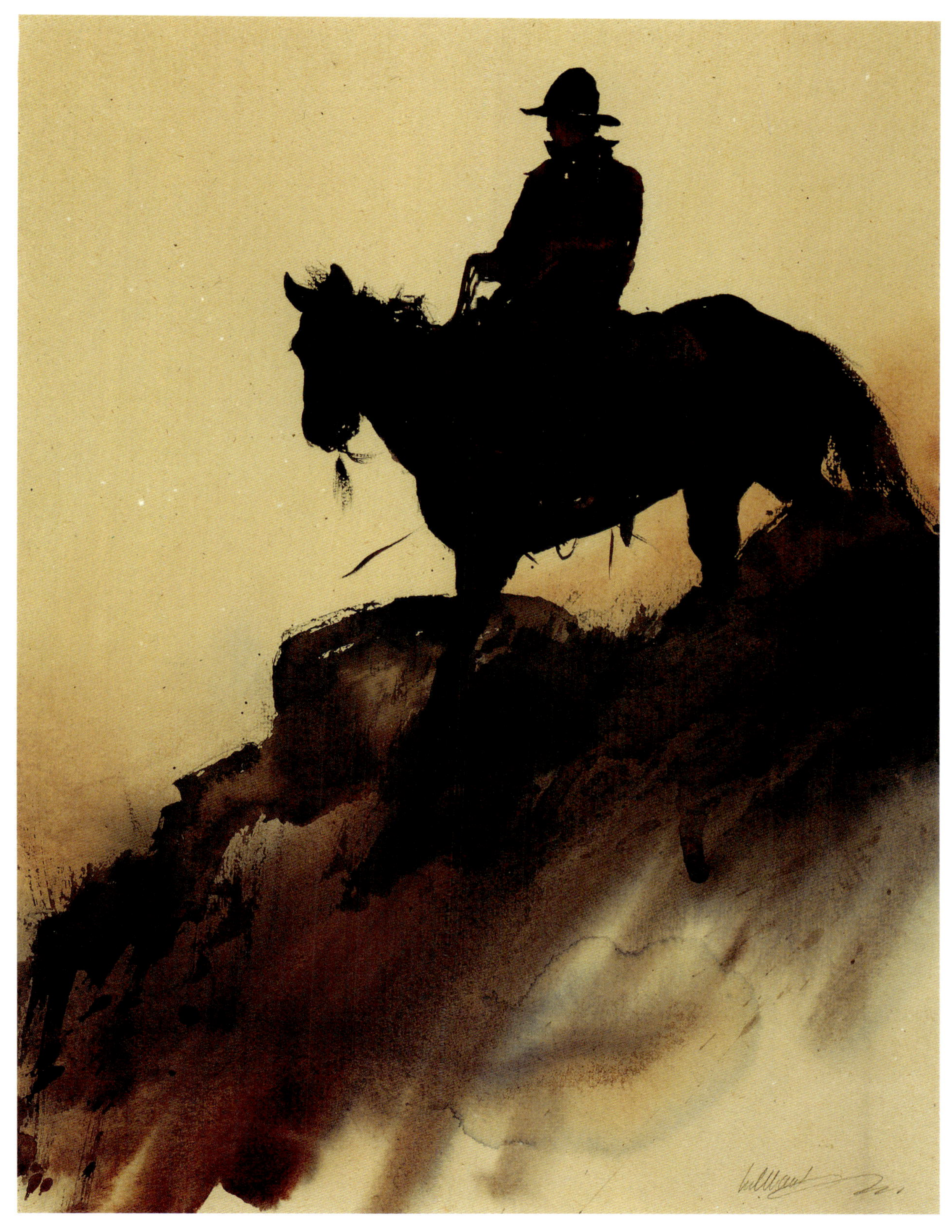

Late in the Day

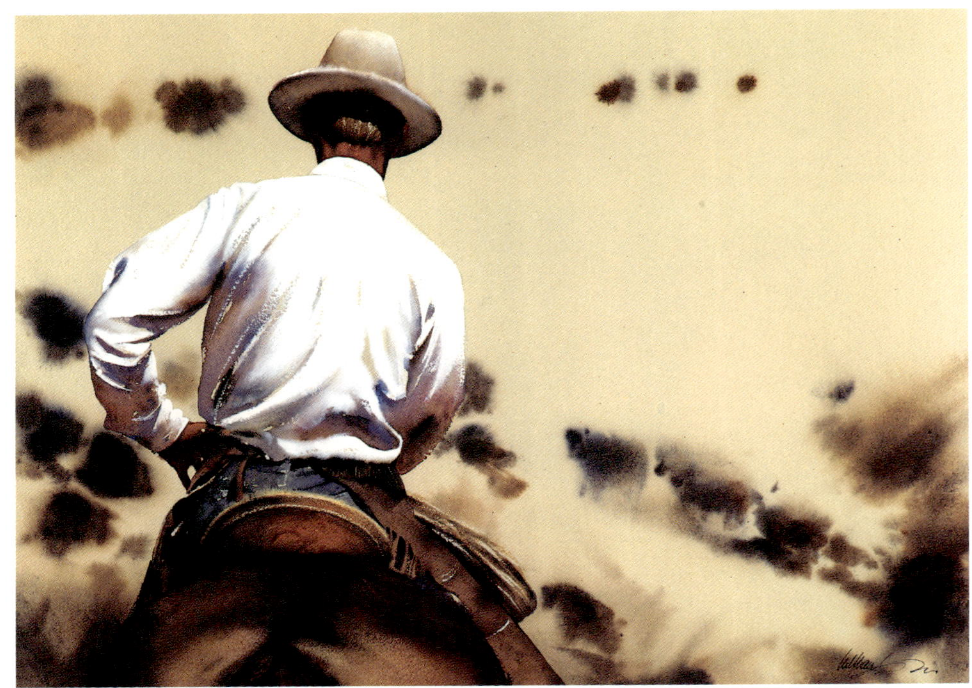

The Sentry

(OPPOSITE)

Cool Water

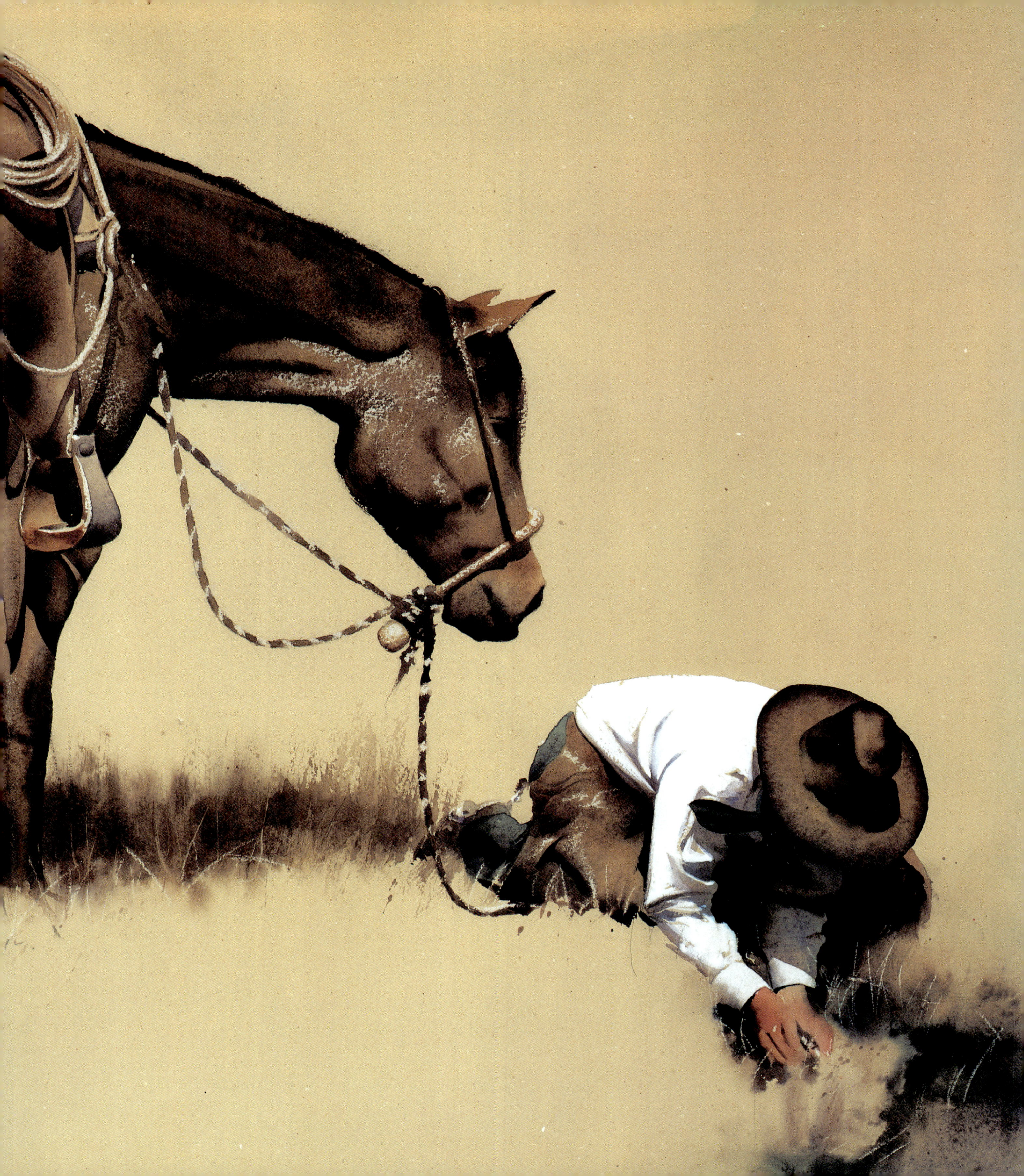

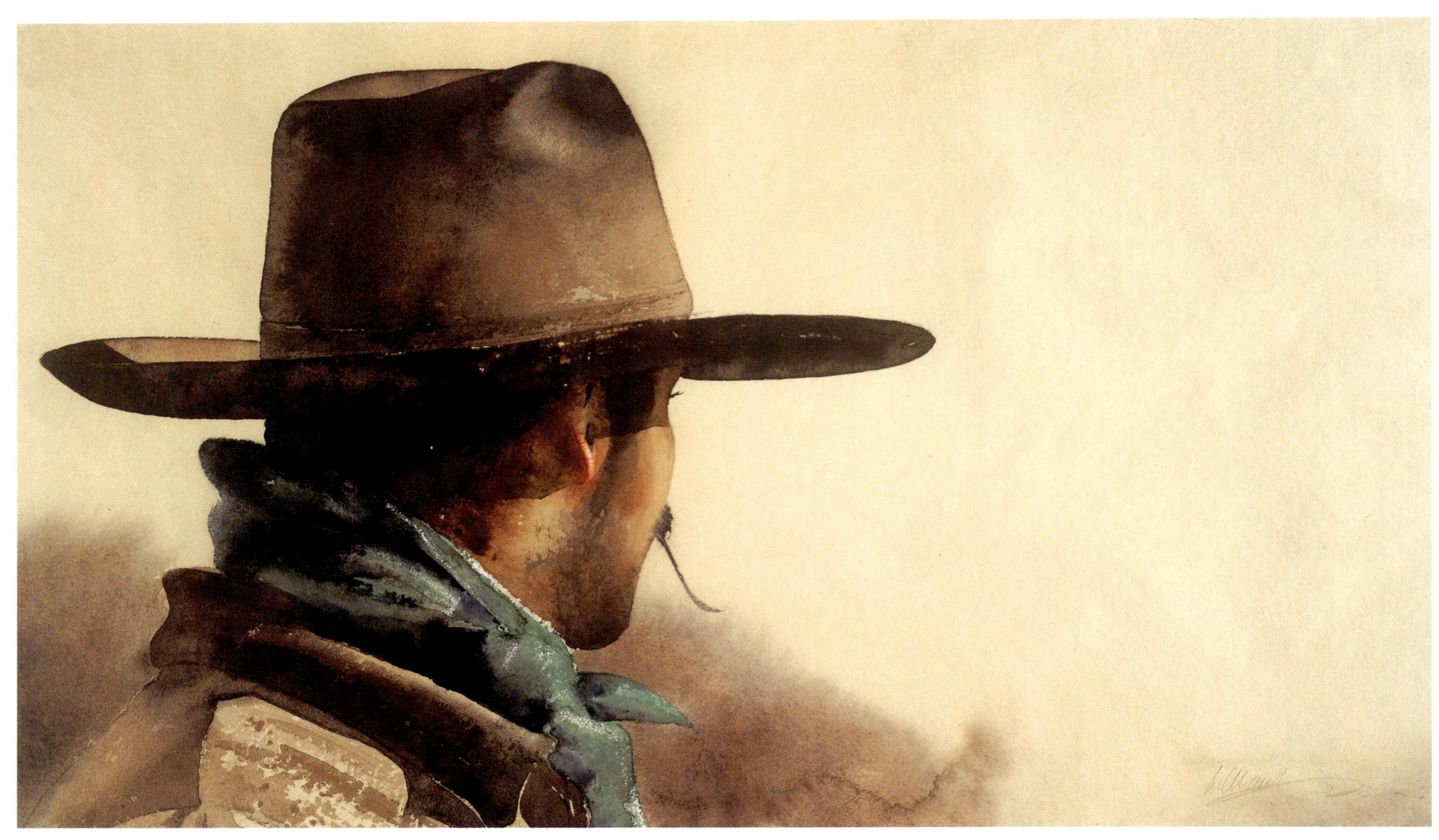

Martin Black

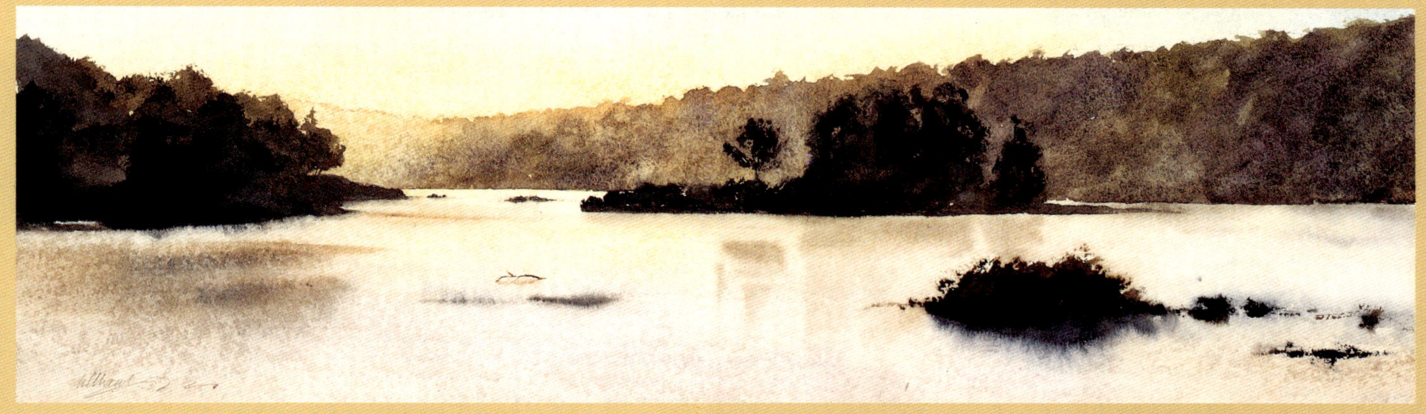

Headwaters

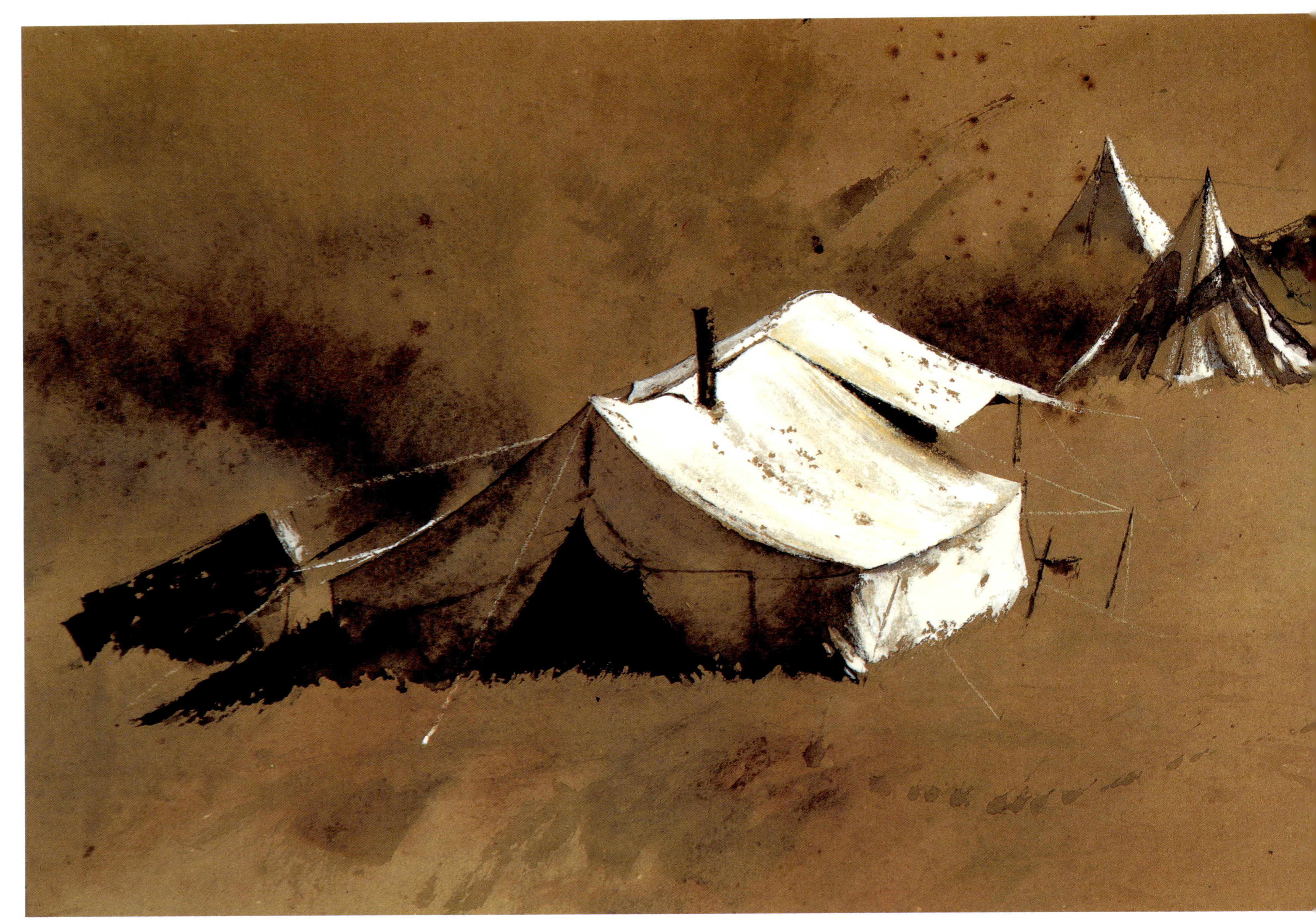

Cow Camp, Columbia Basin

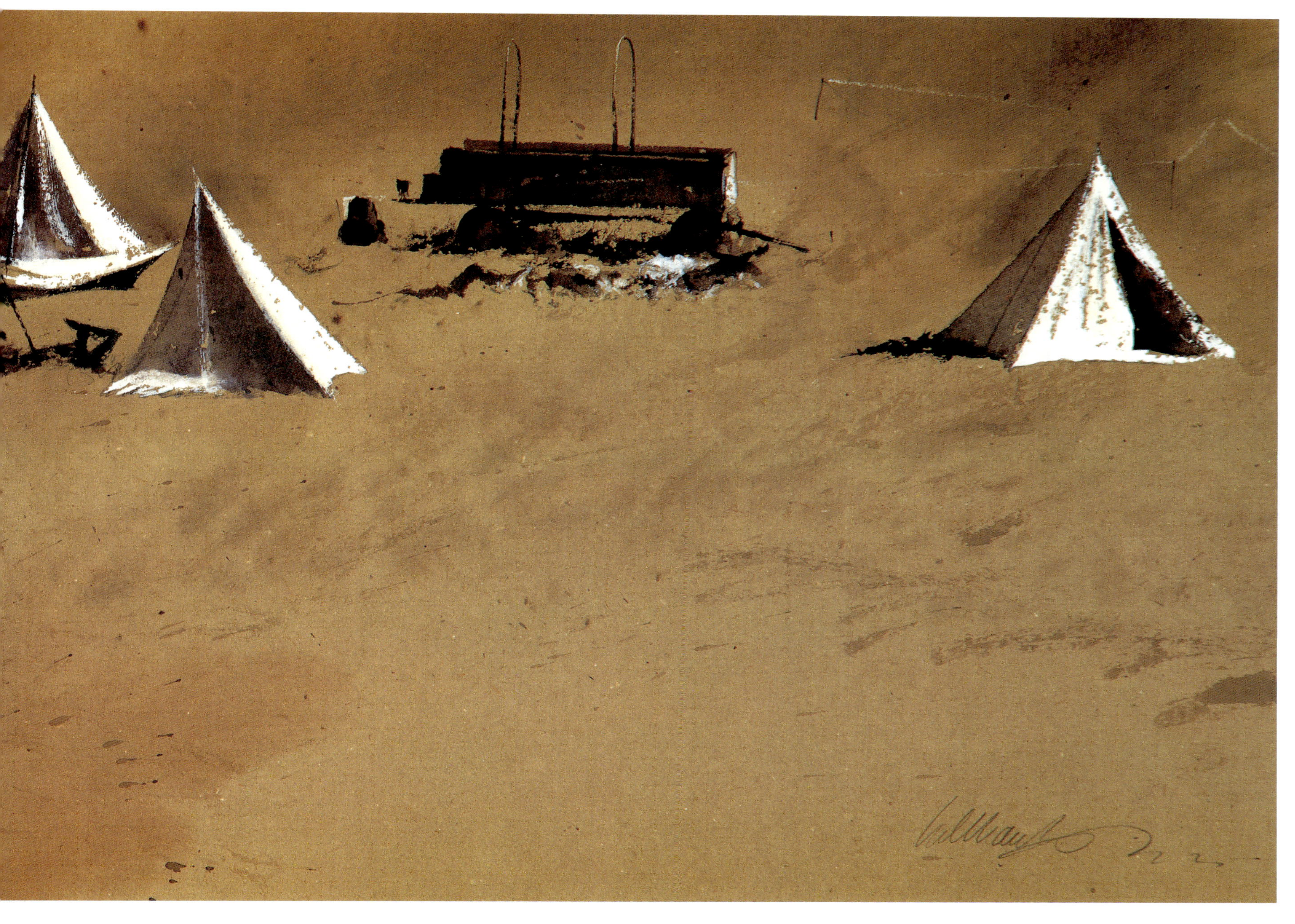

Cow camp is a mobile home base cowboys use when tending the herd. The cook tent (lower left) consists of a wood-burning stove, where everyone congregates, and a cookwagon. The cowboss and jigger boss sit on one side, the cowboys on the other. Each man has a tepee and a bedroll that are carried in a bedwagon, or 'hoodlum.'

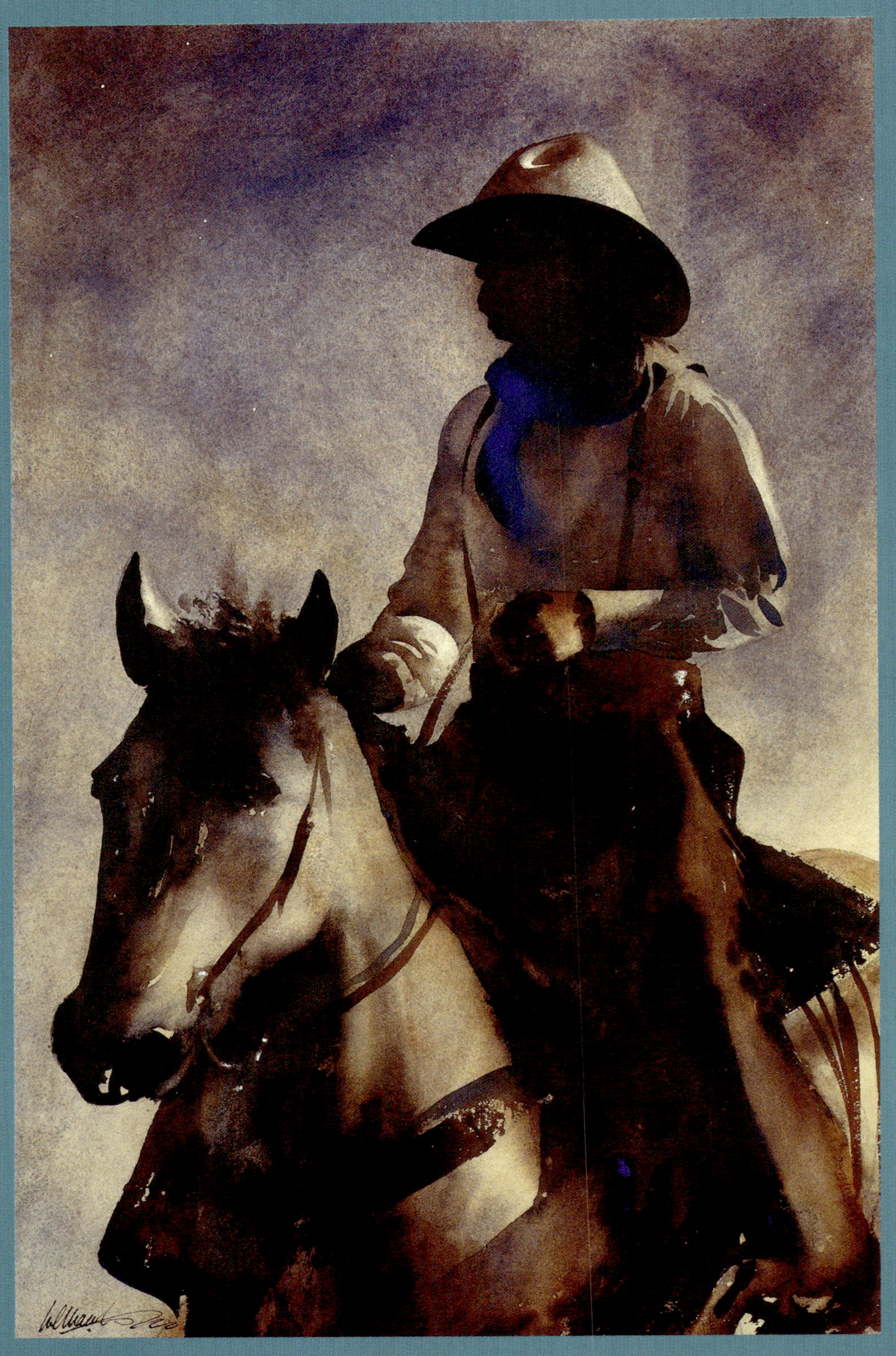

Nightherd

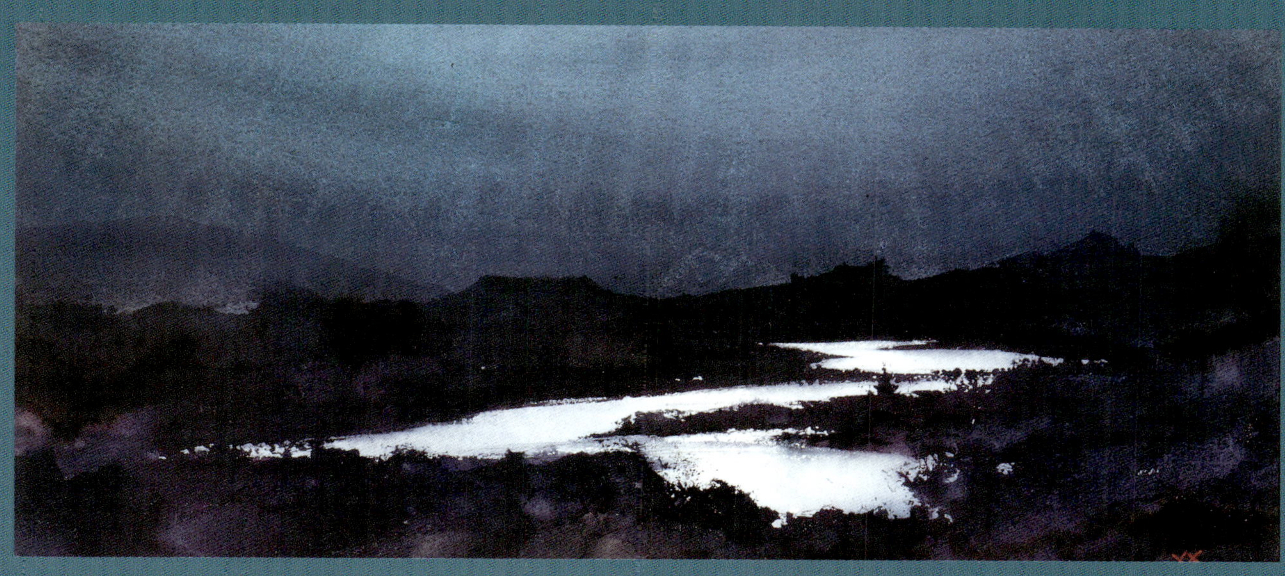

Moonlight on the Colorado

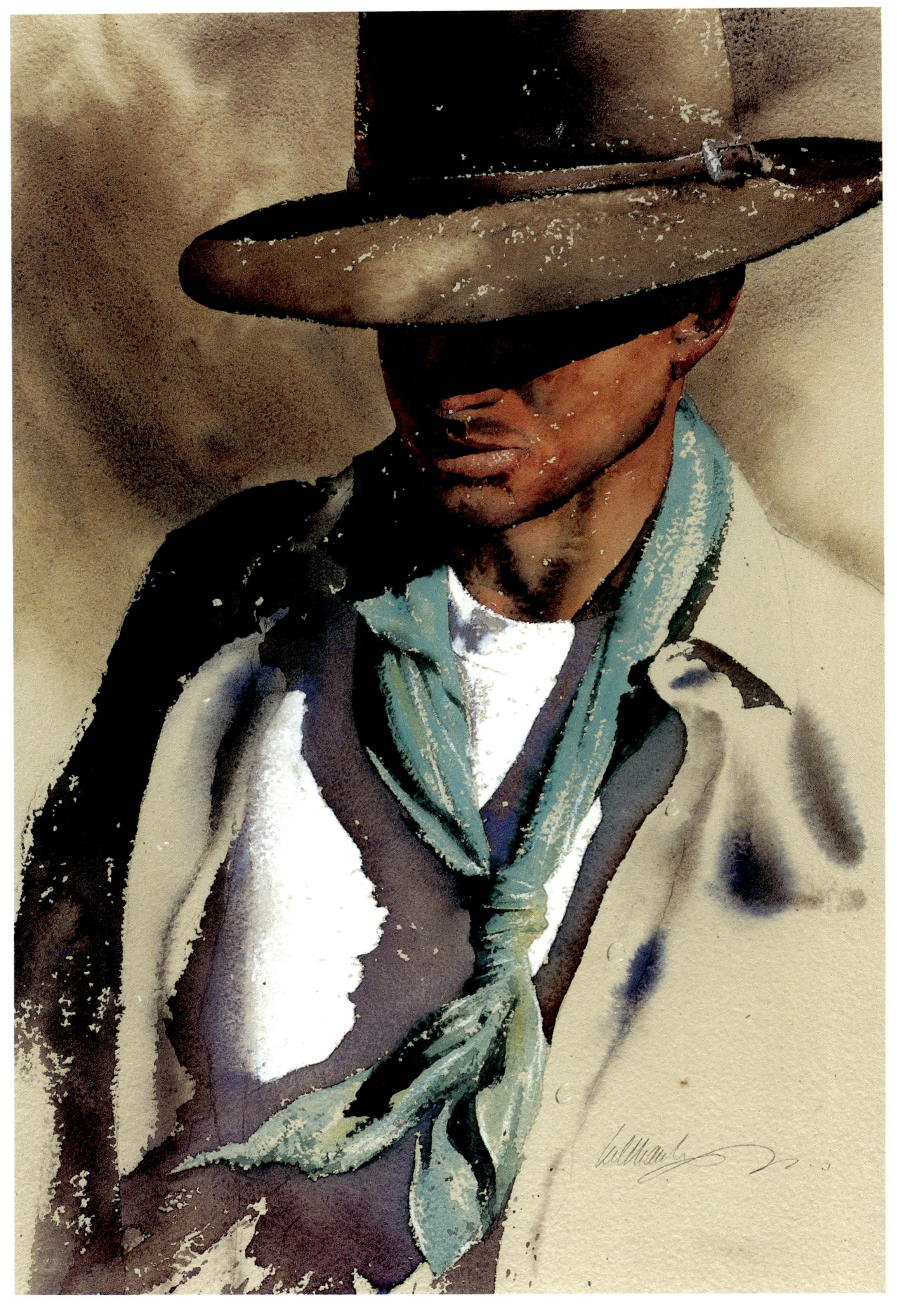

Wash Up

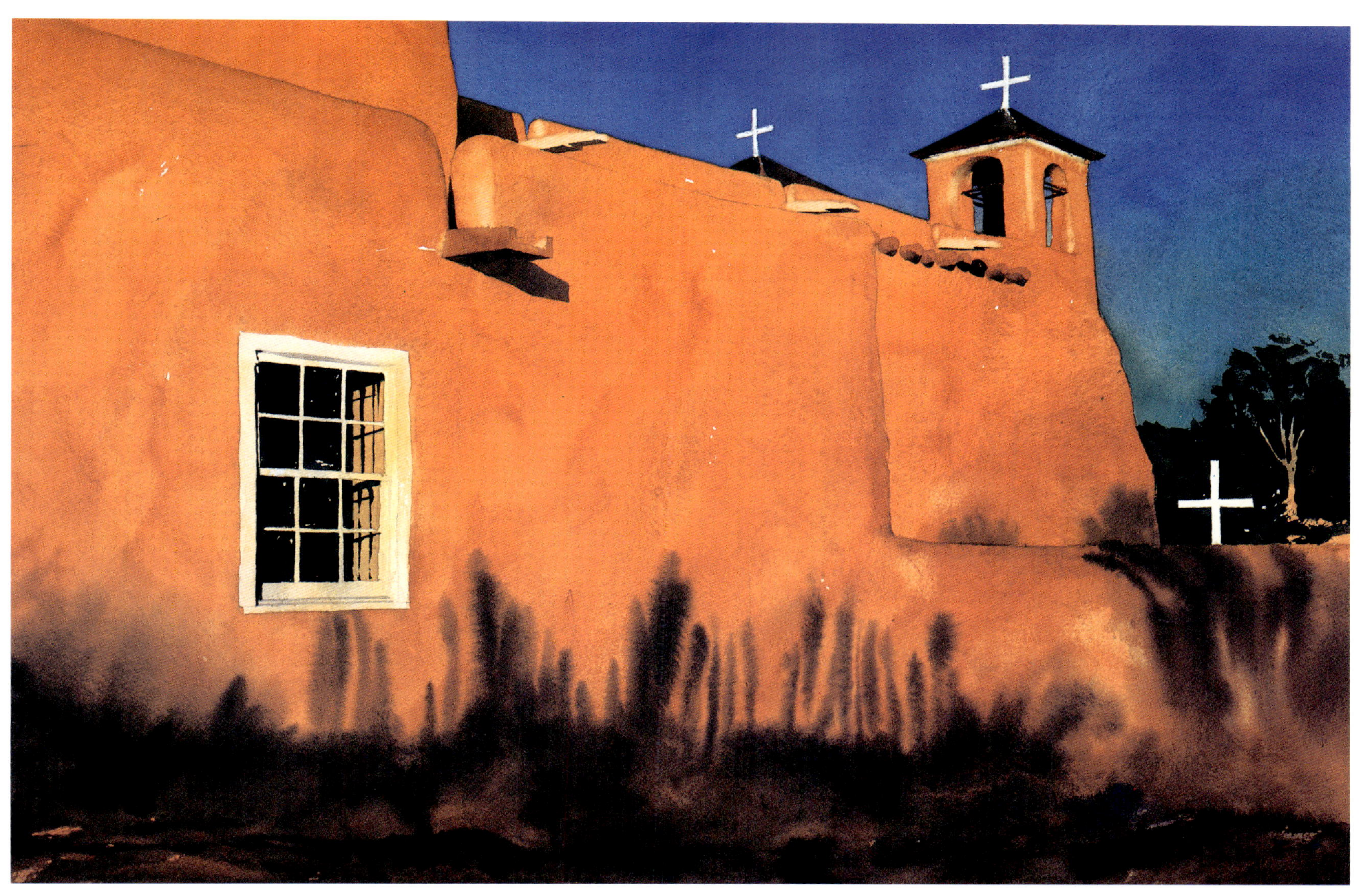

Tres Cruces

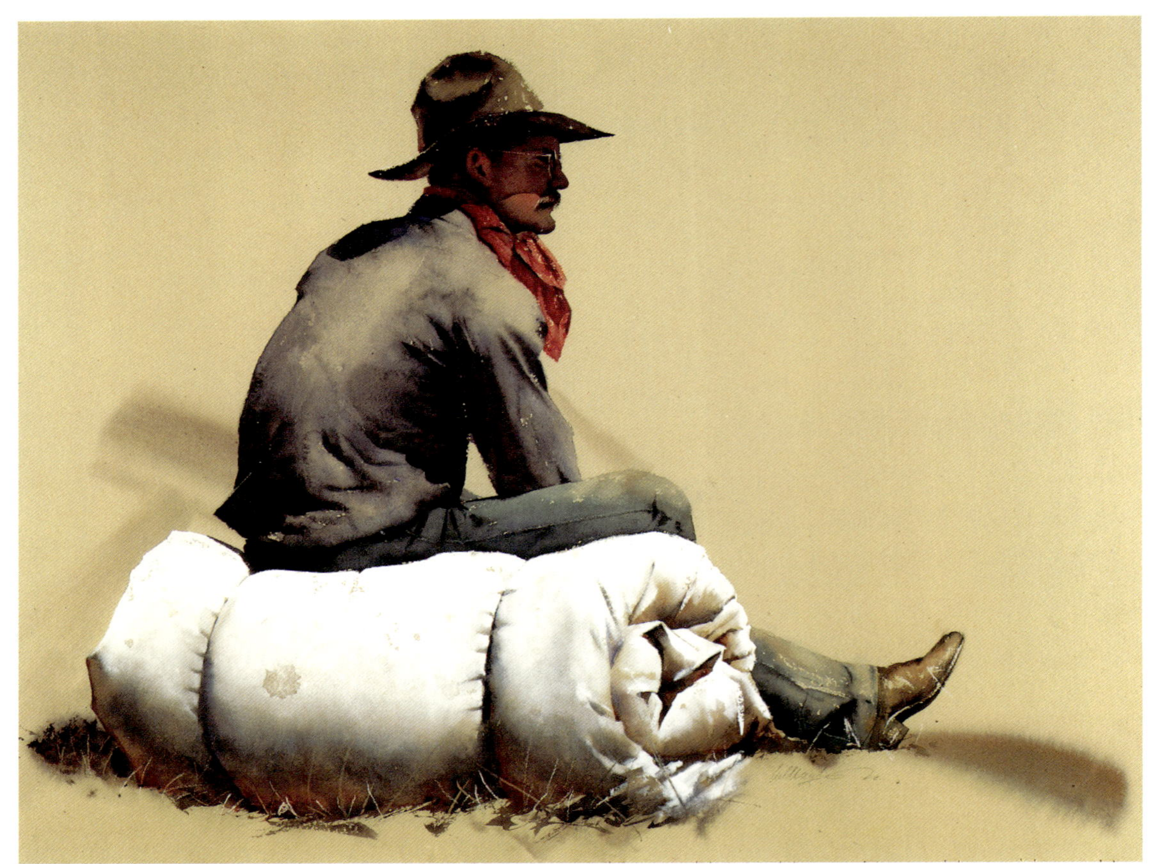

Living Room

(OPPOSITE)

Bucksnort

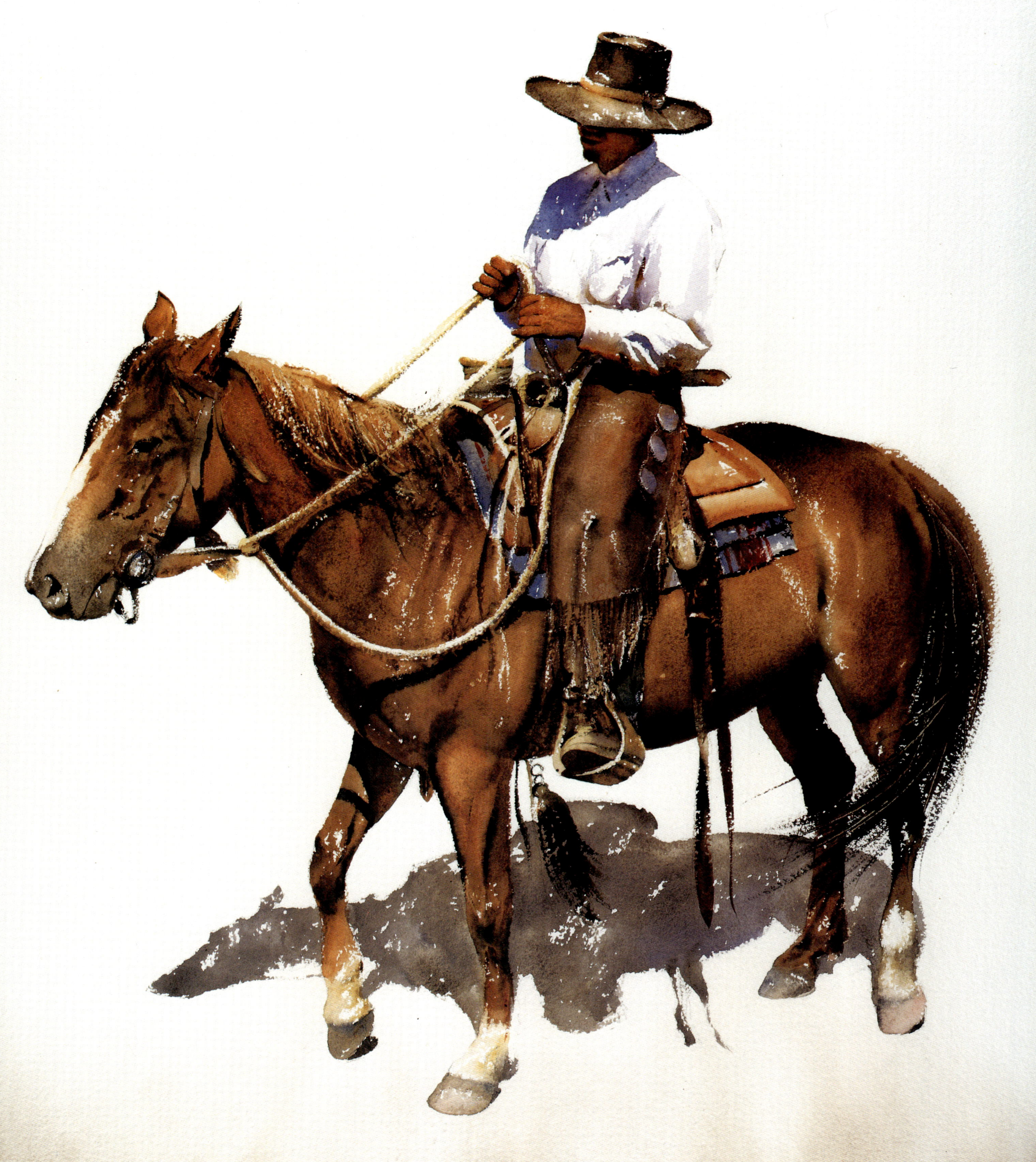

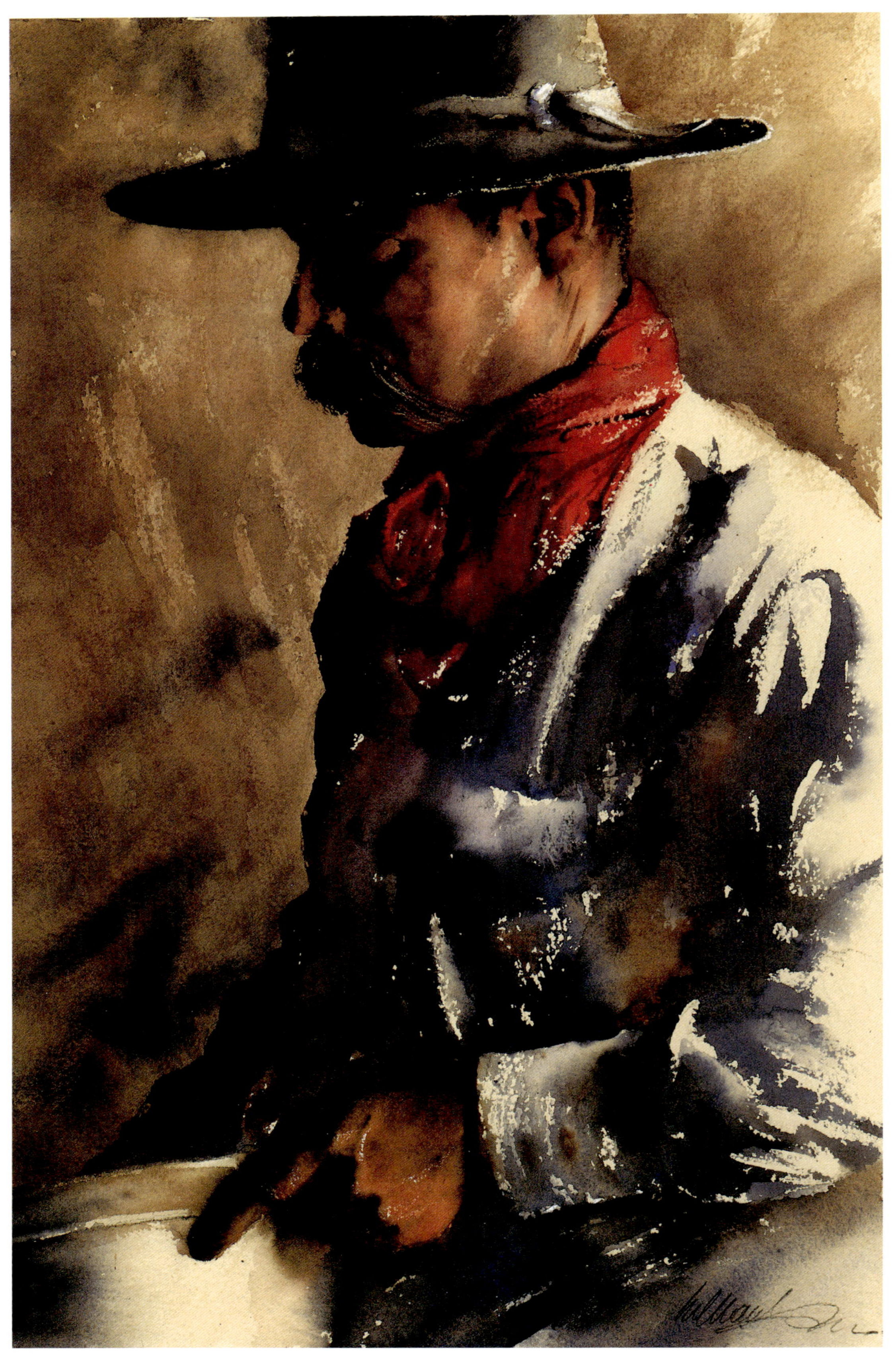

Evening Grain

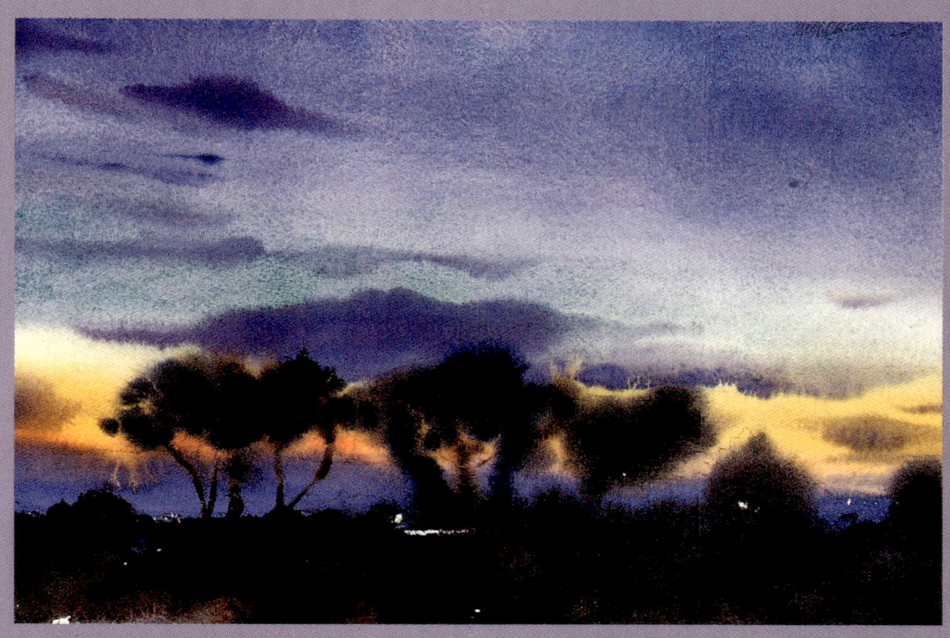

Winecup Headquarters, Before Dawn

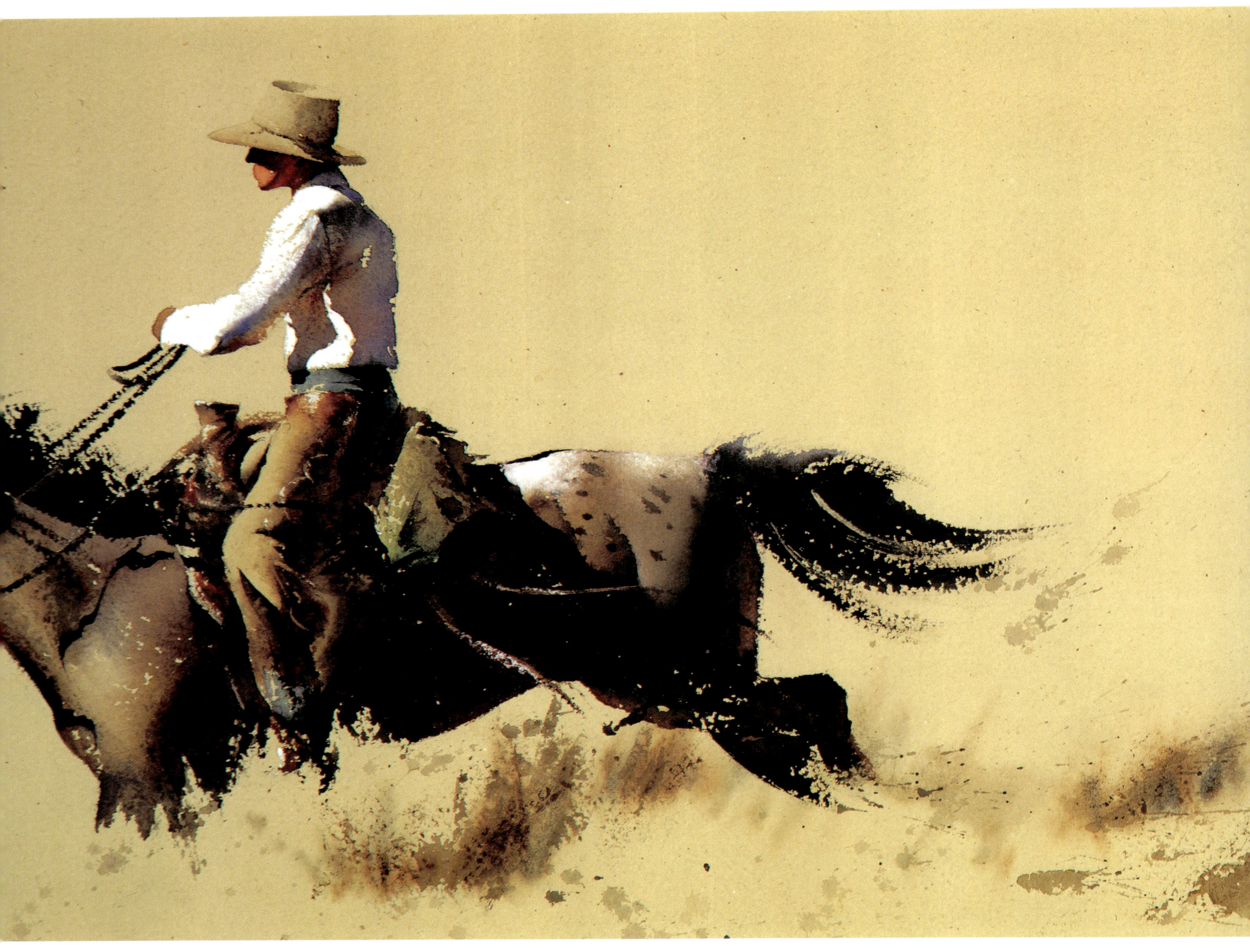

The Fugitive

Tom Dorrance, on the right, is a small man with enormous knowledge. A highly respected horseman, he approaches horse training as a partnership. He makes the *right thing* easy and the *wrong thing* difficult — a philosophy of horsemanship that is also a philosophy of life.

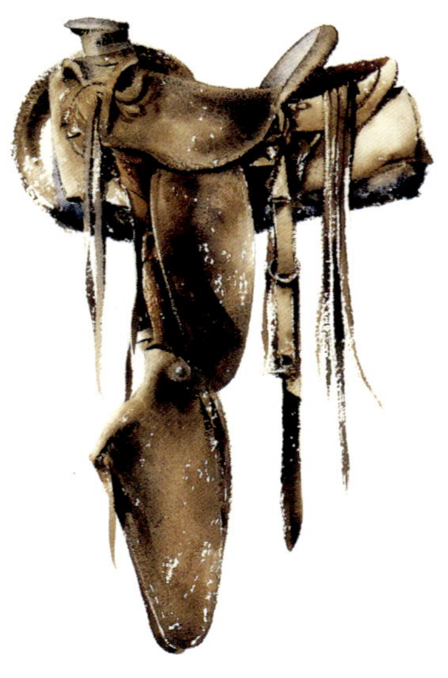

Classic Wade Saddle

(opposite)

The Workshop

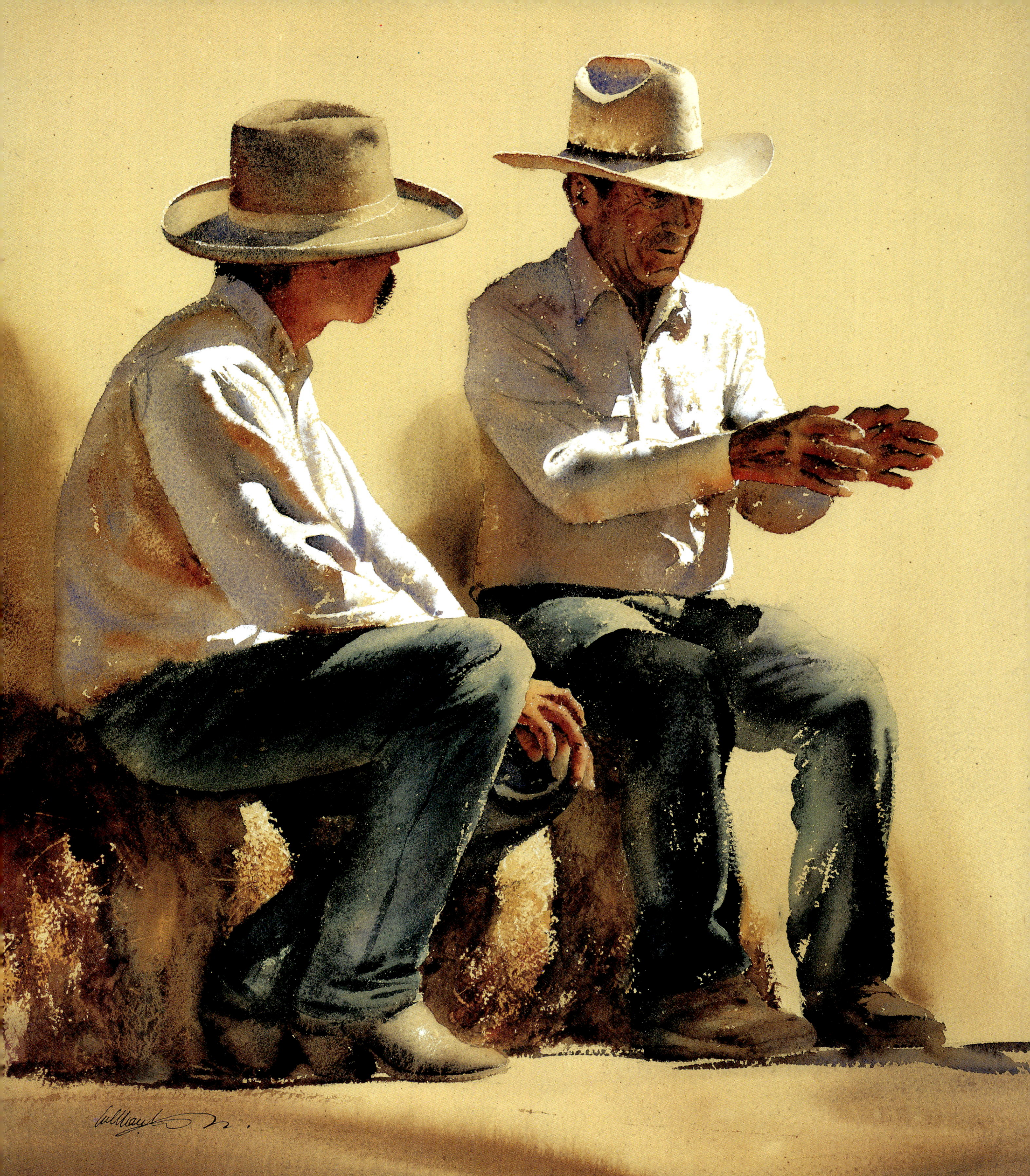

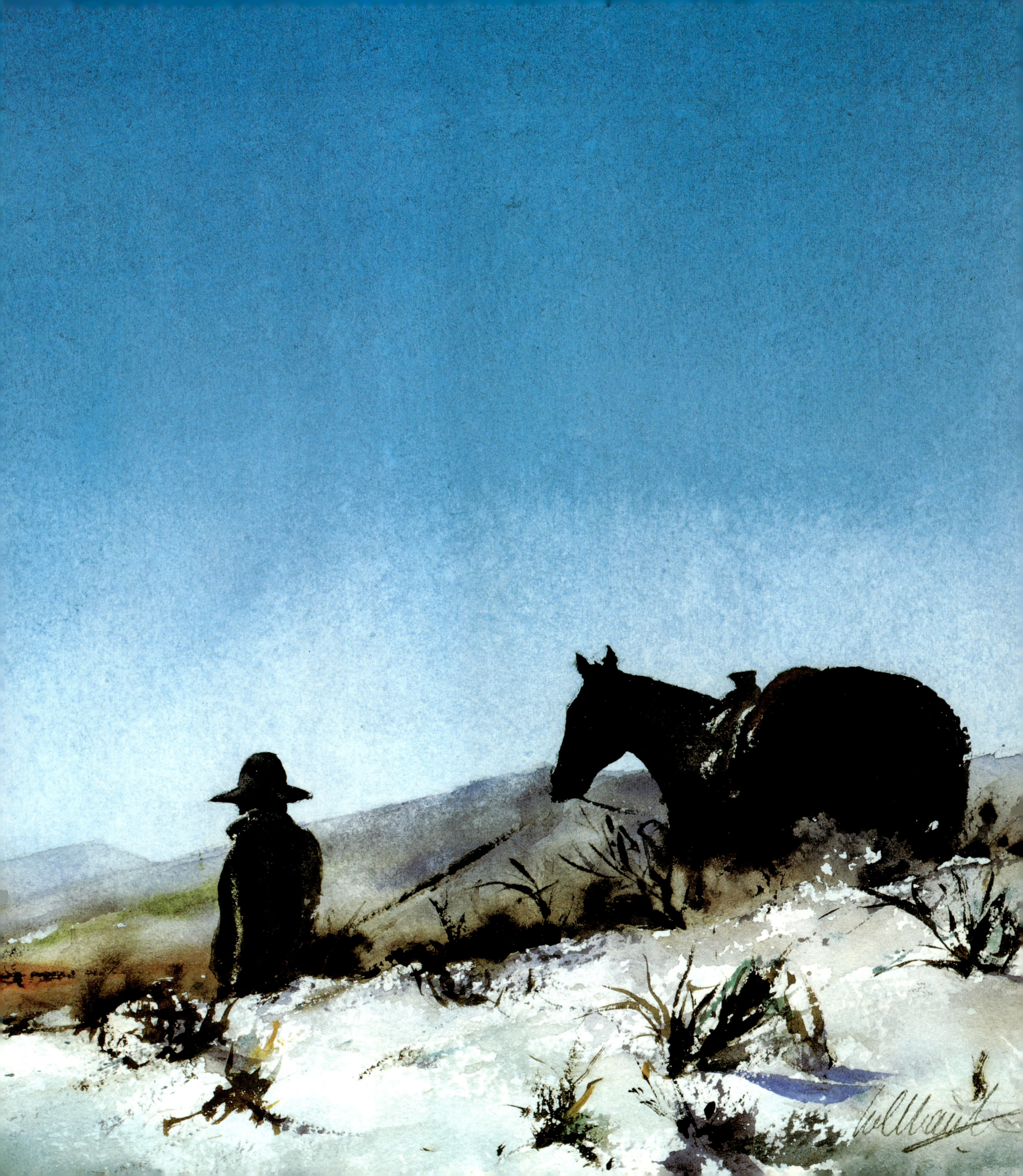

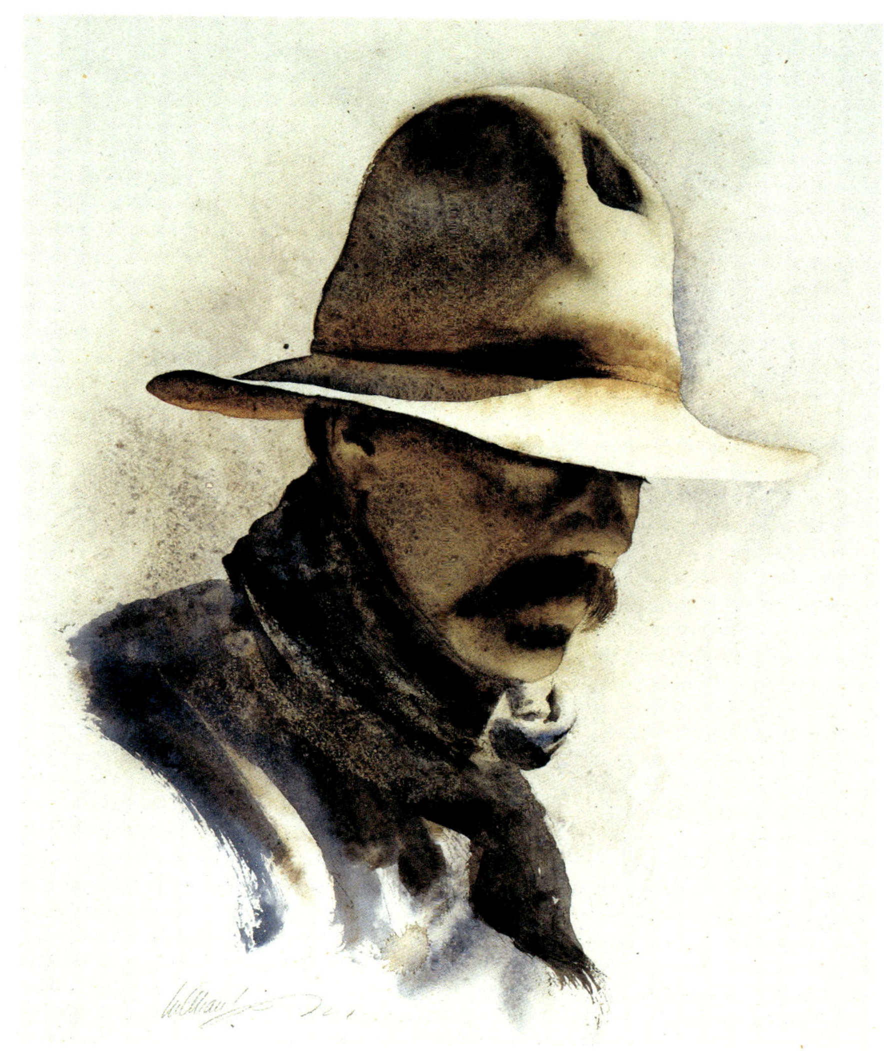

The Specter

(OPPOSITE)

High Noon

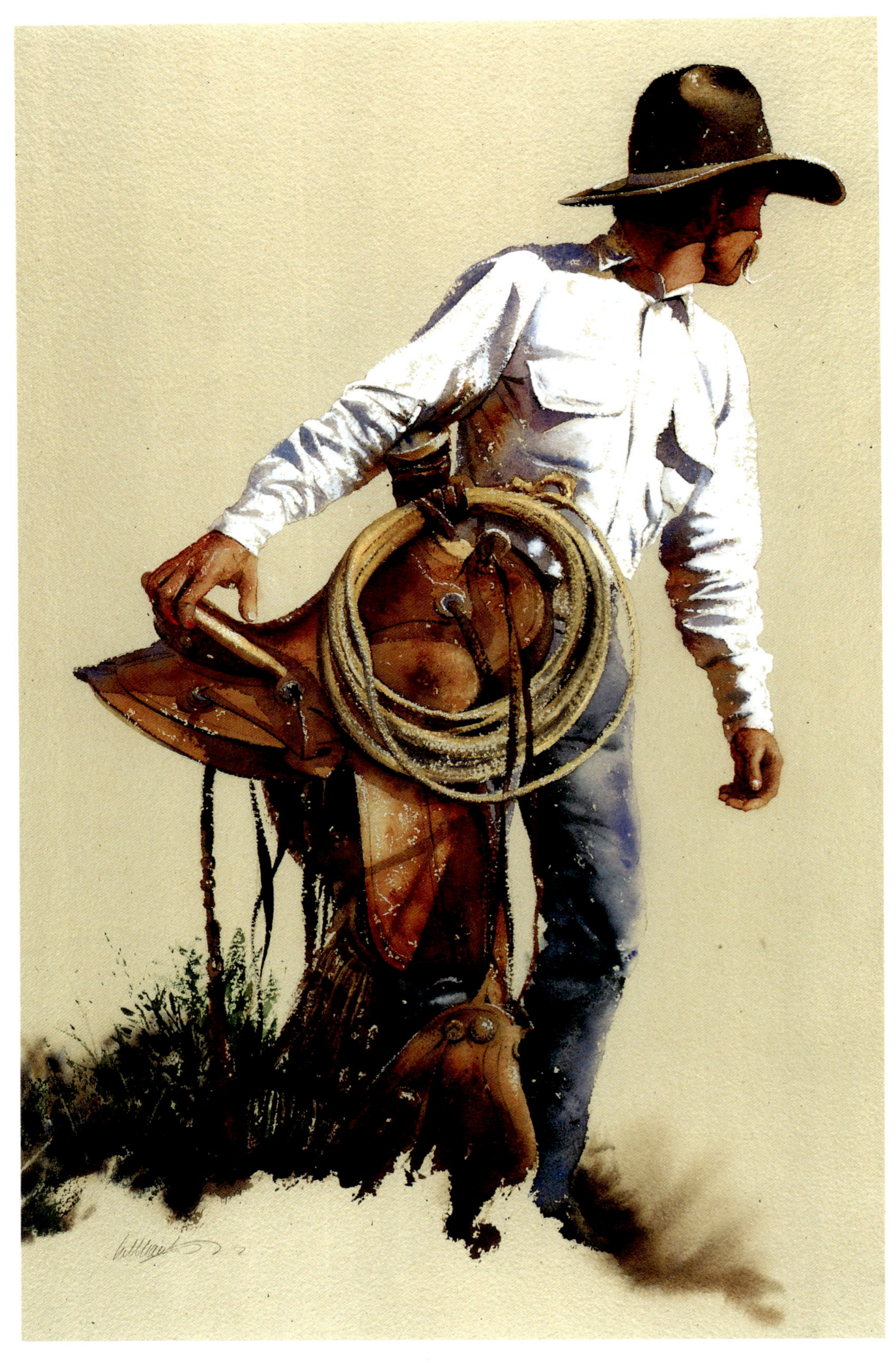

Waddie's Slick Fork

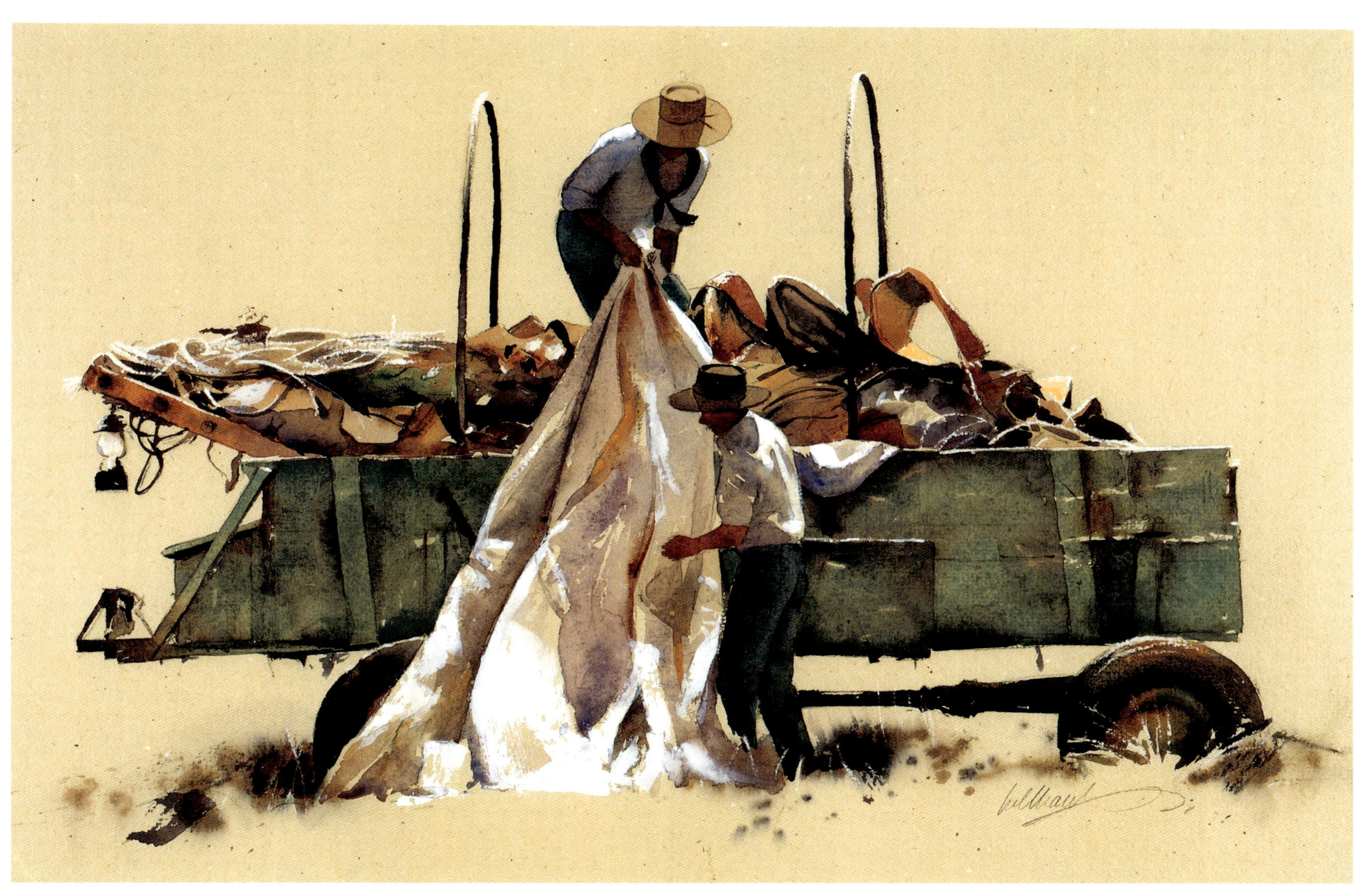

Packing Up the Bedwagon

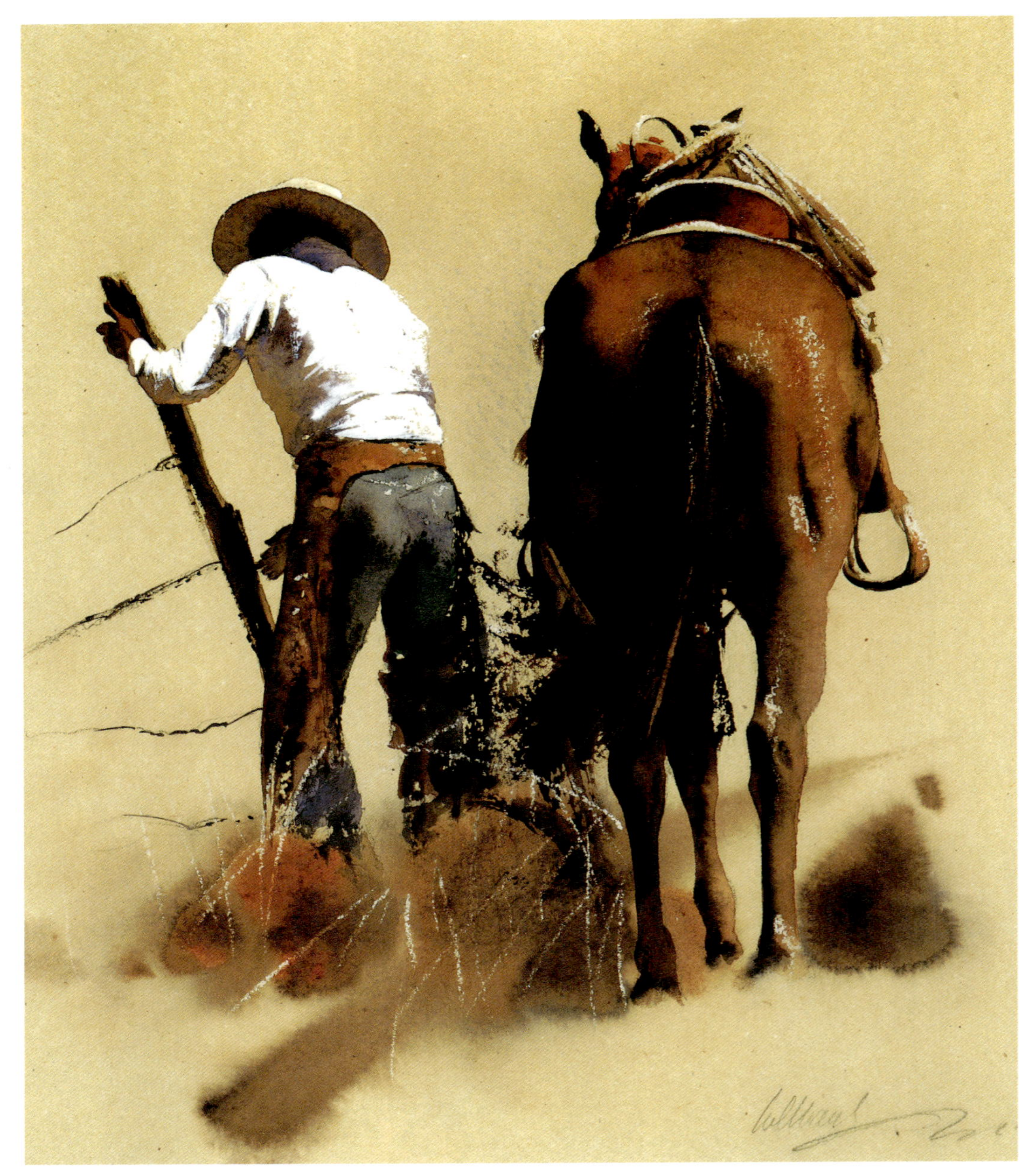

The Back Gate

(OPPOSITE)

Stampede String

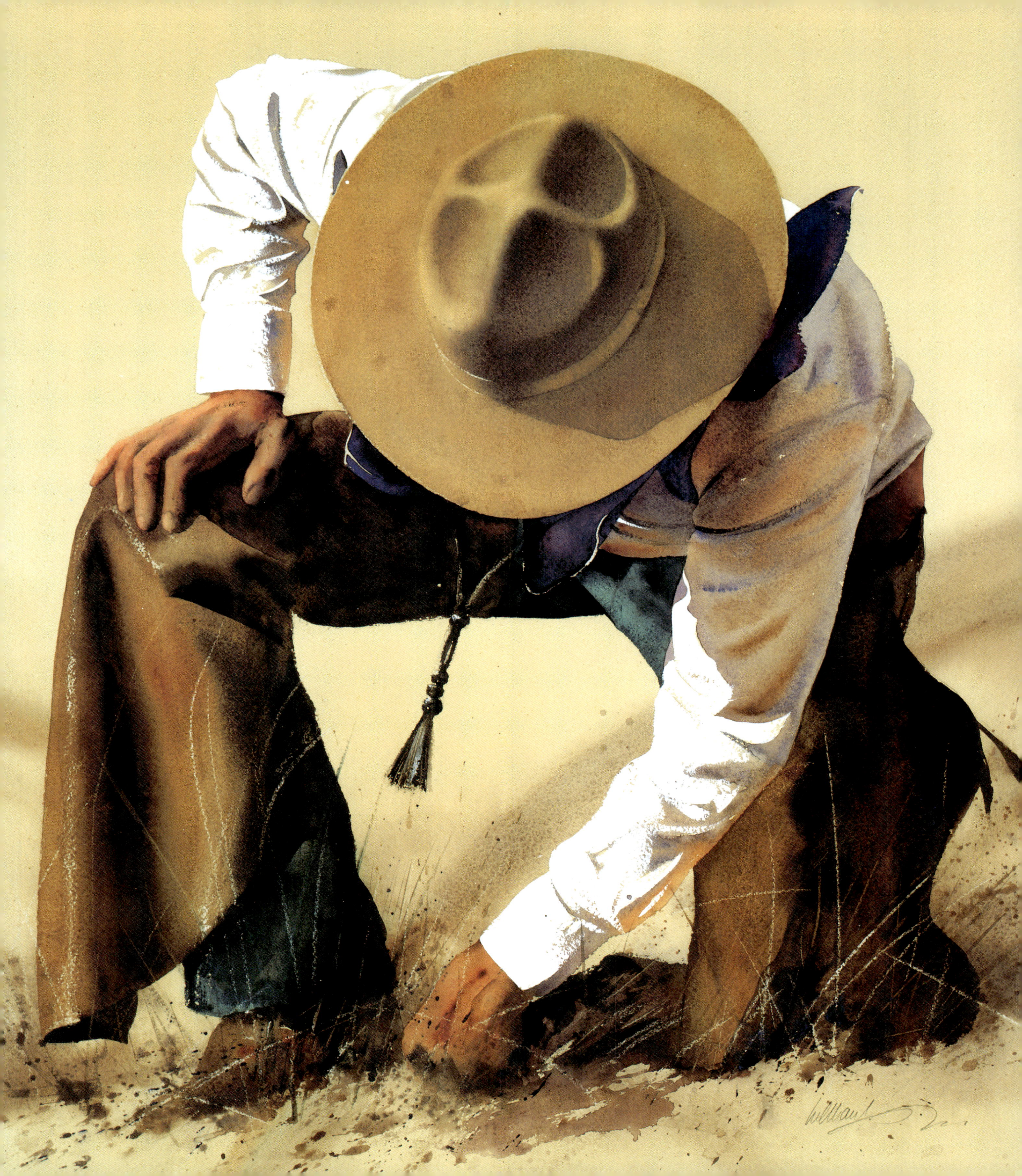

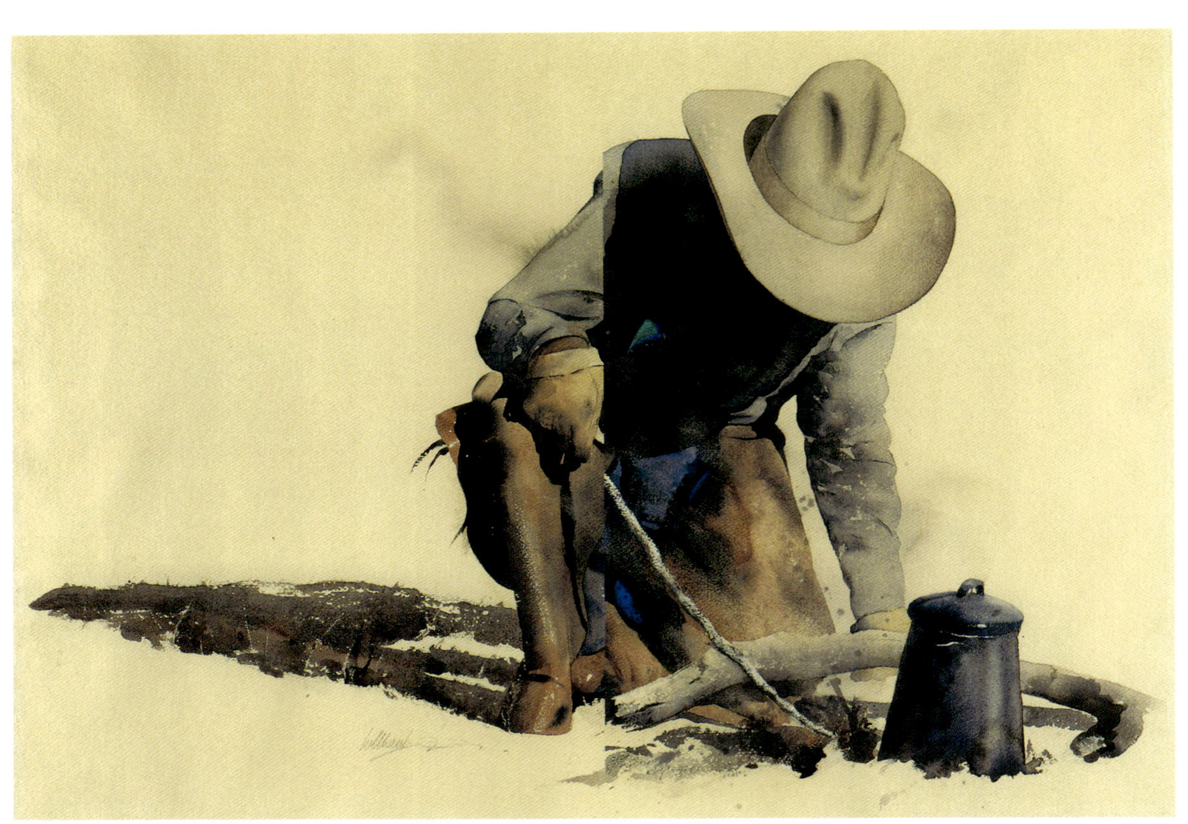

Fire Poker

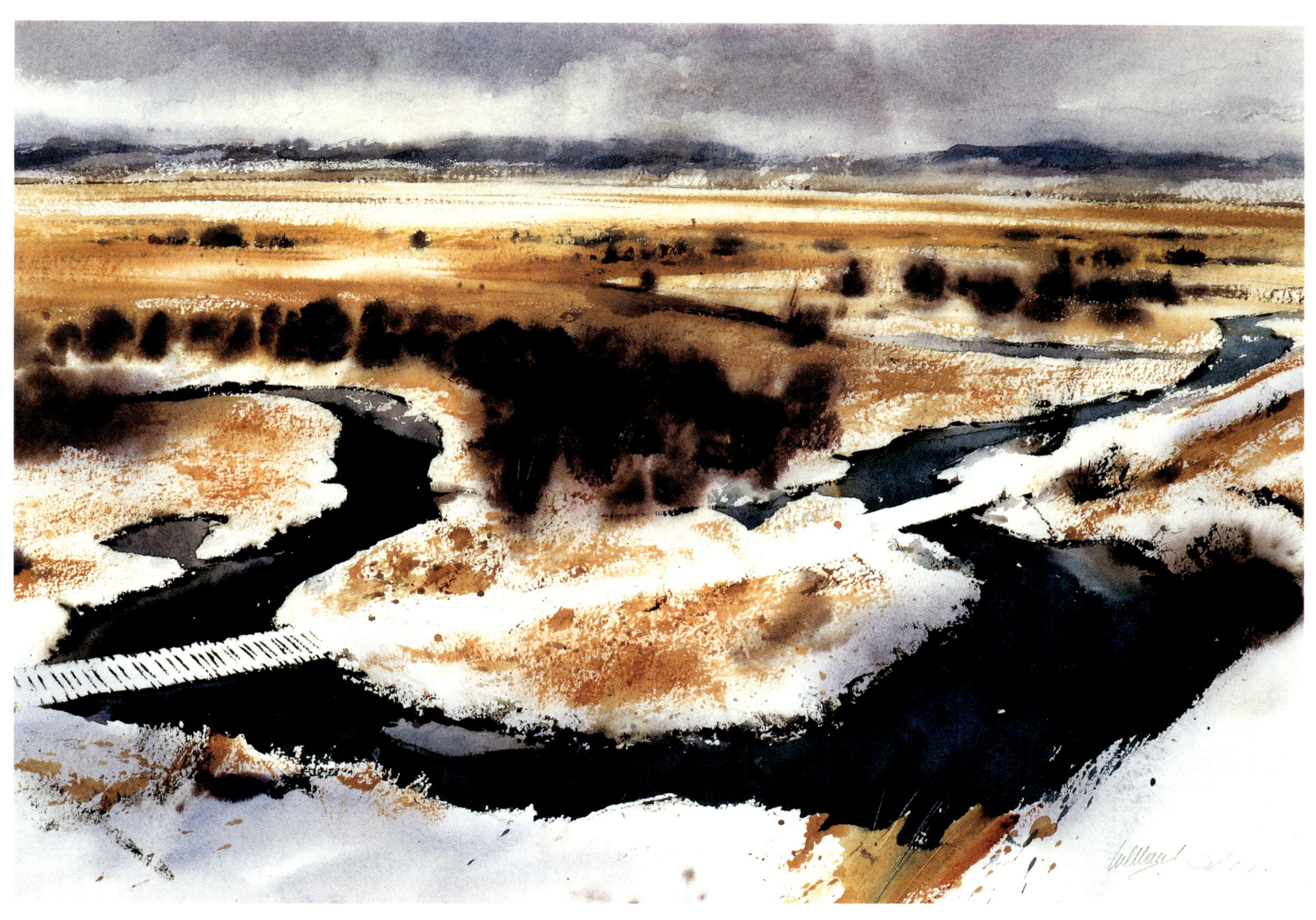

Wyoming

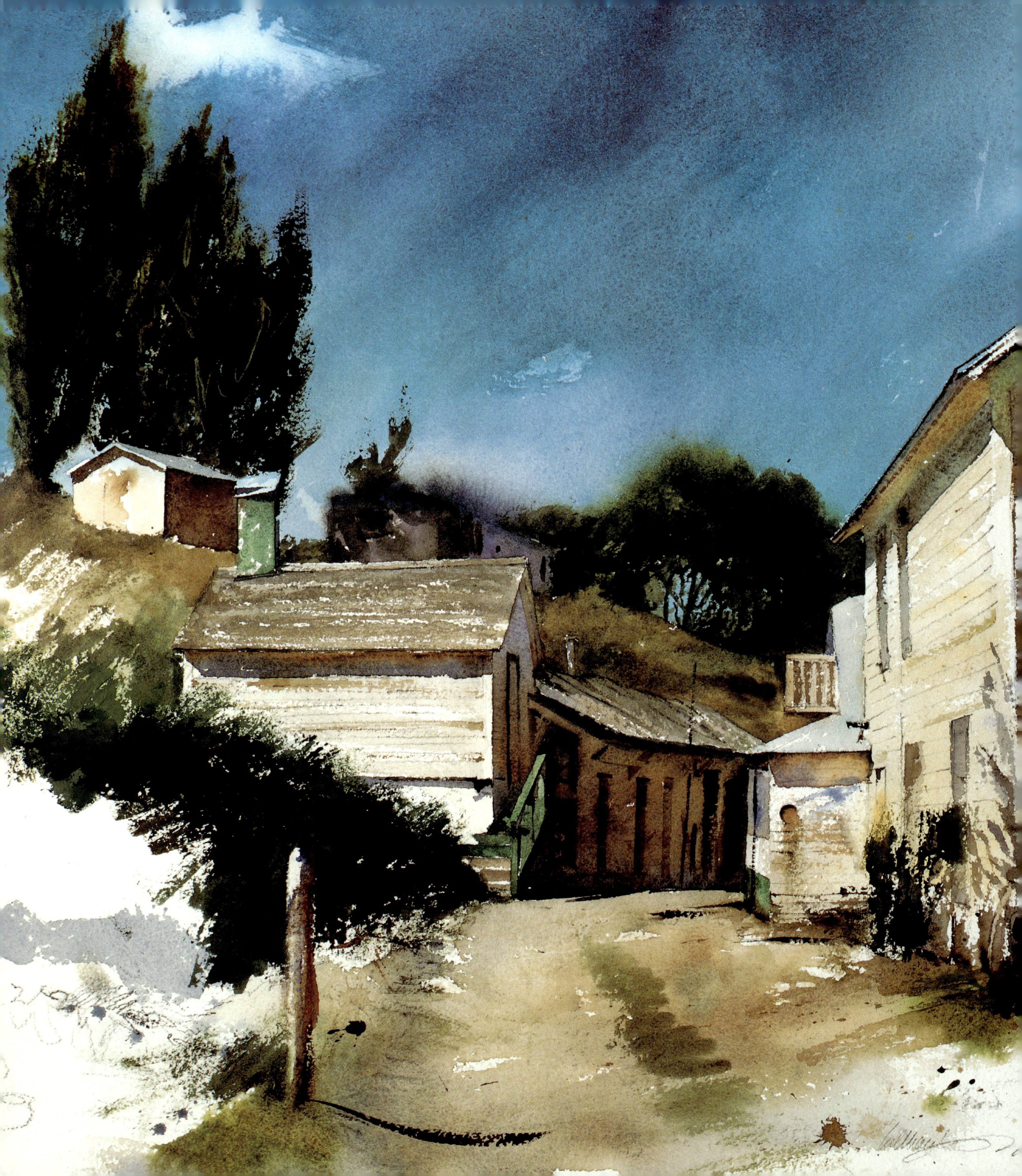

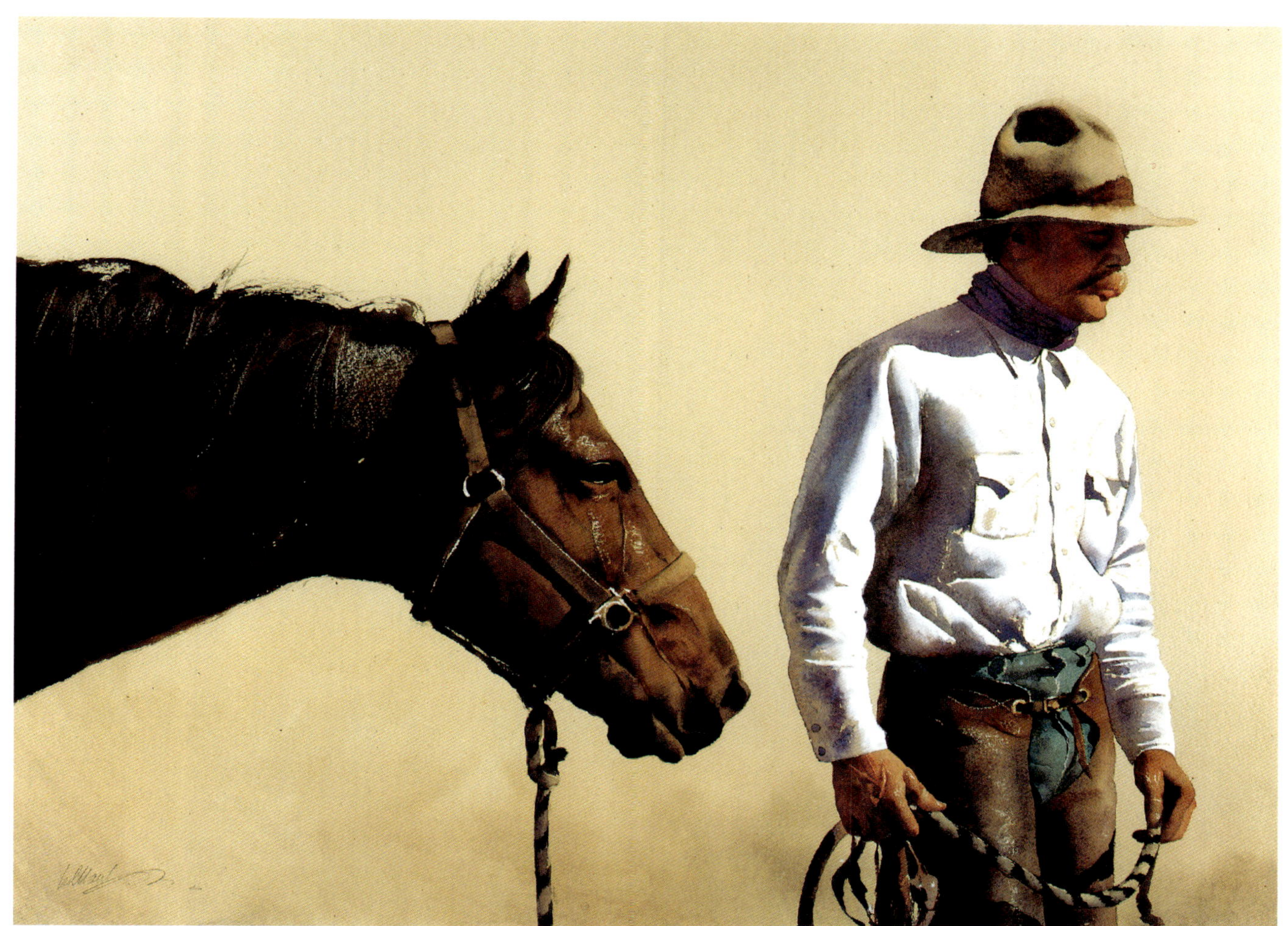

Understood

(OPPOSITE)

Cookhouse, MC Headquarters

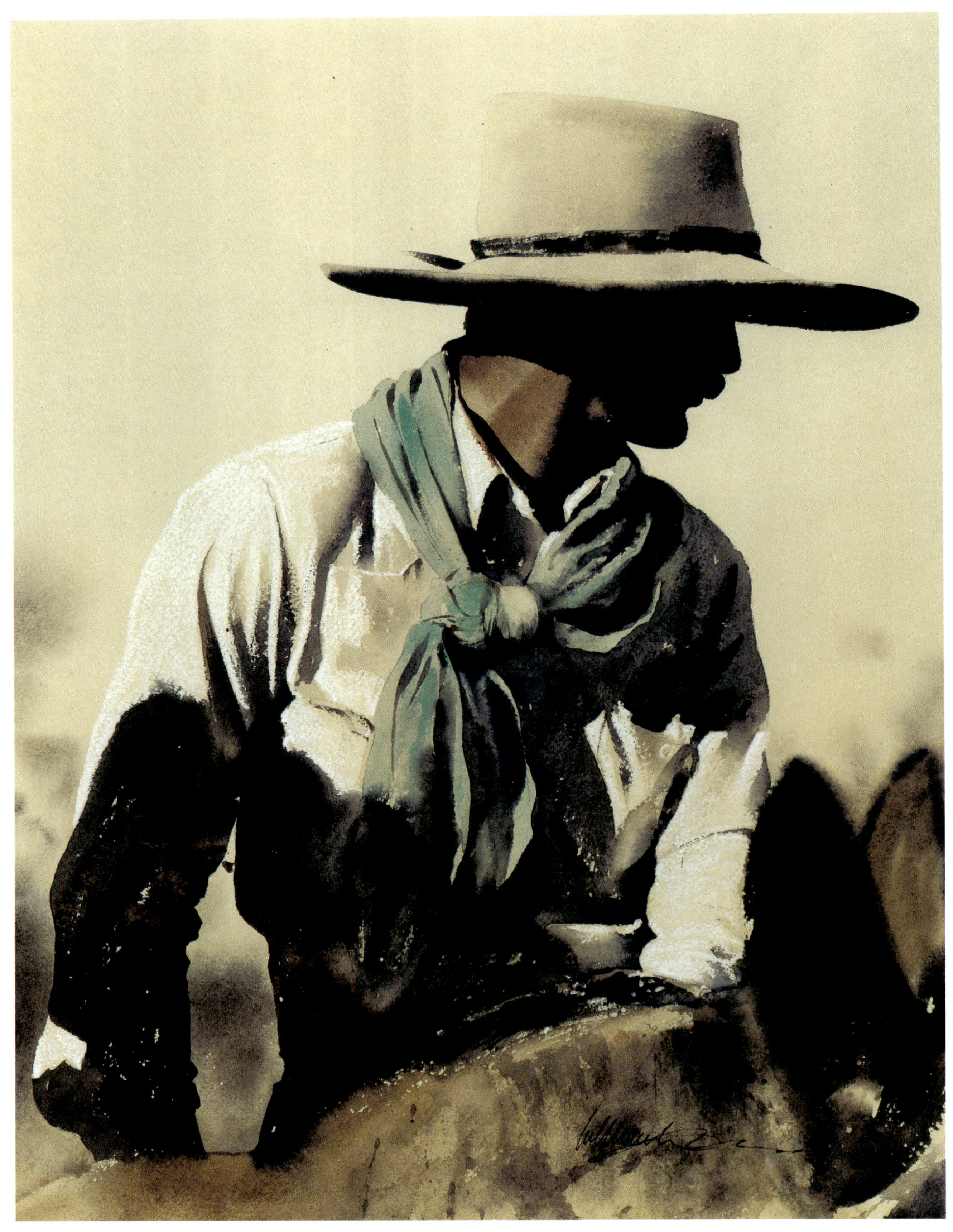

Dallied Up

WILLIAM MATTHEWS was born in 1949 and grew up in San Francisco where he studied briefly at the San Francisco Art Institute, living thereafter as a painter, a designer, and a musician in Europe and the United States. Today, he lives in Evergreen, Colorado, and shows paintings in his own gallery in Denver as well as in many prominent galleries in the United States and Europe.

WILLIAM KITTREDGE grew up on the MC Ranch in southeastern Oregon and worked there until the age of thirty-five, when he embarked upon a new career as a writer. He is the author of two collections of stories, *The Van Gogh Field* and *We Are Not in This Together*; a book of essays, *Owning It All*; and a memoir, *Hole in the Sky*. Mr. Kittredge lives in Missoula, Montana.

DYAN ZASLOWSKY has written about the West for the *New York Times*, *American Heritage*, *High Country News*, *Condé Nast Traveler*, *Wilderness*, and other magazines. *These American Lands*, a conservation history of public land, which she wrote in collaboration with T.H. Watkins in 1986, will be reissued by Henry Holt in 1994. Ms. Zaslowsky lives in Evergreen, Colorado.

LIST OF PLATES

ACKNOWLEDGMENTS

I CANNOT REMEMBER A TIME WHEN I DID NOT think in images, or when image-making was not my obsession. The process speeds up as time runs out. I never painted with the anticipation of producing a book.

Through the years there have been many people who have encouraged and supported me. Many are listed as collectors. Others I want to thank include:

Peter & Peggy Eggers, Bert & Pat Newman, William Channing, Michael Martin Murphey, Seth Milliken, Christopher & Lucy Buckley, Scott Setrakian, Hal Cannon, Teresa Jordan, Bob Russo, Henry Beer, Paul Lohr, David & Kerri Greenberg, Marc Musyl, Carol Curtis, Mike & Ann Moore, Kent & Caroline Rickenbaugh, John & Lynn Grigsby, Michael & Marne Roberts, Senator Alan & Ann Simpson, Pat Duffy, Gibbs Smith, Verushka Chromy, Kurt & Maria Markus, Buffalo Kaplinski, Bill Marlow, Michael Morris, Steven Whatley, Richard Shaw, Michael Lynch, Dyan Zaslowsky, Tim O'Brien, Richard Rasso, Kevin Burke, Leo Kottke, Milton Johnson, Fred Shellman, Barry Poss, Craig Ferguson, Micheál Ó Domhnaill, Tríona Ní Dhomhnaill, Bill Dailey, Sam Provenzano, Ernie Norris, John & Minette Broschofsky, Casey & Jennifer Boone, David Duggan, Kevin O'Farrell, Eugene & Barbara Sternberg, Willis Alan Ramsey, Bruce Wolfe, George O'Neil, Keith Case, Howard & Kathryn Clark, Sandra Wilson, Jack Irwin, Brian Deevy, George Gund, John Hartford, Sally Harvey, Joel & Kate Kopp, Dr. & Mrs. Eugene Kilgore & Family, and John Minford. Also Sheila White, Patricia Childs, Becky Stevens, Christina Johnson, Kim, Cary & Peter Matthews, my mother and father, and Susan Matthews.

Over the years I have been welcomed as a friend by perfect strangers, fed, and bunked. These ranch communities have been oases. I would like to thank the White Horse Ranch, the Spanish Ranch, the IL, the T Lazy S, the ORO, the Quien Sabe and Las Aguilas, the ZX, the MC and Roaring Springs, the YP, the 71, Maggie Creek, the Russell Ranches, the Quarter Circle S, the Winecup, and the Gamble Ranches.

The cowboys have been willing and tolerant subjects, often perplexed by my persistent attention, but their depth and character have constantly amazed me. In particular, I would like to thank Waddie Mitchell, Scott Brown, Randy Rieman, Larry Schutte, Bill Black, Gary MacMahon, Cecil Wetzstein, Jeremiah Watt, Chick Wolf, Randy Stowell, Martin Black, Tom Dorrance, Ron Apodoca, Tom Freeman, Hoot Raney, Bill Maupin, Wade Cooper, Cisco Scott, Pat Cain, Rick Bates, Kent Kraven, Dick Jagels, Jim Andre, Bryan Neubert, Dick Jones, Ross Knox, Randy Everitt, Nathan Kelly, Frank Dominguez, Bryan Joe Hetler, Dean Tobias, John Griggs, Mitch Hagey, Royce Hansen, Wally Byrne, Gabe Nance, Steve Jones, Casey Horg, Paul Summers, Trague Cuthbert, Bill Whitenberg, Lief Smith, Doug Groves, Scott McKay, Gary Stowell, Dave Weaver, Rodger Fisher, Woody Harney, Tom Martin, Manuel Palomino, and Louie Hawkins. I would also like to thank their wives and families, including Colleen Watt and Toni Schutte. There are names I have missed, I'm sure. But to those I have forgotten, please accept my thanks and appreciation.

In addition, I would like to thank Nicholas Callaway and Thomas West for their vision and durability, and especially my old pal, Hans Teensma, for assembling *Cowboys & Images*.

— W.M.

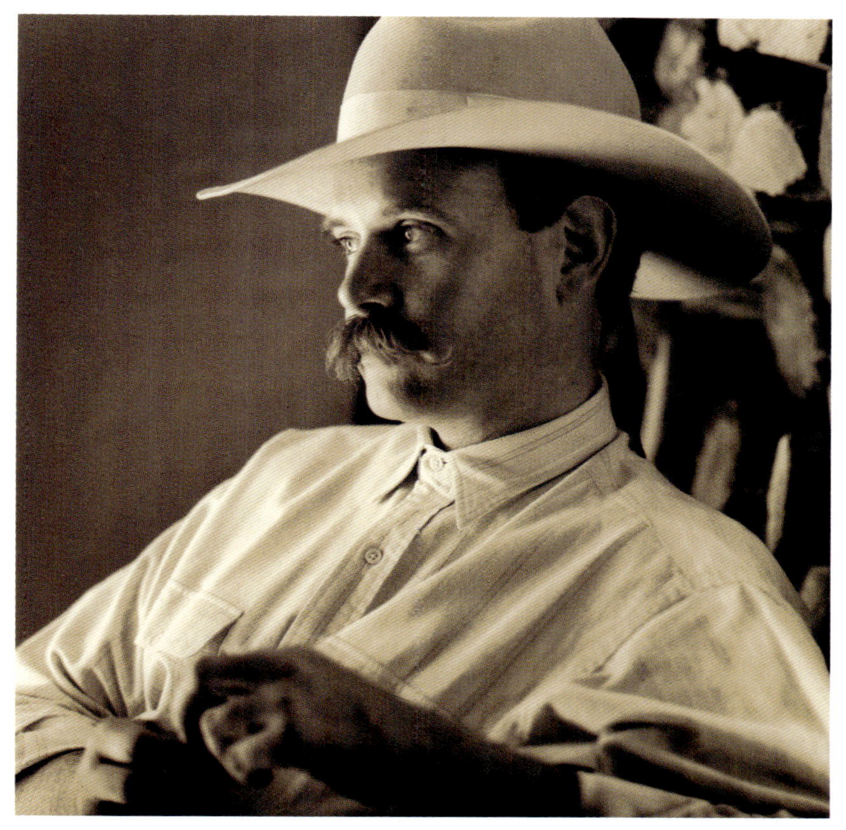

Photograph of William Matthews by Brad Bartholomew

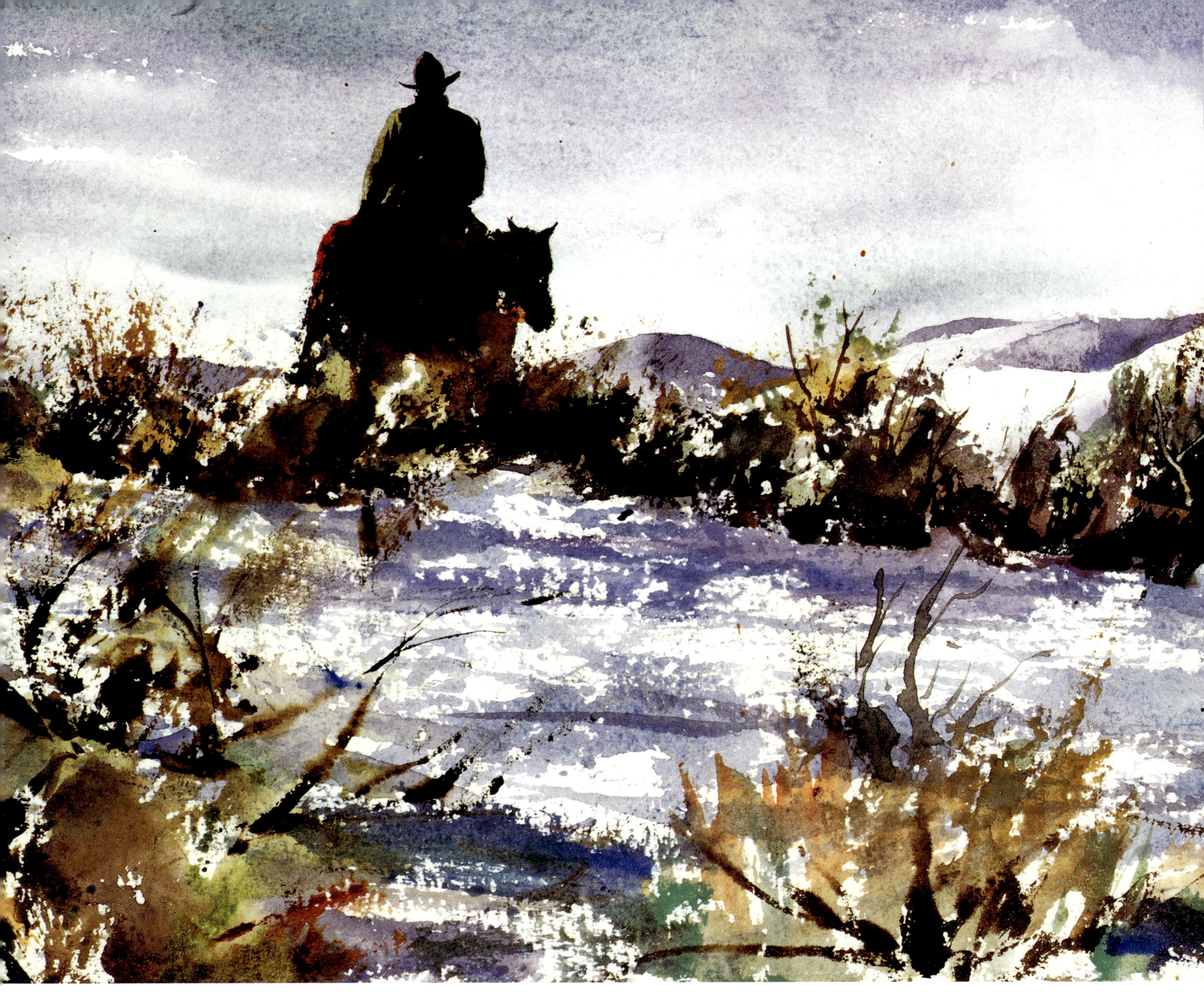

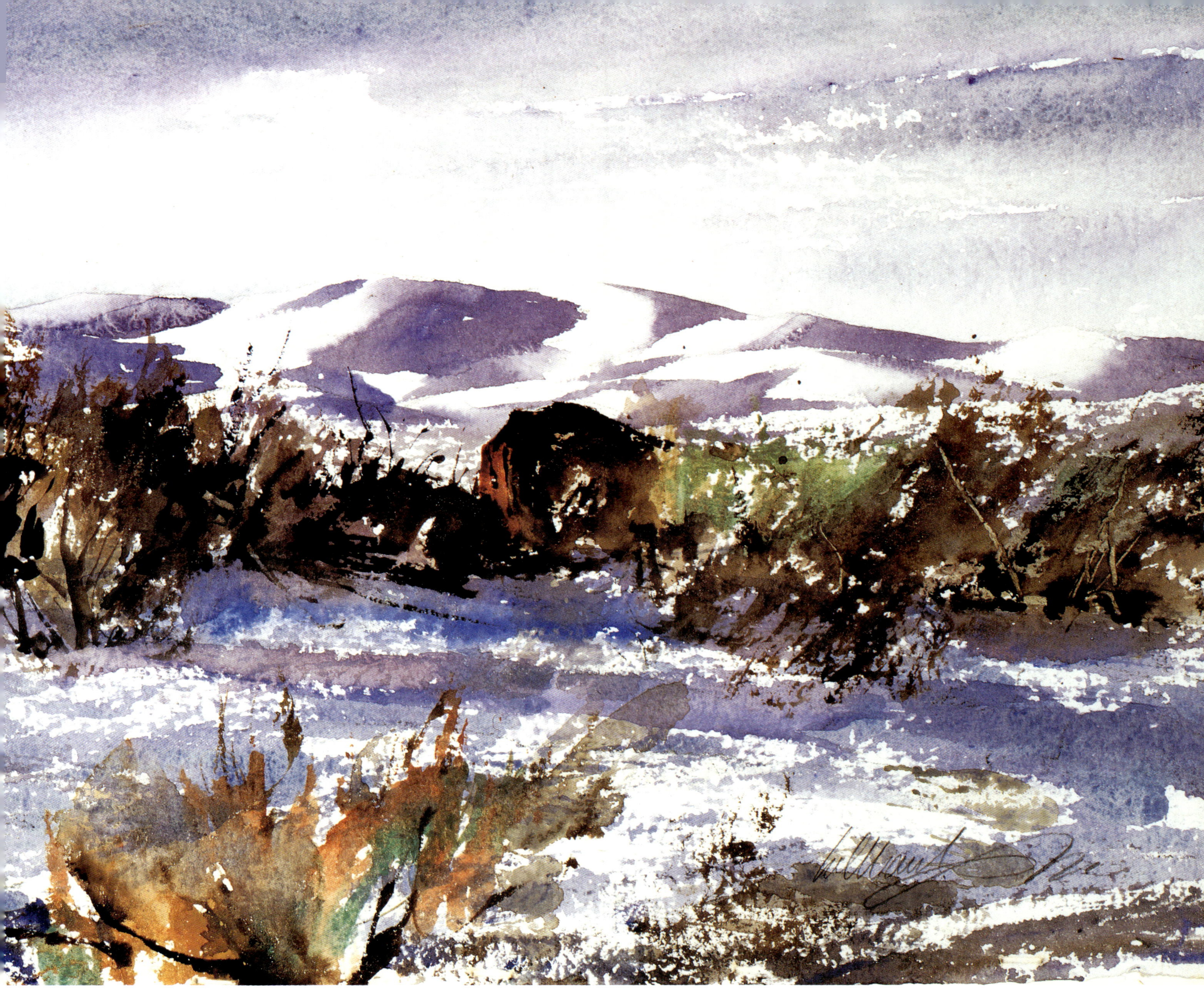

The High Desert

This book was produced by Callaway Editions
under the direction of Nicholas Callaway and Charles Melcher.
The book was edited by Thomas West at Callaway Editions
and designed by Hans Teensma of Impress, Inc.

True Sims was production director at Callaway Editions,
and was assisted by Ivan Wong, Jr., José Rodríguez, and Toshiya Masuda.
Barbara Bergeron and Christy Goldfinch proofread the copy.

Caroline Herter supervised the publication of *Cowboys & Images*
at Chronicle Books, with assistance from Sarah Malarkey.

Becky Stevens, Patricia Bosworth Childs, and Sheila White
researched and organized the book for the William Matthews Gallery.

Most of the copy transparencies were shot by
Cies-Sexton and James Milmoe in Denver, Colorado.

Color separations were made by Palace Press International (Singapore).
Typesetting was by Jeff Potter of Impress, Inc.
This book was set in Lanston Kaatskill, a typeface designed by Frederic Goudy
for fine, limited edition book printing work and recently revived
in digitized form for modern electronic publishing.

Cowboys & Images was printed and bound in Hong Kong by Palace Press International.
The reproductions were printed in four-color offset lithography on 140 gr. coated paper.
The essays by William Kittredge and Dyan Zaslowsky were printed on 140 gr. uncoated paper.
The jacket was printed in five colors with a gloss varnish.
The sheets were gathered and smyth sewn in twelve-page signatures,
and cased in T-Saifu cloth.